THE SINGLE-CHILD FAMILY

THE SINGLE-CHILD FAMILY

Edited by
TONI FALBO
The University of Texas at Austin

THE GUILFORD PRESS
New York London

A Division of Guilford Publications, Inc.
200 Park Avenue South, New York, N.Y. 10003

Printed in the United States of America

LIBRARY OF CONGRESS CATALOGING IN PUBLICATION DATA
Main entry under title:

The Single-child family.

Includes indexes.
1. Only child—Addresses, essays, lectures. I. Falbo, Toni. [DNLM: 1. Only child—Psychology. 2. Family characteristics. WS 105.5.F2 S617]
HQ777.3.S55 1984 155.4'42 83-1612
ISBN 0-89862-630-7

To my parents

CONTRIBUTORS

Sally L. Boswell, PhD, Institute for Research on Social Problems, Boulder, Colorado

John G. Claudy, PhD, American Institutes for Research, Palo Alto, California

Sherri M. Condon, BA, Department of Linguistics, The University of Texas, Austin, Texas

Catherine R. Cooper, PhD, Department of Psychology and Division of Child Development and Family Relationships, Department of Home Economics, The University of Texas, Austin, Texas

Toni Falbo, PhD, Department of Educational Psychology, The University of Texas, Austin, Texas

Candice Feiring, PhD, Institute for the Study of Child Development, Rutgers Medical School–UMDNJ, New Brunswick, New Jersey

H. Theodore Groat, PhD, Department of Sociology, Bowling Green State University, Bowling Green, Ohio

Harold D. Grotevant, PhD, Department of Psychology and Division of Child Development and Family Relationships, Department of Home Economics, The University of Texas, Austin, Texas

Phyllis A. Katz, PhD, Institute for Research on Social Problems, Boulder, Colorado

Michael Lewis, PhD, Institute for the Study of Child Development, Rutgers Medical School–UMDNJ, New Brunswick, New Jersey

Mary Sue Moore, PhD, Learning Disabilities Center, The University of Texas, Austin, Texas

Arthur G. Neal, PhD, Department of Sociology, Bowling Green State University, Bowling Green, Ohio

Denise Polit, PhD, American Institutes for Research, Washington, D.C. Current affiliation: Director, Humanalysis, Inc., Jefferson City, Missouri

William E. Snell, Jr., PhD, Department of Educational Psychology, The University of Texas, Austin, Texas
Jerry W. Wicks, PhD, Department of Sociology, Bowling Green State University, Bowling Green, Ohio

PREFACE

When asked to describe the only child, most Americans use such terms as "selfish," "lonely," or "maladjusted." Parents who have only one child are described in similarly negative terms. These parents report tremendous social pressure to have a second child. Their major reason for having this second child is to prevent their first from becoming an only child. Americans apparently believe that sibling relationships are the sole source of experiences conducive to proper social development. Without siblings, a child is expected to become a socially handicapped adult. Consequently, many parents feel obligated to have a second child.

Most of the research reported in this book challenges this negative view of the only child and the necessity of siblings for desirable social development. In the first chapter I have reviewed the psychological and sociological literature concerning only children and their parents. In this review, only children are contrasted to children with siblings in terms of social and intellectual development. In general, the evidence disputes the belief that only children are maladjusted, lonely, or selfish. Only children perform well on intelligence and achievement tests and do not differ consistently from other children in self-esteem or mental health. Only children have been repeatedly found to be less affiliative than others, but this low level of affiliation appears to be caused more by personal preference than by a lack of social skills.

The remaining seven chapters are individual studies that examine a wide range of developmental outcomes as they are affected by sibling absence. These studies cover a major portion of the lifespan, beginning with infancy and ending with middle adulthood.

The mother–infant relationship is the focus of a longitudinal study reported in the second chapter. Candice Feiring and Michael Lewis investigated the disruptions associated with dethronement during the first two years of life by contrasting changes in mother–child behaviors between one- and two-child families.

In the next chapter, Sally Boswell and Phyllis Katz address the influence of siblings on sex-role development during early and middle childhood. Boswell and Katz compared differences in gender-role identity between only children and children with one sibling. They also examined the sex-role attitudes of the parents to determine if one-child parents differed from two-child parents. Boswell and Katz reported that only children were more flexible in gender roles than their peers, perhaps because one-child parents had less traditional sex-role attitudes than parents with two children.

The development of ego identity in adolescence is the topic of Chapter 4, by Catherine Cooper, Harold Grotevant, Mary Sue Moore, and Sherri Condon. Although the authors found no difference between only children and others in terms of role-taking skill or identity exploration, their analysis of family communication patterns points to potential weaknesses in the one-child family. Guided by the work of Minuchin, the Cooper *et al.* chapter describes the types of family communication patterns that foster healthy development in teen-agers and the role of siblings in these communication patterns.

In Chapter 5, written with the assistance of William Snell, I have examined the impact of sibling tutoring on intellectual development. The sibling tutoring factor was invented by Zajonc and Markus to explain the lower-than-expected performance of only children and last-born children on intelligence scores. In this study, two experiments were conducted to determine if the basic process underlying the sibling tutoring factor worked. The weakness of the support provided by both experiments suggests that other factors, such as father absence, famine, unwantedness, or handicaps, may be as plausible explanations of the intelligence discrepancies of only and last-born children as sibling tutoring.

Denise Polit's chapter deals with the double handicap of growing up without siblings and without a father. Her chapter is based on interviews she conducted with mothers of one, two, or three children. Surprisingly, Polit discovered that the one-parent, one-child family was associated with positive outcomes for both mother and child, especially in comparison to the outcomes of single-parent families with two or three children.

Chapter 7, by John Claudy, is based on a longitudinal survey of high school students across the United States and on an 11-year follow-up of these individuals. Claudy contrasted the intellectual performance and personal preferences of children of one-child families to those of children of two-child families. Only children compared favorably to individuals from two-child families, especially in intellectual performance and educational attainment. Although individuals from one-child families expressed greater preferences for solitary activities than did their peers, their success at marriage was as great as that of individuals from two-child families.

Finally, the chapter by Theodore Groat, Jerry Wicks, and Arthur Neal compares the adult outcomes of individuals from one-child families to those of individuals from larger families. The research reported in this chapter was based on a national sample of individuals ranging in age from 15 to 44. Individuals from single-child families were generally found to be similar to others in terms of marital stability and fertility and to attain higher educational levels. Therefore, Groat *et al.* conclude that the adult outcomes of only children are not much different from the outcomes of children from larger families.

Recognition is given to the Center for Population Research (CPR) of the National Institute for Child Health and Human Development for funding most of the research reported in this book. In particular, I am grateful for the efforts of Dr. Gloria Kamenske in focusing CPR's attention on the need for more research on the one-child family.

Toni Falbo
Austin, Texas

CONTENTS

·1·

ONLY CHILDREN: A REVIEW

TONI FALBO

Most Americans feel that parents ought to provide their children with at least one sibling. According to a Gallup poll taken in 1972, a large majority of white Americans think that an only child is disadvantaged and that the two-child family is ideal (Blake, 1974). Thompson (1974) points out that only children are popularly viewed as "generally maladjusted, self-centered and self-willed, attention-seeking and dependent on others, temperamental and anxious, generally unhappy and unlikeable, and yet somewhat more autonomous than a child with two siblings" (pp. 95–96). In fact, the general opinion regarding only children is so negative that the most commonly cited reason for having a second child is to prevent the first from being an only child (Solomon, Clare, & Westoff, 1956).

In recent years much research has investigated the consequences of growing up without siblings. In general, these studies conclude that only children are no worse off than their counterparts with siblings and that only children compare quite favorably to other children in some ways. This book is devoted to disseminating much of this recent research. This chapter reviews the previous literature on only children, beginning with a brief description of the historical context of the only child and then turning to the psychological theories and research relevant to evaluating the only child.

HISTORICAL CONTEXT

In the United States during the period between 1920 and the early 1940s, the percentage of women with one child in their completed

Toni Falbo. Department of Educational Psychology, The University of Texas, Austin, Texas.

family rose from about 20% to 30%. This trend reversed when World War II ended. During the postwar baby-boom period, the percentage of women with one child decreased to about 15%. This high fertility pattern began to change around the mid-1960s, and by the mid-1970s the percentage of women who had only one child returned to the level of the 1920s. There is speculation that among families forming during the early 1980s the proportion of one-child families will be as high as it was during the Depression (around 30%). Therefore, it appears that the United States is repeating the cycle of low fertility that occurred during the 1920–1940 period.

This earlier increase in the percentage of one-child families has been attributed largely to economic factors (Falbo, 1982). However, the present increase in the number of only children has been attributed to four factors: (1) advances in contraceptive technology, (2) increased employment of women, (3) inhibiting economic factors, and (4) increased marital instability. The first of these factors, contraceptive technology, has provided men and women with greater control of their fertility and thus has allowed them to postpone or prevent childbearing. The last three factors are reasons families currently have for postponing or preventing the arrival of additional children. There is evidence that two of these reasons, women's employment and marital instability, are associated with the one-child family. Women who have one child are more likely to be employed outside the home than women with more than one child (DeJong, Stokes, & Hanson, 1980). In addition, evidence from a variety of sources indicates that only children are more likely to come from single-parent families (Blake, 1981; Claudy, Farrell, & Dayton, 1979; Falbo, 1978b). However, it is unknown at present whether one-child families are especially affected by current economic conditions, although it is possible that one of the reasons women with one child are more likely to be employed outside the home is that their families have greater financial problems than families with more than one child.

Some evidence suggests that many parents who have only one child do not feel entirely comfortable with the size of their family. For example, Polit (1980) has reported that a sizeable number of the one-child mothers she interviewed, regardless of their current marital status, expressed the wish that they had had a larger family. Likewise, Lewis (1972) reported that women who involuntarily had one child were more unhappy with their fertility outcome than were women with two or three children or women who had voluntarily chosen to have only one child. Beyond this, one is left to speculate about the consequences of involuntarily having a single child. It seems likely that a woman who involuntarily had only one child would be disappointed by her low fertility and that this disappointment would influence her parenting. For example, it is easy to imagine such a mother overprotecting, overindulging, or expecting too much from her only child. In contrast, one would expect a voluntary one-child mother to be less likely to overprotect, overindulge, or expect too much from her child, because she would lack the frustration driving the behavior of the involuntary one-child mother.

Given the recent increase in women's participation in the labor force and advances in contraceptive technology, it seems likely that the proportion of voluntary one-child families will be greater during the early 1980s than it has been in previous generations. This enhanced voluntarism among one-child mothers may result in the production of a group of only children who are markedly different from their predecessors. For this and other historical reasons, such as wars, economic depressions, and changes in societal values, the results of research on past generations of only children and their mothers may not represent the current generation. With this caution in mind, let us proceed with a review of the literature on only children.

CAUSAL MODELS OF HUMAN DEVELOPMENT

Given the strong popular aversion to having or being an only child (Blake, 1974; Thompson, 1974), one can assume that the American public regards the presence of siblings as essential to normal human development, especially social development.

Many psychologists agree with these popular notions. For example, Zajonc and Markus (1975) have devised a model of intellectual development that explains discontinuities in the performance of only and last-born children in terms of their lack of a younger sibling to tutor. However, psychologists have applied additional causal models to explain the development of only children. For example, parental characteristics associated with the single-child family, such as father absence or enhanced parental attention, have been used to explain some of the differences found between only children and others. In particular, Falbo (1978b) has explained some of the IQ discontinuities of only children in terms of the higher incidence of father absence in this group. Similarly, Kidwell (1978) has suggested the enhanced attention parents pay to an only child as an explanation for the finding that only children perceive their parents more affectionately than do first-born children.

Of course, the major psychological models used in this context have been those associated with birth order. That is, the interaction of siblings, as determined by their order of birth, has been both theoretically and empirically linked to the development of many significant personality characteristics. Only children have been variously dealt with in these birth-order models. Sometimes they are combined with first borns (e.g., Crandall, Katkovsky, & Crandall, 1965); sometimes they are separated into a distinct category (e.g., Toman, 1969); and sometimes they are regarded as similar to last borns (e.g., Zajonc & Markus, 1975). Only children are difficult to categorize, because they represent a family size (the one-child family) as well as a birth order. Therefore, their presence in a sample has generally posed difficulties for investigators who have attempted to consider birth order and family size simultaneously. In such studies, only children have had to be combined with first- or last-born children.

The following review surveys a wide range of topics, from intelligence to affiliativeness. The causal models associated with each topic are described in terms of popular notions, sibling absence, parental characteristics, and birth order.

INTELLIGENCE

Several large-scale studies of the relationship between IQ and family size have found these variables to be inversely related (Belmont & Marolla, 1973; Breland, 1974; Claudy, 1976). On the basis of this negative relationship, one would expect only children to have the highest IQ of all because they come from the smallest family size. Unfortunately, only children have frequently been found to score lower than expected (Belmont & Marolla, 1973; Breland, 1974; Zajonc & Markus, 1975).

The best-known model used to study both the general relationship between family size and IQ and the specific performance of only children is the confluence model (Zajonc & Markus, 1975). This respected ("Zajonc Defuses IQ Debate," 1976) and popular (Zajonc,

1975) model states that intelligence develops as a function of a combination of factors, including the child's maturation and experience within the family. As children grow older, they become capable of more and more sophisticated intellectual activities, partially because of maturation and partially because of interaction with the environment. The confluence model proposes that the child's environment is largely defined by the family. Thus it is through the child's experiences within the family that family size affects intelligence.

The confluence model posits that intellectual development is largely determined by the level of intelligence present within the family. The level of intellectual functioning of a family is defined operationally as the average of the combined absolute intelligence scores of all family members. Absolute intelligence is the upper level of intellectual operations that an individual can perform when tested and is uncorrected for age. Therefore, since children have lower absolute intelligence levels than adults, the intellectual environment of a family is greater the more adult and fewer child members it has.

The original tests of the model assumed that each family consists of two adults with average adult intelligence and a specified number of children with varying ages and age gaps between siblings. In simplified form, the confluence model represents the intellectual level of a two-adult, no-child family as

$$\frac{100 + 100}{2} = 100$$

After the birth of the first child, the intellectual level of the family changes drastically. As a newborn, the first child's intelligence is close to zero. Applying the simplified version of the confluence model, we can see that the arrival of the first child depresses the overall intellectual environment of the family:

$$\frac{100 + 100 + 0}{3} = 66.6$$

As children grow older, their absolute intelligence increases. Giving the child of 5 years an absolute intelligence of 30, and applying the simplified confluence model, we can see that the overall intellectual level of the family has improved:

$$\frac{100 + 100 + 30}{3} = 76.6$$

Now, if the parents have another child, the arrival of the newborn means that the intellectual level of the family is less than after the arrival of the first child:

$$\frac{100 + 100 + 30 + 0}{4} = 57.5$$

Thus, one would predict that if this second child were the last, he or she would attain an intellectual level lower than that of the first-born child.

If one parent dies soon after the birth of the second child, the intellectual level of the family declines from 57.5, as described above, to

$$\frac{100 + 30 + 0}{3} = 43.3$$

Consequently, the confluence model predicts that the loss of an adult member lowers the overall intellectual environment of the family, thereby depressing the intellectual development of family members who are children. In this fashion, the confluence model explains the frequent finding that children from single-parent families score lower on IQ tests than children from two-parent families of comparable size (Biller, 1974; Blanchard & Biller, 1971; Broman, Nichols, & Kennedy, 1975; Carlsmith, 1964; Lynn, 1974; Sutton-Smith, Rosenberg, & Landy, 1968). However, one should note that research on father absence generally has been criticized for methodological flaws (Herzog & Sudia, 1968; Marino & McCowan, 1976; Shinn, 1978).

In addition to explaining the effects of such variables as family size and father absence on intellectual development, the confluence model explains why several large-scale surveys of young adults have found that only borns do not fulfill the expectation that they will have the highest IQs. Zajonc and Markus (1975) combined the only-child discontinuity with the additional finding that last borns also demonstrated a decline in IQ performance relative to expectation. Since both only and last borns have no younger siblings, Zajonc and Markus decided that this lack caused the discontinuity. Therefore, the sibling tutoring factor was added to the confluence model. It was argued that having a younger sibling gives the older child the opportunity to tutor and that tutoring a younger sibling benefits intellectual development.

Originally, Zajonc and Markus (1975) represented the sibling tutoring factor as a zero or a 1. Zeros were added to equations representing only and last-born children, whereas 1's were added to all other birth order–family size cases. More recently, Zajonc, Markus, and Markus (1979) elaborated the confluence model to accommodate the finding that the relative scores of only children and of first- and second-born children of two-child families change as a function of age. Among older subjects (17 years or older), the intelligence scores of first borns of two-child families have been repeatedly shown to surpass those of only children. Among younger subjects, only children demonstrate no such IQ loss (Barnes, Fisher, & Palmer, 1979; Fowler & Richards, 1978; Steelman & Mercy, 1980).

Zajonc *et al.* (1979) explained these age shifts in terms of the differential gains and losses brought about by the combination of the sibling tutoring factor and the entry of a new sibling into the family. Their argument is that the presence of a younger sibling at first has a negative effect on the intelligence of the first-born child, because the newborn lowers the average intellectual level of the family. However, as the second-born child matures, he or she contributes positively to the intellectual development of the first born because the younger sibling is present to be tutored. This second factor accumulates over time, so that the maximum benefits derived from this tutoring accrue to the older siblings during their adolescence. In short, during childhood, younger siblings cost more than they benefit intellectual development in earlier borns. Beginning with adolescence, the presence of young siblings benefits the intellectual development of older siblings by providing them with the opportunity to tutor.

TESTS OF THE CONFLUENCE MODEL

The original test of the confluence model, conducted by Zajonc and Markus (1975), consisted of a correlation between two curves, both representing the relationship between family size and intelligence. One curve was based upon aggregate data and the second was produced by a simulation of the model. With the addition of the sibling tutoring factor to the simulated data, these two curves shared about 97% of their variance (Zajonc & Markus, 1975).

Unfortunately, a subsequent test of the confluence model found that it accounted for only about 2% of the variance in predicting children's IQ scores. Using regression equations representing the confluence model, Grotevant, Scarr, and Weinberg (1977) substituted actual IQ scores of all family members for the simulated ones used by Zajonc and Markus. Grotevant *et al.*'s (1977) results suggest that the confluence model may explain the relationship between family size and IQ at the aggregate but not the individual level.

More recently, two large-scale studies have cast even more doubt on the family configuration and intelligence relationships that formed the basis of the confluence model. For example, Galbraith (1982) attempted to find a negative relationship between family size and the American College Testing Program Examination (ACT) scores of 10,925 undergraduates. In addition, Galbraith attempted to find a positive relationship between sibling age spacing and ACT scores. In neither case was he able to find a statistically significant relationship. Similarly, Rodgers (in press) found that neither family size nor sibling age spacing shared a significant amount of variance with the intelligence scores of 581 children (ages 7–13 years).

In contrast, Brackbill and Nichols (1982) examined relationships between several family configuration variables and widely used measures of intelligence and achievement. They found some evidence of the existence of the relationships explained by the confluence model in their sample of 47,000 children (ages 4 and 7 years). In particular, Brackbill and Nichols reported a significant association between sibling age spacing and both intelligence and achievement. Wider spacing was associated with higher intelligence and achievement. However, wider spacing was found to ameliorate the effects of large family size (as predicted by the confluence model) only for the achievement scores of whites, not of blacks. Similarly, Brackbill and Nichols reported that before socioeconomic factors were controlled, children without fathers scored significantly lower than did children with fathers in both intelligence and achievement. However, when socioeconomic factors were controlled, the direction of this relationship reversed in four out of the five remaining significant (but extremely small) correlations. This means that father absence alone was sometimes found to be positively related to achievement and intelligence levels for both whites and blacks. More important for the purposes of the present chapter, Brackbill and Nichols tested the sibling tutoring hypothesis by examining the scores of only children. They reasoned that if the proposed importance of the sibling tutoring factor is correct, only children should score lower than would be expected from family size alone. Their results only partially supported this expectation: For both blacks and whites, only children scored significantly worse than expected on achievement but not on intelligence tests.

Additional tests of the sibling tutoring factor have also produced mixed support. Falbo and Snell (1982) simulated sibling tutoring among 152 pairs of female undergraduates. The tutors were seniors and the tutees were freshmen; the tasks covered were either spatial or verbal in nature. Both spatial and verbal ability tests were given before, at the midpoint, and after the ten-day training session. The results indicated that simply teaching someone younger does not produce a significantly greater change in either abilities or task performance than being taught or teaching oneself the same tasks. Even when relatively inactive tutors were eliminated from the sample, neither their abilities nor their skills were improved beyond levels achieved by tutees or self-teaching peers.

If the Falbo and Snell (1982) and Brackbill and Nichols (1982) studies provide only qualified support for the sibling tutoring effect, it may be advisable to reconsider some of the alternative explanations for the IQ discontinuities of only and last-born children. Indeed, Zajonc and Markus (1975) were the first to speculate about this. They suggested two explanations: degree of wantedness and incidence of congenital handicaps. Zajonc and Markus suggested that there might be a higher incidence of unwantedness or handicaps among only and last borns and that this difference could lead only and last borns as a group to score lower than expected on intelligence measures. Unfortunately, Zajonc and Markus chose not to include these alternatives in their model, because no information was available on the incidence of unwantedness or congenital handicaps in the general population. Lack of information about the incidence of sibling tutoring, however, did not prevent them from including the sibling tutoring factor in their model. In fact, there is evidence that last borns are more likely to be unwanted (Westoff & Ryder, 1977) and that unwanted children score lower on school achievement than do wanted children (David, 1981). Furthermore, there is some evidence that parents whose first child is born with a handicap tend to stop their family at one child (Collins, 1982).

In addition, two alternative explanations for the only/last born handicap have been suggested. Blake (1981) has proposed that the only/last born handicap found in the original Dutch data used by Zajonc and Markus can be attributed to the increased likelihood that these individuals were affected by the 1944–1945 Dutch famine. She argues that these only or last borns were the last to be born in their families because their parents were particularly affected by the famine. Because of this deprivation during their prenatal or infancy periods, these only and last borns were likely to suffer from intellectual deficiencies as young adults.

The second alternative explanation offered for the intelligence discontinuity of only and last borns involves father absence (Falbo, 1978c). One of the strengths of the confluence model was its ability to explain why children with one parent frequently are found to have lower intelligence levels than children with two parents (Biller, 1974; Blanchard & Biller, 1971; Broman, Nichols, & Kennedy, 1975; Carlsmith, 1964; Lynn, 1974; Sutton-Smith, Rosenberg, & Landy, 1968). According to United States census data, however, father absence is more common among women with one child in their completed family than among women with more than one child (Falbo, 1978b). Zajonc and Markus (1975) chose to ignore this possible explanation for the IQ discontinuity of only children. In contrast, Claudy, Farrell, and Dayton (1979) used this information as the basis for a reanalysis of data that had previously supported the only-child discontinuity. They found that when individuals from single-parent families were eliminated from their sample, the only-born discontinuity in intellectual abilities disappeared. In fact, Claudy *et al.* found that only children in this revised sample scored significantly better than individuals from two-child families on 25 of the 32 possible tests. Only children scored lower than individuals from two-child families on 3 of these tests and no differently on the remaining 4 tests. This explanation may also apply to last-born children, although comparable census information about them is unavailable. The argument for the applicability of the father-absence explanation to last-born children is that last borns may be the last child born in the family because the parents' marriage ended, either through divorce or death.

In summary, the current status of our knowledge about the intelligence of only children is uncertain. The reasons for the inconsistent results probably lie in the various confounding factors (father absence, socioeconomic status) not controlled for in the various studies. At present, the confluence model is the most important model available in the literature to explain the origins of the relationships between an array of family configuration factors and intelligence. However, recent investigations of this model have cast doubt on the basic associations between specific family configuration factors and intelligence that serve as the basis of the model. Further, because the sibling tutoring factor has only qualified empirical support, other reasons why only children do not consistently have the highest IQ of all children have been proposed and empirically supported. Therefore, the validity of the confluence model, especially in explaining the performance of only children, is currently in doubt.

ACHIEVEMENT

Compared to intelligence, the picture of the achievement of only children is clear. Disproportionate numbers of first and only borns have been found among eminent men (Ellis, 1904), the faces on the covers of *Time* (Toman & Toman, 1970), and psychologists (Roe, 1953). Furthermore, several birth-order studies of achievement have found that both first-born and only-born individuals perform better academically than others (Guilford & Worcester, 1930; Jones, 1954; Lees & Stewart, 1957; Oberlander & Jenkin, 1967; Skouholt, Moore, & Wellman, 1973). More recent studies that have made comparisons on the basis of family size have found only borns to compare favorably to people from larger families. For example, Blake (1981) found that only-born men attain higher levels of education and occupational prestige than men from larger families, especially families containing four or more children. Claudy *et al.* (1979) also found evidence that only children are more academically oriented in high school and that later, as adults, only children obtain more education than individuals from two-child families. Consistent with these findings, Falbo (1981) found that, among undergraduates, only and first borns have higher educational aspirations than do later borns.

Searches for the psychological factors that account for this achievement effect have focused on the special relationship only and first-born children have with their parents. Achievement motivation had been thought to originate in the high standards for mature behavior that parents impose on their children at relatively early ages (Rosen & D'Andrade, 1959; Winterbottom, 1958). This approach to explaining achievement motivation is relevant here because there is evidence that first-born and only-born children receive greater pressure for more mature behavior from parents than do later-born children (Clausen, 1966; Kammeyer, 1967). In support of the achievement motivation explanation, Sampson and Hancock (1967), Angelini (1967), and Rosen (1961) found that first-born and only-born children scored higher on need-for-achievement tests than did later borns. However, not everyone has found such an effect in need-for-achievement data (e.g., Rosenfeld, 1966).

There is one factor unique to only children that might enhance their achievement: their uninterrupted relationship with their parents. The acquisition of adult-like behavior is probably accelerated in only children because they have solely adult models of behavior in their family environments. Children with siblings are exposed to both child and adult models of behavior and this may slow these children's acquisition of adult-like behavior. Guilford and Worcester (1930) support this speculation, reporting that only children are more adult-oriented than are children with siblings. Further, several investigations suggest that only children have a special relationship with their parents. Gewirtz and Gewirtz (1965) found that mothers of only children interacted with their children twice as much as did mothers of last-born children. Lewis and Kreitzberg (1979) found that only children experienced more parent–child interaction than did first-born or later-born children. In addition, as reported earlier, Kidwell (1978) found that only children perceive themselves as having more affectionate relationships with their parents than do first borns.

Another factor that contributes to the achievement of only and first-born children is their strong tendency to take responsibility for outcomes First-born and especially only-born children have been found to have a more internal locus of control than do later borns (Crandall, Katkovsky, & Crandall, 1965; Falbo, 1981). To date, there has been little adequate explanation for this finding. Crandall *et al.* explain their result as attributable to the tendency of first borns to take care of their younger siblings. Although this explanation is plausible for first borns, it fails to explain the fact that Crandall *et al.*

found that both first-born and only children have a more internal orientation than do later borns. Perhaps the special relationship only children have with their parents is responsible for their strong internality. Because only children receive their parents' full attention, they may receive more immediate and consistent reinforcement for their acts than do children with siblings. This enhanced parental attention may facilitate the development of an internal locus of control.

In summary, onlies, like first borns, have been found to be overrepresented among achievers. Further, only borns have been found to attain higher educational levels than others. The reasons for this high achievement appear to be related to the special parent–child relationships onlies, and to some extent first borns, have. The parent–child relationships are thought to produce high levels of achievement motivation and an internal locus of control in children.

SELF-ESTEEM

On the basis of the common stereotype about them, one would expect only children to have unrealistically high self-esteem. Early research tended to support this notion. Fenton (1928) and Goodenough and Leahy (1927) compared teacher ratings of only versus nononly children and found that only children scored higher on the traits of "conceit" and "self-confidence."

More recent studies of the self-esteem of only children have resulted in a mixed picture. The mixed results have yielded a variety of interpretations, emphasizing both parents and siblings as contributing factors.

For example, Zimbardo and Formica (1963) based their research on social comparison theory, which states that one's level of self-esteem is determined by the results of one's comparison between oneself and others. Zimbardo and Formica reasoned that first and only borns compare themselves to their parents (an adult to child comparison), whereas last borns compare themselves to their older siblings (a child to child comparison). Because the difference between adults and children is greater than differences between children, Zimbardo and Formica argued that only and first borns acquire lower levels of self-esteem than do last borns. Unfortunately, the empirical test of this prediction obtained supportive results that were only of borderline significance. Later, Kaplan (1970) had more success. He found that last borns were more likely to be in the high self-esteem group than were middle or first and only borns. Further analysis of Kaplan's findings, however, indicated that the effect was true only for white males from high social class groups.

Other authors have argued that onlies and firstborns should have higher self-esteem than middle and last borns, because first and only borns receive more unconditional positive regard from their parents than do later borns. Some support for this prediction was found by Coopersmith (1967). He found that only- and first-born adolescent males were overrepresented in his high self-esteem group. Similarly, Rosenberg (1965) reported that only borns were more likely to be classified as having high self-esteem than were nononly borns. However, further analysis of Rosenberg's data indicated that this apparent difference between only and nononly borns existed mainly for males, especially Jewish males.

The most recent study of the self-esteem of only children found that last borns scored significantly less well than first borns and that middle and only borns scored between these two extremes (Falbo, 1981). Further, the self-esteem of only borns was not significantly different from the self-esteem of all the nononly categories. In explaining this result, Falbo (1981) revised the social comparison rationale initially proposed by Zimbardo and Formica. According to this revised view, children develop their sense of personal worth by comparing themselves to their siblings (if they have siblings), not to their parents, as Zimbardo and Formica proposed. Because older siblings are generally more capable, larger, and more skilled, than younger siblings, first borns come to regard themselves more favorably than do their siblings, and therefore they develop the most positive self-esteem. Conversely, last borns have the least favorable comparison to their siblings, and they therefore develop the least positive self-esteem. Finally, both only and middle borns develop moderate levels of self-esteem, but for different reasons. Middle borns compare negatively to their older siblings but positively to their younger siblings, and this mixed comparison leads middle borns to acquire moderate levels of self-esteem. In contrast, only children do not experience a sibling comparison, and consequently their self-esteem development is unaffected by the comparison process. Therefore, they also develop a moderate level of self-esteem.

Falbo (1981) also reported that only borns may be more self-centered than others. Using a single questionnaire item that asked respondents to estimate how often others had told them that they thought only of themselves, Falbo found that these estimates were higher among only borns than among any nononly category, including first borns. However, the scores of onlies on this item did not differ from the scores of individuals from two-child families. In fact, differences between onlies and others only began to emerge with later-born individuals from families with three or more children. While these results are provocative in view of the only-child stereotype, they do not tell us whether onlies are in fact more self-centered than others. Although such an interpretation is the most obvious one, it is also possible that other people tell onlies that they are self-centered because the stereotype establishes an expectation that alters their perceptions of the only child's behavior. It is possible that the stereotype sets up an expectation for selfish behavior that produces its own confirmation, a process similar to that described by Snyder and Swann (1978) and Snyder, Tanke, and Berscheid (1977) as the self-fulfilling prophecy.

In summary, various studies of the self-esteem of only children have placed this value above, below, and even at par with that of others. This disparity of results is probably attributable to several causes, including the nature of the self-esteem measurement, the age of the subjects, and the effects of stereotype-produced expectations.

INTERPERSONAL ORIENTATION

The popular view of only children suggests that they have a particularly undesirable interpersonal orientation. Because of this popular concern, psychologists have paid considerable attention to this aspect of the only child's personality. The results of these investigations are mixed, but they generally vindicate the only child.

A recent study (Snow, Jacklin, & Maccoby, 1981) examined the sociability of 101 33-month-old children and found that onlies at this age behaved more assertively and positively toward a peer than did later-born children. Snow *et al.* explained this difference in terms of the greater parental attention given to only and first borns than to later borns. In contrast, the weaker sociability found among later borns was explained in terms of undesirable sibling interactions. That is, later borns were thought to develop an aversion to others because they were more likely to be victims of these sibling interactions.

Various studies of the peer popularity of older children portray only children as like first borns or like last borns. In a study of sociometric choices within the classroom, Miller and Maruyama (1976) found that last borns were selected more frequently as playmates and as someone to sit close to than were only and first borns. Likewise, teachers of these students rated later borns as more sociable than only or first borns. Miller and Maruyama suggested that because only and first borns do not have older siblings, they acquire more autocratic, less interactive interpersonal styles and that this has negative consequences for peer popularity. However, contradictory results about only children were observed in an earlier study of peer popularity. Sells and Roff (1963) obtained likeability ratings from same-sex grade school classmates and found that only and last borns received the highest ratings. Given the mixture of results about only children, it is difficult to draw a conclusion about their reception among their peers.

If only children have seriously defective social skills, one would expect them to have a negative mental health record. In general, on a variety of mental health variables, no differences have been found between only and nononly children (Burke, 1956; Howe & Madgett, 1975). In fact, there is some evidence that only children are underrepresented among psychiatric or other clinical clients (Blatz & Bott, 1927; Corfield, 1968; Kurth & Schmidt, 1964; Tuckman & Regan, 1967). However, there is also evidence that only children are more likely to be referred for clinical help (Hough, 1932; Ko & Sun, 1965) and for repeat visits to the clinic (Howe & Madgett, 1975). In all three of these studies, however (Hough, 1932; Howe & Madgett, 1975; Ko & Sun, 1965) the investigators suggested that the most important reason for this relatively high referral and repeat rate was the overprotective attitude of the parents.

One area of interpersonal functioning that has produced a fairly consistent finding about only children is affiliativeness. Early research in this area focused on parent–child interactions. Schachter (1959) argued that onlies and first borns affiliate more during times of stress than do later borns because only- and first-born infants receive more immediate attention when they cry than do later borns. According to Schachter, mothers of first and only borns are more anxious about their babies and therefore respond more promptly to them than to subsequent children. By the time mothers have their second child, their greater experience with babies reduces their anxiety; consequently, they respond less promptly to the cries of the later-born children. Schachter posited that this differential mothering brought about the expectation among only- and first-born adults that other people will be comforting during times of stress. Schachter's early experiments supported this prediction, and the general effect has been replicated in field studies (Hoyt & Raven, 1973) as well as with role-playing techniques (Greenberg, 1967).

In other types of affiliation, however, the accumulating evidence suggests that only children are less affiliative than others, including first borns. Only children have been found to belong to fewer organizations (Blake, 1981; Falbo, 1978a), report having fewer friends (Falbo, 1978a), visit friends and relatives less often (Blake, 1981), and have a less intense social life (Claudy, Farrell, & Dayton, 1979) than others. Consistent with these results, Rosenfeld (1966) compared the need-for-affiliation scores of first and only borns and found first borns to have significantly higher needs for affiliation than only borns. Nonetheless, only children do not appear to suffer from this relatively low affiliation. Among undergraduates, only children reported having numbers of close friends that were comparable to those reported by nononly borns (Falbo, 1978a). Further, only-born undergraduates have been found to be no lonelier than their nononly-born counterparts (Falbo, 1981). Similarly, among adults, only borns express a level of life satisfaction and general happiness that is no different from that of others (Blake, 1981).

The cause of this low affiliativeness among only borns has been explained by the relatively large amounts of affection they receive from their parents. Specifically, Connors (1963) argued that because only children suffer less affection deprivation from their parents than do children with siblings, only children are less motivated to affiliate with others. In a study designed to test the hypothesis that there is a linear continuum of affectional deprivation that goes from only child to last-born child, Connors (1963) was able to support this hypothesis and also to demonstrate an inverse relationship between affection deprivation and affiliation. Therefore, only children may be less affiliative and yet no lonelier than others because of the strong and unbroken parental affection they receive during childhood.

In summary, it appears that only children may be less affiliative than others, but this difference may result from their lack of affection deprivation rather than from their lack of social skills. The mental health record of only children appears to be reasonably good. There are contradictory results regarding the peer popularity of only children.

SUMMARY AND CONCLUSIONS

This chapter has reviewed areas of knowledge about only children that have received some research attention. Certainly, the topics covered here do not exhaust the areas of interest about only children and their families. In particular, we need more longitudinal studies involving the effect of siblings on the development of social skills. In addition, we need to examine the consequences of having no siblings on events of later life, such as caring for elderly parents or coping with widowhood. Much valuable research remains to be done.

This chapter has discussed in detail the most important model that has been used to describe the intellectual development of the only child, the confluence model. After this model was published, the case of the only child appeared closed: Several large-scale surveys had found only children to score less well on intelligence tests than expected. However, more recent investigations have found that only children live up to expectations on intelligence tests, if not on achievement tests (Brackbill & Nichols, 1982). Therefore, the intellectual development of only children is again a topic of discussion. The reasons for these varying results consist of a wide range of confounding variables, including wantedness, father absence, and famine.

The achievement of only children as adults appears to be relatively high, especially in the educational domain. The cause of this high achievement may be related to the greater ability of one-child parents to finance the education of their children (Bayer, 1967; Schooler, 1972). Nonetheless, the cause emphasized in this review was the special relationship only children have with their parents. The unbroken attachment between onlies and their parents, their more adult-oriented home environment, and the high standards set by one-child parents probably all contribute to the facilitation of achievement among only children.

The self-esteem of only children has been repeatedly investigated, usually as part of birth-order studies. Despite the attention paid to this topic, little consistent information has emerged. For example, only children have been found to resemble first borns in having higher (Coopersmith, 1967) as well as lower (Zimbardo & Formica, 1963) self-esteem than others. Solving the self-esteem puzzle will probably require extensive research.

The research on the interpersonal orientation of only children has produced some fairly consistent findings. Recent research with very young children suggests that onlies may have more social skills than children with siblings, especially later-born children. The mental health picture of only children is also positive. Several studies indicate that only children are underrepresented among psychiatric or other clinical clients. Further, many disparate studies of only children agree that only children demonstrate a consistent pattern of affiliativeness. During times of stress, only and first borns appear to be more likely to affiliate with others. Otherwise, only borns appear to affiliate less than others, even though this lowered affiliativeness does not result in increased loneliness or unhappiness for only borns.

Many years ago, Schooler (1972) published a critique of birth-order research that outlined several reasons why birth-order studies produce inconsistent results. Schooler argued that many studies that found specific birth ranks to be overrepresented among special populations, such as alcoholics, schizophrenics, or National Merit Scholars, have generally made the mistaken assumption that birth rank was the cause of the alcoholism, schizophrenia, or scholastic achievement. Schooler demonstrated that many of these findings evaporated when family size, parental education, and the incidence of birth ranks within a comparable normal population was considered. According to Schooler, birth rank *per se* was frequently not the cause of the obtained differences. Other family factors produced an apparent birth-order result. Schooler argued that as long as investigators assume that any observed difference between birth ranks is caused by birth rank and not by other factors, this area of research will continue to be characterized by mixed and often contradictory results.

Similarly, it is argued here that as long as investigators assume that any difference obtained between only borns and others is produced by the only child's lack of siblings, we can expect to continue to produce inconsistent results about only children. Factors other than sibling absence bring about many so-called only-child characteristics. In particular, characteristics of parents and their relationship with their children should be measured and considered. Also, it seems likely that, because of cohort effects, differences found in previous generations may not be repeated within the current generation of only children. The current increase in the number and proportion of parents who voluntarily have only one child should lead to changes in the characteristics of only children as a group. These changes are for future research to uncover.

REFERENCES

Angelini, H. B. Family structure and motivation to achieve. *Revista Interamericana de Psicología*, 1967, *1*(2), 115–125.

Barnes, J., Fisher, J., & Palmer, M. Family characteristics and intellectual growth: An examination by race. *Educational and Psychological Measurement*, 1979, *39*(3), 625–636.

Bayer, A. E. Birth order and attainment of the doctorate: A test of economic hypotheses. *American Journal of Sociology*, 1967, *72*, 540–550.

Belmont, L., & Marolla, F. A. Birth order, family size, and intelligence. *Science*, 1973, *182*, 1096–1101.

Biller, H. B. *Parental deprivation*. Toronto: Lexington Books, 1974.

Blake, J. Can we believe recent data on birth expectation in the United States? *Demography*, 1974, *11*, 25–44.

Blake, J. The only child in America: Prejudice versus performance. *Population and Development Review*, 1981, *1*, 43–54.

Blanchard, R. W., & Biller, H. B. Father availability and academic performance among third grade boys. *Developmental Psychology*, 1971, *4*, 301–305.

Blatz, W. E., & Bott, E. A. Studies in mental hygiene of children: I. Behavior of public school children—a description of method. *Journal of Genetic Psychology*, 1927, *34*, 552–582.

Brackbill, Y., & Nichols, P. L. A test of the confluence model of intellectual development. *Developmental Psychology*, 1982, *18*(2), 192–198.

Breland, H. M. Birth order, family configuration, and verbal achievement. *Child Development*, 1974, *45*, 1011–1019.

Broman, S. H., Nichols, P. L., & Kennedy, W. A. *Preschool IQ: Prenatal and early development correlates*. New York: Wiley, 1975.

Burke, M. O. A search for systematic personality differentiate of the only child in young adulthood. *Journal of Genetic Psychology*, 1956, *89*, 71–84.

Carlsmith, L. Effect of early father absence on scholastic aptitude. *Harvard Educational Review*, 1964, *34*, 3–21.

Claudy, J. G. *Cognitive characteristics of the only child*. Paper presented at the convention of the American Psychological Association, Washington, D.C., 1976.

Claudy, J. G., Farrell, W. S., & Dayton, C. W. *The consequences of being an only child: An analysis of Project TALENT data* (Final Report No. NO1-HD-82854). Washington, D.C.: Center for Population Research, National Institutes of Health, December 1979.

Clausen, J. A. Family structure, socialization, and personality. In L. W. Hoffman

& M. L. Hoffman (Eds.), *Review of child development research* (Vol. 2). New York: Russell Sage Foundation, 1966.

Collins, M. S. *Parental reactions to a visually handicapped child: A mourning process.* Unpublished doctoral dissertation, The University of Texas at Austin, 1982.

Connors, C. K. Birth order and needs for affiliation. *Journal of Personality*, 1963, *31*(3), 409–416.

Coopersmith, S. *The antecedents of self-esteem.* San Francisco: Freeman, 1967.

Corfield, V. K. The utilization of guidance clinic facilities in Alberta, 1961. *Alberta Psychologist*, 1968, *9*(3), 15–45.

Crandall, V. C., Katkovsky, W., & Crandall, V. J. Children's beliefs in their own control of reinforcement in intellectual–academic achievement situations. *Child Development*, 1965, *36*, 91–109.

David, H. P. Unwantedness: Longitudinal studies of Prague children born to women twice denied abortion for the same pregnancy and matched controls. In P. Ahmed (Ed.), *Coping with medical issues: Pregnancy, childbirth, and parenthood.* New York: Elsevier, 1981.

DeJong, G. F., Stokes, S., & Hanson, S. L. *Long term consequences of childlessness and one child on labor force participation, mobility aspirations, and occupational attainment of married women* (Third Progress Report, Contract No. N1-HD-92807). Washington, D.C.: National Institute of Child Mental Health and Human Development, 1980.

Ellis, H. A. *A study of British genius.* London: Hurst & Blackett, 1904.

Falbo, T. Only children and interpersonal behavior: An experimental and survey study. *Journal of Applied Social Psychology*, 1978, *8*, 244–253. (a)

Falbo, T. Reasons for having an only child. *Journal of Population*, 1978, *1*, 181–184. (b)

Falbo, T. Sibling tutoring and other explanations for intelligence discontinuities of only and last borns. *Journal of Population*, 1978, *1*, 345–364. (c)

Falbo, T. Relationships between birth category, achievement, and interpersonal orientation. *Journal of Personality and Social Psychology*, 1981, *41*(1), 121–131.

Falbo, T. Only children in America. In M. Lamb & B. Sutton-Smith (Eds.), *Sibling relationships: Their nature and significance across the lifespan.* Hillsdale, N.J.: Erlbaum, 1982.

Falbo, T., & Snell, W. E. Experimental tests of the sibling tutoring factor. *Texas Population Research Center Papers*, 1982 (Series 4). Austin, Tex.: Population Research Center, University of Texas, 1982.

Fenton, N. The only child. *Journal of Genetic Psychology*, 1928, *35*, 546–556.

Fowler, P. C., & Richards, H. C. Father absence, educational preparedness, and academic achievement: A test of the confluence model. *Journal of Educational Psychology*, 1978, *70*(4), 595–601.

Galbraith, R. C. Sibling spacing and intellectual development: A closer look at the confluence models. *Developmental Psychology*, 1982, *18*(2), 151–173.

Gewirtz, J. L., & Gewirtz, H. B. Stimulus conditions, infant behaviors, and social learning in four Israeli child-rearing environments: A preliminary report illustrating differences in environment and behavior between "only" and "youngest" child. In B. M. Foss (Ed.), *Determinants of infant behavior* (Vol. 3). New York: Wiley, 1965.

Goodenough, F. L., & Leahy, A. M. The effect of certain family relationships upon the development of personality. *Journal of Genetic Psychology*, 1927, *34*, 45–71.

Greenberg, M. S. Role playing: An alternative to deception: *Journal of Personality and Social Psychology*, 1967, 7(2, Pt. 1), 152–157.

Grotevant, H. D., Scarr, S., & Weinberg, R. A. Intellectual development in family constellations with adopted and natural children: A test of the Zajonc and Markus model. *Child Development*, 1977, *48*, 1699–1703.

Guilford, R. B., & Worcester, D. A. A comparative study of the only and nononly child. *Journal of Genetic Psychology*, 1930, *38*, 411–426.

Herzog, E., & Sudia, C. Fatherless homes: A review of research. *Children*, 1968, *15*(5), 177–182.

Hough, E. Some factors in the etiology of maternal over-protection. *Smith College Studies of Social Work*. 1932, *2*, 188–208.

Howe, M. G., & Madgett, M. E. Mental health problems associated with the only child. *Canadian Psychiatric Association Journal*, 1975, *20*(3), 189–194.

Hoyt, M. P., & Raven, B. H. Birth order and the 1971 Los Angeles earthquake. *Journal of Personality and Social Psychology*, 1973, *28*, 123–128.

Jones, H. E. Environmental influence on mental development. In L. Carmichael (Ed.), (*Manual of child psychology* (2nd ed.). New York: Wiley, 1954.

Kammeyer, K. Birth order as a research variable. *Social Forces*, 1967, *46*, 71–80.

Kaplan, H. B. Self-derogation and childhood family structure. *Journal of Nervous and Mental Disease*, 1970, *151*, 13–23.

Kidwell, J. S. Adolescents' perceptions of parental affect: An investigation of only children vs. first-borns and the effect of spacing. *Journal of Population: Behavioral, Social, and Environmental Issues*, 1978, *1*(2), 148–166.

Ko, Y., & Sun, L. Ordinal position and the behavior of visiting the child guidance clinic. *Acta Psychologia Taiwanica*, 1965, 7, 10–16.

Kurth, E., & Schmidt, E. Multidimensional examinations of stuttering children. *Probleme and Efgebnisse der Psychologie*, 1964, *12*, 49–58.

Lees, J. P., & Stewart, A. H. Family or sibship position and scholastic ability: An interpretation. *Sociological Review*, 1957, *5*(2), 173–190.

Lewis, E. J. Psychological determinants of family size: A study of white middle class couples ages 35–45 with zero, one, or three children. *Proceedings of the 80th Annual Convention of the American Psychological Association*, 1972, 7, 665–666.

Lewis, M., & Kreitzberg, V. S. Effects of birth order and spacing on mother–infant interactions. *Developmental Psychology*, 1979, *15*, 617–625.

Lynn, D. B. *The father: His role in child development*. Monterey: Brooks/Cole, 1974.

Marino, C. D., & McCowan, R. J. The effects of parent absence on children. *Child Study Journal*, 1976, *6*(3), 165–182.

Miller, N., & Maruyama, G. Ordinal position and peer popularity. *Journal of Personality and Social Psychology*, 1976, *33*, 123–131.

Oberlander, M., & Jenkin, N. Birth order and academic achievement. *Journal of Individual Psychology*, 1967, *23*(1), 103–109.

Polit, D. F. *The one-parent/one-child family: Social and psychological consequences*

(Final Report, Contract No. NO1-HD-82852). Cambridge, Mass.: American Institute for Research, 1980.

Rodgers, J. L. Confluence effects: Not here, not now! *Developmental Psychology*, in press.

Roe, A. A. Psychological study of eminent psychologists and anthropologists and a comparison with biological and physical scientists. *Psychological Monographs*, 1953, *67*(2, Whole No. 352).

Rosen, B. C. Family structure and achievement motivation. *American Sociological Review*, 1961, *28*, 574–585.

Rosen, B., & D'Andrade, R. C. T. The psychosocial origins of achievement motivation. *Sociometry*, 1959, *22*, 185–218.

Rosenberg, M. *Society and the adolescent self-image*. Princeton, N.J.: Princeton University Press, 1965.

Rosenfeld, H. Relationships of ordinal position to affiliation and achievement motives: Direction and generality. *Journal of Personality*, 1966, *34*, 467–479.

Sampson, E. E., & Hancock, R. F. An examination of the relationship between ordinal position, personality and conformity: An extension, replication, and partial vertification. *Journal of Personality and Social Psychology*, 1967, *5*, 398–407.

Schachter, S. *The psychology of affiliation*. Stanford, Calif.: Stanford University Press, 1959.

Schooler, C. Birth order effects: Not here, not now! *Psychological Bulletin*, 1972, *78*(3), 161–175.

Sells, B., & Roff, M. Peer acceptance–rejection and birth order. *American Psychologist*, 1963, *18*, 355.

Shinn, M. Father absence and children's cognitive development. *Psychological Bulletin*, 1978, *85*(2), 295–324.

Skouholt, T., Moore, E., & Wellman, F. Birth order and academic behavior in first grade. *Psychological Reports*, 1973, *32*, 395–398.

Snow, M. E., Jacklin, C. N., & Maccoby, E. E. Birth-order difference in peer sociability at thirty-three months. *Child Development*, 1981, *52*(2), 589–595.

Snyder, M., & Swann, W. E. Behavioral confirmation in social interaction: From social belief to social reality. *Journal of Experimental Social Psychology*, 1978, *14*, 148–162.

Snyder, M., Tanke, E. D., & Berscheid, E. Social perception and interpersonal behavior: On the self-fulfilling nature of social stereotypes. *Journal of Personality and Social Psychology*, 1977, *35*(9), 656–666.

Solomon, E. S., Clare, J. E., & Westoff, C. F. Social and psychological factors affecting fertility. *The Milbank Memorial Fund Quarterly*, 1956, *34*, 160–177.

Steelman, L. C., & Mercy, J. Unconfounding the confluence model: A test of sibling size and birth order effects on intelligence. *American Sociological Review*, 1980, *45*, 571–582.

Sutton-Smith, B., Rosenberg, B. G., & Landy, F. Father-absence effects in families of different sibling compositions. *Child Development*, 1968, *40*, 1213–1221.

Thompson, V. D. Family size: Implicit policies and assumed psychological outcomes. *Journal of Social Issues*, 1974, *30*, 93–124.

Toman, W. *Family constellation: Its effects on personality and social behavior.* New York: Springer, 1969.

Toman, W., & Toman, E. Sibling positions of a sample of distinguished persons. *Perceptual and Motor Skills*, 1970, *32*, 825–826.

Tuckman, J., & Regan, R. A. Size of family and behavioral problems in children. *Journal of Genetic Psychology*, 1967, *111*(2), 151–160.

Westoff, C. F., & Ryder, N. B. *The contraceptive revolution.* Princeton, N.J.: Princeton University Press, 1977.

Winterbottom, M. R. The relation of need for achievement to learning experiences in independence and mastery. In J. W. Atkinson (Ed.), *Motives in fantasy, action, and society.* Princeton, N.J.: Van Nostrand, 1958.

Zajonc defuses IQ debate: Birth order work wins prize. *APA Monitor*, May 1976, p. 1.

Zajonc, R. B. Birth order and intelligence: Dumber by the dozen. *Psychology Today*, January 1975, 37–43.

Zajonc, R. B., & Markus, G. B. Birth order and intellectual development. *Psychological Review*, 1975, *82*, 74–88.

Zajonc, R, B., Markus, H., & Markus, G. B. The birth order puzzle. *Journal of Personality and Social Psychology*, 1979, *37*(8), 1325–1341.

Zimbardo, P., & Formica, R. Emotional comparisons and self-esteem as determinants of affiliation. *Journal of Personality*, 1963, *31*, 141–162.

·2·

ONLY AND FIRST-BORN CHILDREN: DIFFERENCES IN SOCIAL BEHAVIOR AND DEVELOPMENT

CANDICE FEIRING
MICHAEL LEWIS

INTRODUCTION

It is often claimed that a child receives differential treatment and experience within the family system as a function of ordinal position (e.g., Miley, 1969; Schachter, 1959; Warren, 1966). Some of the more obvious factors that might contribute to differential experiences associated with birth order are parental involvement with the child, availability of parental resources, and interaction and competition among siblings. The effect of birth order on the socialization process has traditionally centered on the parent–child relationship (e.g., Clarke-Stewart, 1973; Jacobs & Moss, 1976; Lewis & Kreitzberg, 1979; Rosenberg & Sutton-Smith, 1969), although more recently the role of the sibling has been given increased attention (Abramovitch, Corter & Lando, 1979; Cicerelli, 1975; Dunn & Kendrick, 1979; Falbo, 1980).

Although birth order has been a topic of interest to psychologists for more than a century (e.g., Galton, 1874), the greatest impetus to the systematic study of birth order effects was provided by Schachter (1959). Schachter observed that under anxiety-provoking conditions, first-born female subjects were more likely to seek out the company of others than were later-born female subjects. Speculating on the nature of this difference, Schachter suggested that through his or her initial experience as the sole focus of parental love and

Candice Feiring and Michael Lewis. Institute for the Study of Child Development, Rutgers Medical School–UMDNJ, New Brunswick, New Jersey.

attention the first born comes to associate the reduction of needs, particularly the reduction of pain and fear, with the presence of others. Later-born children do not enjoy the experience of being the exclusive and constant focus of their parents' attention. Consequently, they have to acquire strategies for tension reduction through their own efforts. In addition, the birth of a younger sibling reduces the first born's status as the primary focus of parental attention and motivates the first born to seek attention, approval, and support from others. Schachter argued that as a consequence of being first born, in later life an individual manifests greater affiliative dependence on others and becomes more conforming to the influence of others than do later born children.

Until recently, research on the effects of family constellation since Schachter's original publication has been characterized, in general, by the following features: (1) the failure to examine only children separately from first borns with younger siblings (e.g., Greenberg, 1967; Hoyt & Raven, 1973; Toman & Toman, 1970), and (2) a strong reliance on the use of adult subjects, usually undergraduates, to form conclusions about behavioral consequences of birth order.

The view that the early experiences of only children and of children with siblings need to be studied separately is supported by Eiduson's (1976) work on the dynamics unique to the one-child family. According to Eiduson, certain family features are important for the only child's development, because from a theoretical perspective they presage unique characteristics of the child's personality. The family environment of the only child is viewed as closely bound and circumscribed. Eiduson asserts that the most salient aspect of the only child's socialization is that there is only one child to absorb parental attention and interest.

The parents' emotional and intellectual investment and sole concern for the only child's needs sets into motion dependency behavior between parents and child. In the only-child family, parents and child remain closely involved with each other, since there is no sibling to dilute parental attention. The parents have the opportunity to spend more time with the child and to take an interest in the child's every experience. The parents are especially sensitive to the impact they have as parents shaping the child's growth and perceive themselves as particularly responsible for what happens to the child.

In the only-child family environment the child is encouraged to become socialized early and rapidly. The only child, like all first-born children, enters an adult household oriented to adult interests, activities, and friends. Eiduson (1976) finds that in only-child families parents expect the child to adjust to them rather than orienting their own life styles toward the child. Her data suggest that parents' personal, social, and economic existence changes very little with the advent of one child, especially as compared to the home that has two or three children. Households with more than one child are rated as more child- than adult-oriented.

As only borns cannot experience loss of parental attention due to the birth of a sibling, they are not exposed to a variety of family experiences available to the first born, such as sibling rivalry or sibling play. Interactions between a first-born child and a new sibling as young as 8 months old are found to be complex, varied, and different from the interactions that children have with their parents (Dunn & Kendrick, 1979). The absence of these more reciprocal and egalitarian sibling interactions within the only child's family implies a difference in the only child's and the first born's early concepts of social objects and their functions. In addition, the nature of the child's social network changes with the number of siblings; thus the addition of siblings influences the first child's development from sources beyond the family (Lewis, Feiring, & Kotsonis, in press).

In a seminal paper on social issues involving family size, Thompson (1974) has argued that if family size recommendations are to reflect a greater understanding of the psychological outcomes for children, adults, and society of having one or more children, a greater research effort is needed to distinguish the behavioral and cognitive outcomes for only children and those for children with siblings. Thompson suggests that since first borns experience many events, in particular "dethroning," which only children do not, it is likely that first borns and only children differ in behavioral patterns. In the birth-order literature, the phenomenon of losing status once held alone, that is, as the only child, has been given special focus in regard to the development of the first-born child and has been labeled "dethronement." According to Bossard and Boll (1960), the first born is the sole focus of parental attention until the birth of a second child. First borns, who until the birth of a sibling are only-born children, have supposedly learned to orient themselves to the behavior of their parents while at the same time they have learned to expect their parents to be pliant and accommodating. With the arrival of a second child, first borns experience a loss of status as the only focus of their parents' attention and seek to reassert their claim on that attention in ways labeled as demanding. With the arrival of a second child, the potential for dethronement of the first child is high, especially when the spacing interval between siblings is small. Based on extensive clinical observations in the home, White (1975) asserts that the mother–child relationship is adversely affected by close spacing between the first and second child. Lewis and Kreitzberg (1979), in a home observation study of the mother–child interaction as a function of birth order and spacing, found that spacing played an important role in determining the amount of positive interaction between a mother and her child. Children spaced more than 4 years apart were treated more like first borns than like later borns.

The research of Dunn and her associates (Dunn & Kendrick, 1979, 1980; Dunn, Kendrick, & MacNamee, 1981) has examined how the birth of a sibling affects the relationship between the mother and the first-born child. It was found that the presence of a second-born sibling affected the amount of time the mother had available for interacting with the first born. The presence of the second-born child was associated with a decrease in the frequency of the mother's initiation periods of joint play, attention, and conversational episodes and with an increase in the frequency of prohibitive commands. The behavior of the first born also changed with the addition of a new child to the family. The first born showed an increase in demanding and negative behavior directed at the mother as well as increases in sleeping, toilet, and feeding problems. However, increases in autonomous behavior were also noted. Research conducted by Jacobs and Moss (1976) found that first borns' demand for attention from their mothers was associated with maternal caretaking and social interaction with the second-born child. Taylor and Kogan (1973) found that interactions between mothers and their first-born children were characterized by increased emotional flatness and decreased expressions of warmth following the birth of a sibling. The phenomenon of dethronement, as evidenced by the first-born child's increased demands upon the mother on the birth of a second child, has thus received some research support.

It has been postulated (Falbo, 1977) that the only child's uninterrupted relationship with the parents might enhance achievement.

The intensely focused attention of one-child parents to their child has been demonstrated by Gewirtz and Gewirtz (1965), who found that mothers of only children interacted with their children twice as much as did mothers of last borns. Another study concluded that mothers were more involved with the activities of their first-born and only children than with their later borns (Hilton, 1967).

An important theme in the recent research on only children is the importance of avoiding the negative stereotypes that surround only children and their parents (Falbo, 1979; Thompson, 1974). One-child parents have been stereotyped as being less socially acceptable, more self-centered, immature, and less friendly and good natured than persons who had more than one child (Polit, 1978). Pinner and Thompson (1974) found that the concept of "only child" was rated consistently more negatively on semantic differentials and on the adjective checklist than was the concept of a child with two siblings. Falbo (1979) found that only children reported having fewer friends and belonging to fewer clubs than did individuals with siblings. However, these same only children reported having a comparable number of close friends and leadership positions in clubs. Thus it appears that the nature of the only child's social network is different from that of children with siblings, a finding in agreement with the recent work of Lewis *et al.* (in press).

The inaccurate characterization of the only child as selfish, lonely, and maladjusted may be a central factor in deterring parents from having a single child. In a study by Hawke and Knox (1978), both the positive and negative consequences of having an only child were examined when 102 parents and 105 only children were questioned about their family lives. Of the only children interviewed, 98% stated that there were advantages to being an only child, which included "avoiding sibling rivalry, more privacy, enjoying greater affluence." Parents reported advantages such as having more personal time and having closer relationships with their child. Only children reported disadvantages as well, and spoke of missing the companionship of a sibling and feeling extra pressure to succeed. Parents reported walking "a tightrope . . . between healthy attention and overindulgence" and having trouble facing criticism from the outside world for being too "selfish" to have more than one child.

Determining the characteristics and experiences of only and first-born children would thus seem important in order to provide valid information for those seeking and offering family planning counseling as well as for the conceptualization of child development. Although recent research efforts in the area of family constellations have addressed some issues relevant to the behavior of first borns and only children, relatively little empirical information regarding the early differences between children with and without siblings is available. Since a clearer understanding of the sources of differences between families with only and first-born children can emerge, particularly through observation of very young children in interaction with their parents, our research emphasizes the differences between only and first-born children in the context of the early mother–child relationship in the first 3 years of life.

In examining our data on the social behavior of first-born and only children and their mothers, we were interested in the determinants of development within and across age levels. Generally, determinants of development have been classified as endogenous, that is, residing in processes internal to the organism, or as exogenous, that is, residing in the environment (Lewis & Starr, 1979). At a given age or in assessing the stability of individual differences over the course of development it is difficult to disentangle the contributions of endogenous and exogenous processes (Kagan, 1971). Although it is fruitless to argue that one class of variables operates to the exclusion of the other, our task is to determine the relative contribution of both endogenous and exogenous influences and of their interaction to the emergence of a particular response pattern or developmental sequence in first-born as compared to only-born children.

The endogenous sources for differences between only and first-born children involve the characteristics of the children themselves. For example, first-born and only children may be different because of variations in temperament or personality factors. The model of the passive child who is socialized by responding to the environment, in particular the young child responding to the parents, has been fairly well refuted (Bell, 1971; Lewis & Rosenblum, 1974). The effect of the child on parent–child interactions has been observed to vary with such factors as the child's sex (Lewis, 1972; Parke & Sawin, 1975), age of child (Harper, 1975), and temperament (Carey, 1970; Chess, Thomas, & Cameron, 1976; Feiring & Lewis, 1980). A study conducted by Van den Berg and Oechsli (1980) suggests that the physical attributes and development of only and first-born children may be different. Data based on developmental examinations at 5 years of age indicated that only borns have higher heart rate and systolic pressure than first borns. Only borns were also reported to need fewer hours of sleep and to be less easily tired than first borns. First borns scored lower on physical measures correlated with obesity and were rated as more acceptable in physical appearance than onlies.

One major exogenous source of differences in only and first-born children is related to parental characteristics and behavior. The effect of parents on children has been a major theme in the study of child development since its beginning (Hartup, 1978; Lewis & Goldberg, 1969). Parents have been shown to influence their child's social (Clarke-Stewart, 1973, 1978; Lamb, 1976; Lewis & Rosenblum, 1979) as well as cognitive development (Lewis, 1976). In a study by Falbo (1978a), several differences between mothers of only children and mothers of two or more children were examined in an attempt to determine the reasons why mothers decided to have just one child. Mothers of only children were twice as likely to have had complications during pregnancy and were more likely to have an unstable marriage than were mothers of two or more children. Consequently, differences in only and first-born children may be caused by their parents' beliefs about such issues as family planning, marriage, pregnancy, and child-rearing practices as well as differences in patterns of parent–child interaction.

Another exogenous source of difference between only and first-born children is the birth and presence of a second child. In other words, first-born children may be different from only-born children in that they must learn to adjust to the presence of another child into a family in which they had previously been the only child. While only children may experience uninterrupted parental focus, first borns must give up their parents' undivided attention upon the birth of a second child. Dunn *et al.* (1981) showed that after the birth of a second child, first borns show an increase in sleep disturbances as well as an increase in behaviors reflecting independence.

In order to explore some of these endogenous and exogenous factors, the authors examined data from a large longitudinal study of children. These data constitute one of the few research efforts that provide empirical, longitudinal information on the behavior of first- and only-born children and their mothers at early age points. Since a clearer understanding of developmental differences between first-born and only children can emerge through close observation of the infant in interaction with the mother, this study focuses on the inception and growth of social–emotional patterns in the context of the mother–child relationship. Such an approach should provide a firmer and more precise understanding of how and why differences emerge between only and first borns in later life.

METHOD

Considerations in Defining an "Only Child"

A child who has no siblings may be defined as an "only child." Within the class of young children who have no siblings, some will remain onlies, whereas others will be dethroned and will become the first born of two or more children in the family constellation. All the first and only children on whom this chapter is based were part of a larger study of children and their mothers that examined the relationship between birth order, socioeconomic status, and sex on the development of the young child (Lewis, 1978). In order to define our sample more accurately, we utilized information from an interview conducted in the 3rd year of our investigation, in which mothers were asked to provide us with up-to-date information about children born into the family since the beginning of the study and plans for future children. In the current report, an "only child" is defined retrospectively as a child who did not acquire a sibling during the course of our 3½-year investigation, whereas a "first-born" child is defined as a child who did acquire a sibling at some point during the investigation.

Defining the Sample

Fifty-six first-born children were observed at 3, 12, and 24 months of age. The sample consisted of 21 only children (children who did not acquire a sibling in the first 48 months of life) and 35 first-born children (children who acquired a sibling between the ages of 24 and 36 months). Of the 21 only children, 12 were female and 9 were male. Of the 35 first-born children, 16 were female and 19 were male. It should be noted that all the analyses comparing only and first-born children at 3 and 12 months were retrospective in nature. That is, in reality, all the children were only borns, (had no siblings) at 3 and

12 months of age. By 24 months of age, 10 children had already become first borns, and the remainder of the sample of first borns acquired siblings by or soon after 36 months of age.

Observation and Recording of Mother–Infant Interaction

Age 3 Months: Home Observation

Each mother–infant pair was observed in the home for a 2-hour period while the infant was awake. Preparatory to observation, the observer briefly explained the purpose of the observation, showed the mother the material being used, tried to put the mother at ease, and instructed the mother to continue with her normal routine and ignore the observer. Upon completion of the 2 hours of observation mothers were given a general-information questionnaire concerning the child's history, parental demographic characteristics, and issues pertaining to childbirth and family planning.

Infant behaviors coded at 3 months were (1) eyes closed, (2) vocalization, (3) extra movement, (4) fret/cry, (5) feed—bottle, (6) feed—spoon, (7) play—object, (8) play—person, (9) play—self, (10) smile/laugh, (11) burp, sneeze, cough, (12) looking at mother, and (13) sucking—nonfeed. Mother behaviors coded at 3 months were (1) touch, (2) hold, (3) vocalization to infant, (4) vocalization to other, (5) look, (6) smile/laugh, (7) play with child, (8) change diaper/bathe, (9) feed, (10) rock child, (11) read/TV, (12) kiss, and (13) give toy/pacifier.

All behaviors (13 for the mother and 13 for the infant) were coded every 10 seconds on machine-scorable checklists. Primary locations such as crib, lap, floor, and so forth were noted for each 10-second interval. In order to ensure accurate timing for coding behavior, the observer used a small timing device which only she could hear.

Ages 12 and 24 Months: Playroom Observation

At ages 12 and 24 months, mother–infant dyads were observed in a playroom at the laboratory. The dyad was left alone in the 10 × 12-foot playroom, which was marked with carpet squares and contained

13 toys, a chair, a table, and a magazine. The mother and infant were observed through a one-way mirror and videotaped. The observation consisted of a 15-minute free-play period in an unstructured situation in which mother and infant had the opportunity to interact with toys.

While watching the mother–child dyad through a one-way mirror, an observer dictated the ongoing behaviors and interactions on to tape so that these behaviors could later be transcribed and coded on to machine-readable sheets for analysis.

Infant behaviors coded at 12 and 24 months were (1) vocalization, (2) look, (3) smile, (4) touch, (5) fret/cry, (6) seek approval, (7) seek help, (8) gesture, (9) seek proximity, (10) toy/nontoy, (11) move/door, (12) lap, and (13) hold/hug. Maternal behaviors coded at 12 and 24 months were (1) vocalization, (2) look, (3) smile, (4) touch, (5) kiss, (6) hold, (7) give direction, (8) read, (9) seek proximity, (10) toy/nontoy, (11) show toy, (12) manipulate toy, and (13) demonstrate toy. At 12 and 24 months, for analysis purposes, mother behaviors were grouped as proximal (touch, kiss, hold, seek proximity) and distal (vocalize, look, smile, give direction). Infant behaviors were also grouped as proximal (same square, touch, seek proximity, lap, hold/hug) and distal (vocalize, look, smile, fret/cry, gesture).

Coding of Social Interaction Data at 3, 12, and 24 Months

The mother–infant interaction data at all age groups was coded in several ways (Lewis & Lee-Painter, 1974). A distinction was made between behaviors that occurred in interaction (as an initiation or a response) and those that simply occurred. This scheme allowed for the recording of both the frequency and the nature of the mother–infant interactions.

Behavior Frequency and Groups

The first type of coding analysis involved the frequency of behavior occurrences. At 3 months, behaviors were coded in 10-second intervals. Since a given behavior could be recorded only once (as an occurrence, initiation, or response) within one 10-second period, a particular frequency reflects the number of 10-second intervals in which the behavior occurred. At 12 and 24 months, the amount of behavior is reported in terms of the actual frequency, or number of time each behavior occurred over the observation period.

Factor Analysis on Child and Mother Social Behaviors at 3, 12, and 24 Months

In order to characterize social behaviors of mothers and children in terms of general categories, factor analyses were performed on child and mother behaviors separately at each of the 3-, 12-, and 24-month age points. This factor analysis was performed on the total sample of children participating in the longitudinal study, which included, in addition to only- and first-borns, second-, third-, and fourth-born children (Jaskir & Lewis, 1981). Factors that described child and mother behavior patterns at each age level were derived for the total sample and then used to derive scores for the subsample of first-born and only children.

Interactive Analyses at 3, 12, and 24 Months

Deeper levels of coding were employed in an attempt to characterize the nature of mother–infant interaction. One type of interactive analysis involved complex interactions between mother and infant in terms of initiations and response frequency. In the complex interactive analysis, total numbers of interactions as well as maternal initiating and responding behavior were examined. As a result of the complex interactive coding, a selection of interactions that occurred with relatively high frequency was subjected to analysis. These selected interactions were also directed interactions: That is, they were either mother initiated (e.g., mother vocalize—infant look) or infant initiated (e.g., infant fret/cry—mother look) and could be characterized by two-link chains. These selected directed interactions were, like the complex interactions, examined in terms of frequency.

Measurement of the Social Networks of Only and First-Born Children at 36 Months

Although no observations of mother–child interaction were conducted at age 36 months, data were available on the composition of the child's social network for 15 only children and 23 first-born children. Mothers completed an adapted version of the Pattison Psychosocial Network Inventory (Pattison, 1975), on which they listed every person who came into contact (by phone, letter, or face to face) with their child. Mothers specified the sex of each person in their child's network, the frequency with which each person was contacted, and the type of relationship (e.g., brother, aunt, friend, babysitter, etc.) each person had with their child. Networks were analyzed in terms of subcategories of people, such as nonrelative adults, peer friends, and relatives, which were derived from the mothers' reports of their children's contacts.

Two attributes of the network, size and average frequency of contact, were analyzed for each category of persons within the network. The size of a network category was computed by simply adding up the total number of people within that category, regardless of the frequency with which they were contacted. The frequency measure for the network categories provide an indication of the average amount of exposure the child received from network members: the mean number of contacts with people. It should be noted that since the average frequency index is a proportional measure, average frequency scores for network categories can be directly compared regardless of network size. Whether contact was made daily, weekly, monthly, or twice or once a year for each category of person comprising the social network was also analyzed.

THE SOCIAL–EMOTIONAL FUNCTIONING OF ONLY AND FIRST-BORN CHILDREN AT 3, 12, 24, AND 36 MONTHS

Means were generated for the social variables at each age level for only and first-born children and their mothers. Because in most cases the measures on social data were not normally distributed, nonparametric tests were used to examine differences between the first and only classifications. Unless otherwise stated, the Mann–Whitney

U Test was used for comparisons between groups. In the results that follow, data are reported on (1) the mother–infant interaction in the first two years; (2) the birth of a sibling and its effect on the first-born child and the mother from 12 to 24 months; (3) characteristics of the social networks of first and only children at 36 months; and (4) the relationship between early child and mother behavior and later child functioning for first and only groups from 3 to 24 months.

Social Data at 3 Months

Infant Behavior

At 3 months of age, onlies (infants who remained only children as of the 3rd-year visit) showed a tendency to move, cry, and burp and sneeze more than first borns (infants who acquired a sibling before or soon after the 3rd-year visit; see Table 2.1). Of these behaviors only crying approached significance. First borns, on the other hand, showed a tendency to vocalize, play, smile, suck, and be fed by spoon more frequently than only borns. These differences were significant for spoon feeding ($Z = 2.20$, $p = .03$) and approached significance for smiling behavior. First borns play, vocalize, and smile more and cry less than onlies. Taken together, the data suggest that at 3 months first-born children are less fussy and more sociable than those children who will remain onlies at least for the opening 40 months of life. At 3 months of age, there are no statistically reliable differences between only and first-born children on the derived social factor scores.

Maternal Behavior

When their infants are 3 months old, mothers of onlies (mothers who will not have another child at least for 40 months) touch, bathe, rock, kiss, play with, look at, vocalize to the infant, vocalize to others, and read or watch TV more than mothers of first borns; see Table 2.1). Mothers of first borns feed their children more than mothers of onlies. Of these differences, rocking and kissing are significant ($Z = 3.36$, $p = .001$ for rocking; $Z = 2.14$, $p = .03$ for kissing). The data indicate that mothers of onlies are more frequently in proximal contact (touch, rock, kiss, bathe) with their infants than mothers of

Table 2.1. Infant and Maternal Behavior at 3 Months

	TOTAL ($n = 56$)	ONLY BORNS ($n = 21$)	FIRST BORNS ($n = 35$)
	INFANT		
Close eyes	6.59	7.24	6.20
Vocalize	163.2	158.0	166.4
Extra movement	92.5	97.4	89.5
Cry	70.8	83.5	63.2
Feed—bottle	91.4	90.3	92.1
Feed—spoon	22.7	19.5	24.6
Play—object	138.7	132.4	142.4
Play—person	15.7	13.4	17.1
Play—self	15.3	11.0	18.0
Smile	47.5	34.5	55.2
Burp/sneeze	19.0	22.2	17.1
Look	160.5	157.5	162.3
Suck	59.9	50.5	65.5
	MOTHER		
Touch	85.0	98.6	76.9
Hold	230.0	228.1	231.1
Vocalize—infant	260.3	276.1	250.9
Vocalize—other	127.6	146.1	116.6
Look	312.9	330.3	302.5
Smile	96.3	98.0	95.3
Play	41.5	49.7	36.6
Bathe	59.5	65.2	56.1
Feed	114.9	106.8	119.8
Rock	28.8	51.1	15.6
Read/TV	26.3	32.1	22.8
Kiss	13.9	20.2	10.1
Toy	24.0	24.8	23.7

Note. The social data present the mean number of 10-second intervals at which a behavior occurred at least once during the 2-hour observation in the home.

first borns. Mothers of onlies are also more frequently engaged in distal contact with their child (looking and vocalizing) than mothers of first borns). Given the tendency for onlies to cry more, it is not surprising to find that their mothers rock them more than mothers of first borns. It is possible that only infants, because they are more fussy, require or demand more monitoring behavior on the part of the mother. However, mothers of onlies also appear to spend more time vocalizing to others and reading and watching TV, activities that are not infant directed or that indicate that they may be more active in general than mothers of first borns.

At 3 months, the derived social factor scores indicate that mothers of onlies show a tendency to engage in more Social Interaction with their children than mothers of first borns ($t\ (2, 54) = 1.87$, $p < .07$). The data further suggest (although the differences are not statistically significant) that mothers of onlies show more Active Play as well as more Nonattend behavior than mothers of firsts. There are no differences between the mothers on the Caregiving factor. The analysis of individual maternal behaviors indicated that mothers of onlies were more frequently in proximal contact (touch, rock, kiss) and distal contact (look, vocalize) and were more likely to watch TV and vocalize to others than mothers of first borns. Mothers of onlies are more socially interactive both with their infants and with others than mothers of firsts.

Mother–Child Interaction at 3 Months

Only borns initiate interaction more and have mothers who are more responsive than first-born children, although these differences are not significant. However, the data suggest that the responsiveness of the mothers of only borns may be related to the fact that the only-born infants show a tendency to cry more than first-born children. In support of this hypothesis, we find that mothers of onlies are more responsive to infant cry than mothers of first borns. Further, the data suggest that only infants are less responsive in terms of positive social behaviors (as noted previously, they smile and play less). First-born infants smile more and have mothers who are more responsive to their smiling than only-born infants ($Z = 2.18$, $p = .03$).

Social Data at 12 Months

Infant Behavior

At 12 months of age there are no reliable differences between only and first-born children on social behavior frequency data (see Table 2.2), although only-born infants show less Social Play ($t\ (2,51) = 1.86$, $p < .07$) and tend to Comfort Seek less than first borns. Also, first borns tend to be characterized by less Solitary Play than only borns.

Table 2.2. Child and Mother Behavior Frequencies at 12 Months

	TOTAL ($n = 53$)	ONLY BORNS ($n = 21$)	FIRST BORNS ($n = 32$)
	CHILD BEHAVIORS		
Vocalize	20.3	18.0	21.7
Look	13.1	11.2	14.3
Smile	6.0	7.1	5.2
Touch	1.2	1.3	1.2
Cry	.6	.2	.8
Seek approval	.02	.0	.0
Seek help	.1	.14	.0
Gesture	1.2	1.5	1.1
Seek proximity	.6	.3	.8
Toy play	50.0	50.9	49.5
Move door	.1	.14	.1
Lap	.1	.3	.0
Hug	.0	.0	.0
Proximal	11.9	13.5	10.9
Distal	41.1	38.0	43.1
Total social behavior	93.8	91.8	95.2
	MATERNAL BEHAVIORS		
Vocalize	29.5	28.8	30.0
Look	48.4	48.0	48.6
Smile	21.0	19.8	21.8
Touch	2.1	3.0	1.5
Kiss	.04	.05	.0
Hold	.3	.4	.2
Give directions	3.0	2.8	3.2
Read	7.8	4.8	9.7
Maintain proximity	.0	.0	.0
Toy play	13.6	17.0	11.3
Show approval	1.0	1.0	.9
Proximal	2.4	3.4	1.8
Distal	109.7	104.1	113.3
Total social behavior	127.0	126.1	127.7

Maternal Behavior

Mothers of only children touch their infants more ($Z = 3.49, p = .001$) and, in general, are more proximal in their behavior than mothers of first borns ($Z = 2.54, p = .01$). Mothers of onlies also play more with their children than mothers of firsts ($Z = 1.93$, $p = .05$). The data indicate that mothers of onlies smile in response to infant smiling more than mothers of firsts ($Z = 6.32$, $p < .0001$, for infant smile–mother smile; $Z = 6.22$, $p = .03$, for infant smile–mother total).

For derived social factors at 12 months, mothers of first borns show less Proximal Contact ($t\ (2, 51) = 2.03$, $p < .05$) and less Active Play than mothers of onlies. Mothers of onlies show slightly more Directive Play and Distal Contact compared to mothers of firsts.

Mothers of onlies show more proximal kinds of behavior toward their children than mothers of firsts, a pattern that was also in evidence at 3 months. In addition, mothers of onlies play more with their children. Thus, of those behaviors that show significant differences, mothers of onlies direct more of these behaviors toward their children than mothers of firsts at both 3 and 12 months. It is also interesting to note that whereas at 3 months only borns show a tendency to cry more and first borns show a tendency to smile more, these infants differences are absent by 12 months.

Social Data at 24 Months

Infant Behavior

At 24 months first-born infants show a tendency to gesture more than onlies ($Z = 1.73$, $p = .09$). Otherwise, there are no diffrences between onlies and firsts at this age level, except that only infants show more toy play in response to maternal direction giving than do first borns ($Z = 2.52$, $p = .01$).

For derived social factors at 24 months, first-born children show more Comfort Seeking than only-born children, although these differences are not significant. Both first-born and only groups show less Social Play and less Proximal Contact than the total sample of children on whom the factors were derived at 24 months.

Maternal Behavior

Table 2.3 presents maternal behavior at infant age 24 months and indicates that mothers of onlies tend to show more approval than mothers of first borns ($Z = 1.64$, $p = .10$). No other differences in behavior frequency were noted at this age level. However, mothers of

Table 2.3. Child and Mother Behavior Frequencies at 24 Months

	TOTAL ($n = 49$)	ONLY BORNS ($n = 18$)	FIRST BORNS ($n = 31$)
CHILD BEHAVIORS			
Vocalize	37.4	35.8	38.4
Look	18.7	18.8	18.7
Smile	9.2	9.0	9.4
Touch	.6	.6	.7
Cry	.8	.1	1.2
Seek approval	.2	.0	.3
Seek help	.8	.4	.9
Gesture	3.5	2.8	3.9
Seek proximity	.5	.5	.55
Toy play	52.2	53.4	51.5
Move door	.9	.4	1.2
Lap	.8	.1	1.2
Hug	.04	.1	.0
Proximal	17.1	14.9	18.3
Distal	69.7	66.5	71.6
Total social behavior	158.0	125.4	129.5
MATERNAL BEHAVIORS			
Vocalize	44.4	44.1	44.6
Look	45.1	44.9	45.3
Smile	16.6	14.2	18.0
Touch	2.4	2.5	2.4
Kiss	.1	.2	.1
Hold	.4	.3	.5
Give directions	4.9	5.0	4.8
Read	6.1	8.4	4.8
Maintain proximity	.0	.0	.0
Toy play	16.7	17.6	16.2
Show approval	3.0	3.6	2.7
Proximal	2.9	3.0	2.9
Distal	114.0	111.8	115.3
Total social behavior	141.4	142.5	140.7

onlies do show more approval to infant toy play than mothers of firsts ($Z = 2.31$, $p = .02$). For social factors at 24 months, mothers of first borns show more Distal Contact and more Active Play than mothers of only borns, although these differences are not significant.

To summarize briefly, differences between only and first-born children are more evident at very early than at later periods of development. At 3 months of age, only infants cry more and smile less then first-born infants. However, these differences disappeared by 12 and 24 months, and the two groups are very similar in the behaviors observed. Mothers of onlies have more proximal contact with their children than mothers of first borns, a pattern that persists from ages 3 to 12 months. At 24 months, mothers of onlies tend to show more approval, especially of toy play, than mothers of first borns.

The Effect of the Birth of a Sibling

The arrival of a second child creates a high potential for dethronement of the first child, especially when the interval between siblings is small. Although the data analysis discussed previously established several differences between the social behaviors of onlies and first borns, further analyses were deemed necessary in order to examine more closely the consequences of dethronement resulting from the birth of a closely spaced sibling.

For the purposes of these analyses, all first-born children who did not have a sibling at age 24 months and all only borns were compared to first borns who acquired a sibling by age 24 months. Repeated-measures ANOVAs were performed to identify group differences and group $\times$ time interactions between the behaviors at 12 months (at which time no siblings were born yet) and the behaviors at 24 months (siblings had been born within the past year for early first borns of the groups). In addition, discriminant analyses were conducted to help determine whether and how the birth of a sibling affects the first-born child's relationship with the mother.

First Borns with and without Siblings

In general, the data indicate that first-born children who have acquired a sibling by age 2 show a greater tendency to increase dependency behaviors toward their mothers than do children who will become first borns and those who will remain onlies (see Table 2.4). Early first-born children (those with siblings) show a greater increase in seeking help from their mothers (group $\times$ time interaction F (1,46) $= 2.91$, $p \leq .05$) from 12 to 24 months and show more help-seeking behavior (group effect F (1,47) $= 2.03$, $p \leq .10$) than do later first

Table 2.4. Social Data for First-Born Subjects at 12 and 24 Months as a Function of the Birth of a Younger Sibling

	EARLY FIRST BORNS*		LATER FIRST BORNS†	
	12 MONTHS ($n = 8$)	24 MONTHS ($n = 8$)	12 MONTHS ($n = 39$)	24 MONTHS ($n = 39$)
INFANT SOCIAL BEHAVIORS				
Look	13.38	19.63	13.10	18.92
Touch	1.75	1.38	1.28	.49
Vocalize	18.38	37.25	20.87	37.28
Cry	1.63	4.50	.41	.10
Seek approval	0.0	.50	.03	.15
Seek help	0.0	1.50	.08	.64
Gesture	2.13	2.75	1.10	3.77
Seek proximity	1.13	1.38	.59	.38
Toy play	47.00	50.13	50.26	52.56
Door-oriented	.25	2.25	.08	.67
On mother's lap	0.0	.75	.13	.82
Smile	5.63	7.38	6.44	9.59
Proximal behavior	12.50	21.50	12.56	16.10
Distal behavior	41.13	71.50	41.92	69.67
Hold toy	23.13	17.13	21.67	18.36
Explore toy	38.75	55.00	42.44	55.21
Share toy	1.13	4.00	2.08	4.87
MATERNAL SOCIAL BEHAVIORS				
Look	52.13	45.00	47.51	45.59
Smile	26.75	21.88	20.90	15.44
Kiss	0.0	0.0	.05	.13
Hold	.13	.75	.36	.36
Give directions	4.25	5.00	2.77	4.85
Read magazine	6.38	5.13	8.05	6.26
Vocalize	37.38	43.88	27.77	44.28
Toy play	9.00	15.00	15.46	16.48
Show approval	1.38	2.38	.92	3.26
Proximal behavior	2.63	21.50	2.46	16.10
Distal behavior	126.88	118.13	107.00	113.41
Demonstrate toy	7.25	7.00	12.56	8.77
Give toy	1.63	2.13	3.28	2.13
Accept toy	0.0	1.88	.44	2.26
Remove toy	.50	.38	.18	.36
Manipulate toy	1.00	5.88	1.85	5.23
Touch infant	2.50	4.38	2.05	2.07

*Sibling acquired before 24 months.
†No sibling at 24 months.

borns (those without siblings) and onlies. Early first borns also seek more proximity to the mother (group effect F (1,47) = 3.5, $p \leq .06$) compared to later first borns and onlies. Although there is a trend for early first borns to increase their proximity behavior to their mothers from ages 12 to 24 months, later first borns and onlies in contrast show a tendency to decrease their proximity behavior. In addition, early first borns show an increase in crying from 12 to 24 months, while later first borns and onlies show a decrease in this behavior (group × time interaction F (1,46) = 5.74, $p \leq .02$). At 12 months, early first borns show a slight tendency to cry more than later first borns and onlies, whereas by 24 months this difference in cry behavior has become larger (group effect F (1,47) = 4.36, $p \leq .04$). Thus, in a free-play laboratory setting, from ages 12 to 24 months, children who acquire a sibling show an increase in upset and dependency behavior toward their mothers. In addition, data gathered from observation of reunion sessions with mothers after separation indicate that early first borns show a tendency to increase crying from ages 12 to 24 months, whereas later first borns and onlies show a decrease in crying (group × time interaction F (1,46) = 5.55, $p = \leq .02$) over the same period. Early first borns also show a significant decrease in toy play during a reunion with mothers from ages 12 to 24 months, whereas later first borns and onlies show an increase in play (group × time interaction F (1,46) = 6.04, p = .02). In general, these results support the notion that first borns who acquire a sibling, especially with close spacing, experience dethroning, as evidenced by an increase in dependency behavior toward their mothers (Bossard & Boll, 1960; Schachter, 1959; White, 1975). That our findings based on laboratory observation are consistent with the work of other investigators based on home observation (Dunn & Kendrick, 1979) is also notable. The data suggest that even in a laboratory, when the younger sibling is not present, early first borns show more dependency behavior to their mothers than later first borns and onlies at 24 months.

Mothers of Children with and without Siblings

In general, the data indicate that mothers of early first borns show an increase in proximal and a decrease in distal behavior by the time the first child is 24 months old, whereas mothers of later first borns and onlies show the opposite trend (see Table 2.4). Specifically, mothers of early first borns show a tendency to increase touching their children by 24 months, whereas mothers of later first borns and onlies without siblings show no such increase (group × time interaction F (1,46) = 2.5, p = .10). Overall, but especially at 24 months, mothers of early first borns with siblings touch their children significantly more than mothers of later first borns and onlies without siblings (group effect F (1,47) = 4.07, p = .05). In regard to distal behavior (vocalization, looking, smiling, and giving directions) by 24 months mothers of early first borns show more distal behavior compared to mothers of later first borns and onlies (group effect F (1,47) = 4.5, p = .05). However, mothers of early first borns show a tendency to decrease distal behavior, whereas mothers of later first borns and onlies show a tendency to increase distal behavior (group × time interaction F (1,47) = 3.04, p = .09). In general, the data suggest that mothers of first borns who have acquired a sibling by 24 months direct more attention to their children in terms of the amount of touching and distal behavior toward the child. After the birth of a second child, they show a tendency to increase their proximal behavior and decrease their distal behavior to the child, perhaps in response to the early first born child's increased dependency demands at 24 months. In contrast, mothers of later first borns and onlies show an increase in distal and a decrease in touching behavior and have children who demand less and become less upset by the laboratory setting at 24 months. Taken together, the data on mother and child behavior indicate that the birth of a sibling does affect the mother–child relationship in ways consistent with theory.

When two groups are compared in terms of many variables, it is of interest not only to see if they differ significantly but also to understand the nature of the difference. When comparing two groups on a number of variables individually, there is a tendency to distort group differences, especially as the correlation between the variables increases. Discriminant analysis provides a means of examining the nature of group differences in terms of a given set of variables rather than looking at variables separately without regard to partly overlapping information (Tatsuoka, 1970). Consequently, in order to determine what set of variables distinguished first borns with siblings by 24 months from first borns and onlies without siblings by 24 months, we performed discriminant analyses on the social be-

Table 2.5. Discriminant Analysis Distinguishing between First-Born Children Who Acquired a Sibling by 24 Months and First-Born Children Who Did Not Acquire a Sibling on the Basis of Child Social Behavior at 24 Months

ANALYSIS

24-MONTHS CHILD SOCIAL VARIABLES	STANDARDIZED DISCRIMINANT FUNCTION COEFFICIENTS
Smile	−.34
Cry	.97
Seek approval	.62
Seek help	.56
Toy play	.74

CLASSIFICATION*

TOTAL SAMPLE ($n = 49$)	EARLY FIRST BORNS ($n = 9$)	LATER FIRST BORNS ($n = 40$)
77.6%	66.7%	80%

*Percentage correctly classified.

haviors of mothers and children separately. Table 2.5 shows the results of the discriminant analysis on the child variables. Using the child behaviors of crying, seeking approval, seeking help, toy play, and smiling, we found that it is possible to correctly classify 78% of the children. The discriminant function correctly classified 67% of the children with siblings and 80% of the children without siblings. The discriminant analysis indicated that not only dependency behaviors but also toy-play behavior were important in describing the differences between early and later first-born children.

Table 2.6 shows the results of the discriminant analysis on the mothers' social variables. Overall, 86% of the mothers were correctly classified; 100% of the mothers with early first borns and 83% of the mothers of later first borns and onlies were correctly identified. The mothers' behaviors used in the discriminant analysis were proximal behaviors (holding, touching, and kissing), distal behaviors (vocalization and showing approval), and toy play. The results of the discriminant analysis indicated that, based on a diverse set of social behaviors, mothers as a group behaved differently toward their first children depending on whether they had a second child.

Table 2.6. Discriminant Analysis Distinquishing between First-Born Children Who Acquired a Sibling by 24 Months and First-Born Children Who Did Not Acquire a Sibling on the Basis of Maternal Social Behavior at 24 Months

ANALYSIS	
24-MONTHS MATERNAL SOCIAL VARIABLES	STANDARDIZED DISCRIMINANT FUNCTION COEFFICIENTS
Vocalize to infant	.59
Touch infant	1.1
Kiss infant	− .70
Hold infant	.49
Play with toy	− .95
Show approval	− .47

CLASSIFICATION*		
TOTAL SAMPLE ($n = 49$)	EARLY FIRST BORNS ($n = 9$)	LATER FIRST BORNS ($n = 40$)
85.71%	100%	82.5%

*Percentage correctly classified.

In general, the results of the discriminant analyses indicate that at 24 months mothers and children behave differently depending on whether a sibling has been born. These data support earlier findings that the birth of a sibling increases the first born's expressions of dependency and demands for attention from the mother.

Attributes of the Social Network for First and Only Children at 36 Months

Size and Frequency of Contact

Several general differences between the social networks of first-born and only children were found (see Table 2.7). The size of the first borns' networks (controlling for nuclear family size) was significantly larger than that of only borns ($Z = -2.26$, $p = .02$). Whereas only children came into contact with an average of 22.1 people, first borns came into contact with an average of 29.0 people. However, only children tended to have more daily contact with network members, as

Table 2.7. Social Networks at 36 Months as a Function of First- and Only-Born Distinctions

	TOTAL ($n = 38$)	ONLY BORNS ($n = 15$)
Total network (excluding nuclear family)		
Number of people contacted daily	4.53	5.73
weekly	9.45	7.80
monthly	7.47	5.07
twice a year	3.79	2.33
yearly	1.05	1.20
Total network size	26.29	22.13
Average frequency of total network*	3.51	3.67
Friends		
Number of friends contacted daily	1.63	2.33
weekly	3.03	2.33
monthly	1.37	.80
twice a year	.50	.40
yearly	.13	.20
Total number of friends	6.66	6.07
Average frequency of friend contact*	3.72	3.94
Adults (nonrelative)		
Number of adults contacted daily	2.24	2.33
weekly	3.24	2.13
monthly	2.37	1.27
twice a year	.79	.27
yearly	.11	.20
Total number of adults	8.74	6.20
Average frequency of contact with adults*	3.45	3.71
Relatives (excluding nuclear family)		
Number of relatives contacted daily	.66	1.07
weekly	3.18	3.33
monthly	3.74	3.00
twice a year	2.50	1.67
yearly	.82	.80
Total number of relatives	10.89	9.87
Average frequency of contact with relatives*	3.07	3.22

*Average frequency scales: 1 = yearly; 2 = biyearly; 3 = monthly; 4 = weekly; 5 = daily.

indicated by a higher average frequency score for the total network ($Z = -1.66$, $p = .10$). Onlies come into daily contact with an average of 5.7 people, as compared to 3.7 people for first borns ($Z = -2.51$, $p = .01$). First borns experienced contact with more people on a monthly ($Z = -1.83$, $p = .07$) and semiannual ($Z = -2.51$, $p = .01$) basis compared with onlies. Thus, according to their mothers' reports, only children can be characterized as coming into contact with a smaller number of people more frequently than first borns, who come into contact with a larger number of people less frequently.

Peer and Adult Contact

First-born children have slightly more peer friends, an average of 7.0, while onlies have an average of 6.1 friends (however, this difference is not significant). Only children know fewer adults than do first-born children ($Z = -1.80, p = .07$), although only children see these adults more frequently (daily contact $Z = -1.82$, $p = .07$).

Extended-Family Contact

Although first borns overall see slightly more relatives than only children, the difference is not significant. Onlies interact with more relatives on a daily basis than do first-born children ($Z = -1.67$, $p = .10$).

In summary, the first-born child has more friends and relatives and knows a larger number of adults than the only child. The only child knows fewer people but sees them, on the average, more frequently. The data suggest that the only child thus experiences fewer contacts on a more frequent basis than the first-born child. These findings are supported by Falbo (1978b), who found that only-born adults report having fewer total friends but an equal number of close friends, compared to people with siblings. Also, social group research indicates that smaller groups facilitate more frequent contact between group members than do larger groups (Cartwright & Zander, 1968). Such findings suggest that parents who have only one child prefer depth of social contact to breadth and consequently structure their families and their young child's social network to reflect this preference.

EARLY MATERNAL AND INFANT BEHAVIOR AS PREDICTORS OF LATER CHILD BEHAVIOR

In order to understand the development of first-born and only children, it is important to examine how children and parents change over time. Although very short in terms of the entire life span, the first 3 years of life comprise a period of major change during which the child constructs the foundations for social skills. Individual differences in the experience of only and first-born children in regard to the development of social skills have rarely been examined.

In conducting the longitudinal analyses previously described two issues were of central concern. The first was whether differences existed in the relationship between early child behavior and subsequent development for first-born and only children (child→child analyses). We were interested in examining prediction of later social characteristics from earlier social characteristics. The second issue of central concern in the longitudinal analysis was whether differences existed in the relationship between early maternal social characteristics and later child social characteristics for first-born and only children (mother→child analysis).

In order to carry out the child→child and mother→child longitudinal analyses on only-born and first-born groups, it was necessary to generate two correlation matrices: one with the correlations across time for all social factors for first-born children and their mothers, and one for only-born children and their mothers. Each matrix was then examined for significant relationship across time for firsts as compared to only groups. In addition, the correlation matrices were subjected to a Fisher Z transformation, and differences between correlations for first and only groups were tested when appropriate. Social factor scores, rather than individual behaviors, were used in the analysis, in the belief that the findings would be more conceptually comprehensible as well as psychometrically valid.

In the discussion that follows, we present the child→child longitudinal analyses followed by the mother→child analyses. In each case, we attempt to extract patterns of development that were significant (i.e., based on correlations significantly different from zero) and of theoretical interest for first-born and only groups as well as for the sample as a whole. While some interesting patterns and differences did emerge in regard to the development of first-born and only children, we must warn the reader to accept these results with caution. Correlations based on such small numbers of subjects are unstable even when stringent significance criteria are applied (i.e., the confidence interval on the correlation is very wide). However, given the fact that longitudinal data of mother–child interaction for onlies and first borns does not usually come in large sample sizes, we feel that our exploratory analyses yield some interesting findings that merit consideration.

Child→Child Longitudinal Analysis

Early Child and Later Child Social Characteristics

The focus in this analysis was on the relationship between child social factors at 3 months and at 12 and 24 months as well as on the relationship between child social factors at 12 and 24 months.

In terms of the total sample, children who may be characterized as alert at 3 months (i.e., children who vocalize, smile, and look at mother) tend to seek comfort more at 12 and 24 months ($r = .24$, $r = .28$, $p = .05$, for comfort seeking at 12 and 24 months, respectively. In addition, alertness and object play at 3 months are negatively related to solitary exploration at 24 months ($r = -.48$, $p = .001$, for alertness; $r = -.29$, $p = .04$, for object play). The data seem to indicate that, in general, alert infants become more mother-oriented children, as reflected in their tendency to be more inclined to seek comfort and less inclined to explore the environment independently. Both first borns and onlies show this pattern of relationships between early alertness and later comfort seeking and solitary play. However, some interesting differences in the relationships between 3-month and later 12- and 24-month behaviors of first borns and onlies emerge. Figure 2.1 gives the significant relationships between early and later social factors for the first-born and only groups. For first borns, self-stimulation at 3 months is negatively related to social play at 24 months ($r = -.30$, $p = .09$), whereas for only borns this relationship is positive ($r = .54$, $p = .02$; significant difference between correlations $p < .05$). Also, early object play is positively related to social play at 12 months for first borns ($r = .32$, $p = .09$), but not for onlies ($r = -.01$). Thus, first borns who are less self-play oriented and who play with objects earlier in life tend to explore the environment and play with objects later on. Sociable behavior in 2-year-old only children, however, is observed most often in onlies who are more self-oriented (i.e., self-stimulated) as infants.

For the total sample of first-born and only children, comfort seeking at 12 months was found to be positively related to comfort seeking ($r = .40$, $p = .006$) and proximal behavior ($r = .35$, $p = .02$) at 24 months. Comfort seeking at 12 months is also negatively related to solitary exploration ($r = -.40$, $p = .006$) at 24 months. A pattern seems to emerge here, in that toddlers characterized as comfort seekers at 12 months are more likely to be mother oriented at

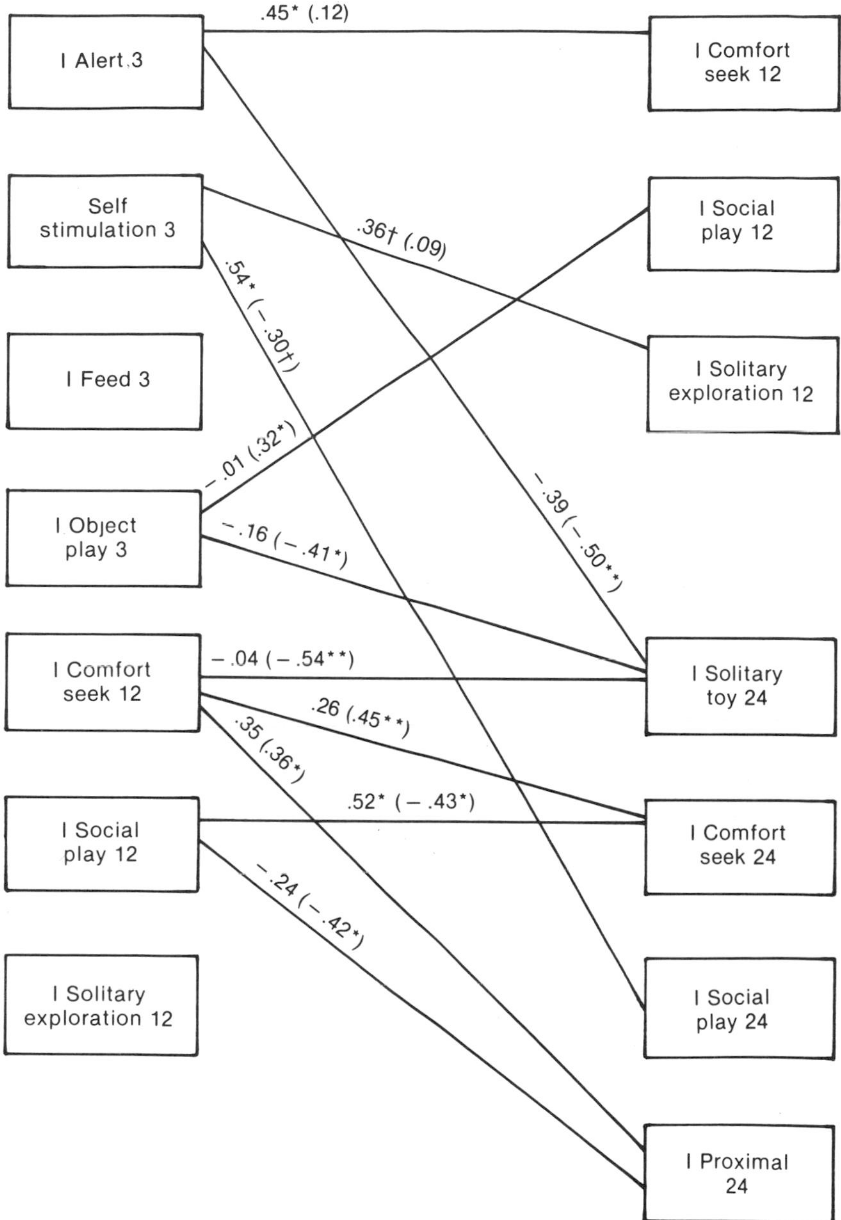

Figure 2.1. Early child social behavior as predictor of later child social behavior: 3→12, 3→24, and 12→24 correlations for onlies and first borns. Correlations for first borns are shown in parentheses following correlations for only borns. Correlations marked † were significant at the .10 level, * were significant at the .05 level, and ** were significant at the .01 level.

24 months as reflected by their tendency to seek proximity and comfort more and do less solitary exploration at 24 months. On the other hand, children who at 12 months are characterized by social play are less likely to seek comfort and proximity at 24 months ($r = -.32$, $p = .03$, for comfort; $r = -.37$, $p = .01$, for proximity). The positive relationships between comfort seeking at 12 months and later comfort seeking and proximity seeking are observed in both firsts and onlies. However, although correlations between first-borns' behaviors closely parallel the trends observed for the total sample at these ages, several of the correlations among only-borns' behaviors are different in magnitude from the relationships observed for firsts and for the total sample. Whereas comfort seeking is negatively related to solitary exploration at 24 months for both firsts ($r = -.54$, $p = .002$) and the total sample ($r = -.40, p = .006$), no such relationship exists for onlies ($r = -.04$). For first borns, as for the total sample, social play at 12 months negatively predicts seeking proximity ($r = -.42, p = .03$) and comfort ($r = -43, p = .02$) from mothers at 24 months. Unlike first borns, onlies' social play at 12 months positively predicts comfort seeking at 24 months ($r = .52$, $p = .03$).

In summary, first borns who are sociable early in life tend to be sociable later on. Also, the more the first borns play, the less likely they are to seek proximity and comfort from the mother at 24 months. On the other hand, only borns who are less sociable at 3 months are the ones who tend to be more sociable at 24 months. In particular, it is the self-stimulating only born, in contrast to the alert, playful first born, who is more social-play oriented at 24 months. Also, early social play for onlies positively predicts comfort seeking from the mother at 2 years, while for firsts and relationship is negative. These findings suggest that first borns show a more consistent developmental path from early sociability to later sociability and from early play to more play and less comfort seeking from the mother. Onlies appear to undergo a developmental transformation from less sociable behavior to more sociable and mother-oriented behavior at 24 months. These patterns are interesting in light of the early mean differences between first borns and onlies at 3 months. Onlies were more fussy than firsts at 3 months and had mothers who were more proximally oriented at 12 months. By 12 months, however, only-born and first-born infants are not different in their social behavior, while their mothers are still different. Perhaps it is the mother's responsiveness to her fussy only-born 3-month-old that somehow influences the transformation from the fussy, self-stimulating only born into a more sociable child at 24 months. It is interesting to note that there are fewer significant relationships between the early behavior and later behavior for onlies than there are for first borns. This suggests that first borns' own early behavior is a good indicator of their later behavior. This is not true for only borns. As we shall see in the mother→child longitudinal analyses, it appears as if mothers' behavior toward onlies is a better indicator of these children's later social behavior.

Early Mother Social Characteristics and Later Child Social Characteristics

This analysis examined the correlations between early maternal social factors and later child social factors for onlies, firsts, and the total sample. Nonattentive mothering at 3 months is positively related to a less maternal orientation in the child at 12 months. Specifically, for the total sample, nonattending at 3 months is negatively related to children's social play at 12 months ($r = -.15$) and comfort seeking at 12 months ($r = -.24$, $p = .08$). Overall, mothers who at 3 months are more sociable to the infant tend to have more mother-oriented children at 24 months. In particular, mothers' active toy play at 3 months is positively related to child comfort seeking at 24 months ($r = .30$, $p = .04$, for the total sample). Also, maternal active toy play at 3 months is positively related to child proximal contact at 24 months ($r = .29$, $p = .04$).

Considering differences between firsts and onlies, onlies had five significant correlations while firsts had one. Specifically, for mothers of firsts nonattending at 3 months tends to be positively related to child solitary exploration ($r = .30$, $p = .10$) at 24 months, whereas this relationship is weak and negative for onlies ($r = -.12$). For onlies but not firsts, maternal social interaction at 3 months is positively related to infant comfort seeking at 12 months ($r = .45$, $p = .06$; $r = -.08$; for onlies and firsts, respectively) and negatively related to solitary exploration at 24 months ($r = -.44$, $p = .07$; $r = .04$; for onlies and firsts). Also, for onlies but not for firsts, mothers' caregiving at 3 months is positively related to infant comfort seeking at 12 months ($r = .43$, $p = .05$; $r = -.06$; for onlies and firsts) but negatively related to social play at 24 months ($r = -.65$, $p = .005$; $r = .02$; for onlies and firsts). Thus, early maternal involvement predicts the development of comfort seeking in only-born children. This tendency for early maternal social interaction and caregiving to be positively predictive of only borns' comfort seeking is not evidenced by the first-born group.

Active maternal toy play at 12 months is positively predictive of social play at 24 months for only children but not for firsts ($r = .45$, $p = .07$; $r = .17$; for only and first borns, respectively). Moreover, 12-month maternal active toy play for onlies is also positively related to child proximal behavior at 24 months, but this relationship does not exist for firsts ($r = .47$, $p = .05$; $r = -.04$; respectively). These data indicate that for onlies, but not for firsts, maternal active toy play at 12 months is related to later child social orientation to the mother.

In summary, early maternal toy play and social interaction are positively predictive of later social play and interaction in children, whereas early nonattending maternal behavior leads to a less mother-oriented child. The relationship between early maternal involvement (as characterized by caregiving and social interaction) and later child sociability with the mother is noted for only-born mother–child dyads as compared to first-born dyads. The data indicate that for onlies, later child social characteristics are more closely related to early maternal social characteristics than to child characteristics. The pattern of significant correlations suggests that the behavior of mothers has more impact on only children's development than on that of firsts. This may be attributable to the fact that onlies are more fussy as infants and demand more early maternal attention and intervention. Increased maternal involvement seems to lead to changes in the onlies' social behavior from a less sociable to a more sociable individual. In contrast, first-born infants tend to be more sociable at 3 months than onlies, and this early first-born sociability is positively predictive of later sociability. In general, first borns' early characteristics are more closely related to later social characteristics than are early maternal characteristics. Perhaps mothers of firsts may have less influence on their infants' social development, because, compared to onlies, the infant's behavior does not require as much maternal intervention or involvement in order to produce a more sociable child.

SUMMARY AND CONCLUSIONS

Data were obtained on four sets of issues related to first and only borns: (1) mother–child social interaction in the first two years of life, (2) the birth of a sibling and its effect on mother–child interaction, (3) social networks of children at 36 months, and (4) the relationship between early mother–child interaction and later child functioning. The findings regarding first- and only-born children are reviewed here.

Mother–Child Interaction from 3 to 24 Months

Differences between only and first-born children are most evident at early age points, when only borns are fussier and less sociable than firsts. By 2 years of age, however, onlies and firsts are very similar in their social interaction with their mothers. Mothers of only borns have more proximal contact with their children, especially in the first 12 months of life, and at 24 months they show more approval to their children than do mothers of firsts. Overall it appears that at 3 months, mothers of onlies respond to their fussy infants with more proximal, caretaking behaviors than do mothers of first borns. Consequently, at 3 months, there is an appropriate match between fussy infants and attentive, soothing maternal behavior. By 12 months, mothers of only borns are still more proximal in their behavior than mothers of firsts, although the infants no longer behave differently.

The data suggest that both endogenous and exogenous factors may contribute to differences between only and first born children. These factors, alone or in combination, may contribute to differences in mother–only-born-child dyads. Considering endogenous sources of difference, only borns may have a different temperamental–biological disposition, as evidenced by their tendency to cry more and smile less than first-born infants. In regard to exogenous sources of differences, mothers of only borns may be more involved in the parenting role and may focus more attention on the child than mothers of first borns, as evidenced by their greater interaction, proximal contact, and approval of their child.

The Birth of a Sibling

The birth of a sibling may be one of the major contributing exogenous factors to differences between only and first-born children. Our findings suggest that the birth of a sibling affects the security of the mother–child dyad and that birth of a sibling disrupts the mother–first-born-child interactions, at least initially. The mother–child dyad, when a sibling is born by 24 months, is characterized by less play, more upset, and more proximal and dependency types of behavior than the mother–child dyad when no sibling is born into the family. Consequently, it does appear probable that the first born's experience of dethronement from only-child status may engender differences between only and first-born children.

Social Networks at 3 Years of Age

Our data suggest that only children and first borns have different types of social networks. First borns have larger social networks than onlies. Only borns tend to have fewer friends and adults in their networks, although they do see the adults they know more frequently than do firsts. Consequently, the nature and type of contact available to the child may be an important exogenous source of differences between only and first borns. At age 3, the child's network is to a great extent controlled by the parents (Lewis *et al.*, in press). The early pattern shown in our data of only children knowing fewer people but seeing them more frequently may lead to a similar pattern when the only child becomes an adult (Falbo, 1978b), even though the individual's network is no longer constrained by parental contacts.

Early Social Behavior and Later Child Development

Our findings indicate that for first-born children early child social characteristics are the best predictors of subsequent social development. For firsts, sociable infants become sociable children. On the other hand, the best predictors of only children's subsequent social development seem to be the social characteristics of the mother. Only infants who are not sociable at 3 months become more sociable at 24 months, and the data suggest that the mothers of onlies help bring about this transformation. In particular, mothers of onlies who are more involved with their infants' activities have more sociable children later on. In general, the longitudinal analyses were enlightening as to the determinants of development for first and only borns. Of particular note was the pattern of correlation, which indicated that the social development of first borns seems to be more clearly affected by their own behavior. In contrast, the social development of only borns appears to be more closely related to the social behavior of their mothers.

Taken together, our findings indicate several possible sources of variation for differences between first-born and only children. Differences in child and maternal social behavior, differences in family situation (e.g., presence or absence of a sibling), differences in social networks, and differences in the course of development in regard to parent and child influences are all areas that our data show to be probable sources of differences between only and first-born children. Although our findings are based on a small sample, the opportunity to observe mothers and children longitudinally over the first three years of life has enabled us to obtain insight into the characteristics at various age points and the changes over time in the development of only and first-born children.

ACKNOWLEDGMENTS

Data collection and preparation of this chapter was supported by Grant NO1-HD-82849 from the Center for Population Research, NICHD, to Michael Lewis.

The authors appreciate the assistance of Linda Wellman and John Jaskir in compiling and analyzing the data.

REFERENCES

Abramovitch, R., Corter, C., & Lando, B. Sibling interaction in the home. *Child Development*, 1979, *50*, 997–1003.

Bell, R. Q. Stimulus control of parent or caretaker behavior by offspring. *Developmental Psychology*, 1971, *4*, 63–72.

Bossard, J. H. S., & Boll, E. S. *The sociology of child development.* New York: Harper, 1960.

Carey, W. B. A simplified method for measuring infant temperament. *The Journal of Pediatrics*, 1970, *77*, 188–194.

Cartwright, D., & Zander, A. (Eds.). *Group dynamics: Research and theory.* New York: Harper & Row, 1968.

Chess, S., Thomas, A., & Cameron, M. Temperament: Its significance for early schooling. *New York University Education Quarterly*, Spring 1976, pp. 24–29.

Cicerelli, V. G. Effects of mother and older siblings on problem-solving behavior of the younger child. *Developmental Psychology*, 1975, *11*, 749–756.

Clarke-Stewart, K. A. Interaction between mothers and their young children: Characteristics and consequences. *Monographs of the Society for Research in Child Development*, 1973, *38* (Serial No. 153).

Clarke-Stewart, K. A. And daddy makes three: The father's impact on mother and young child. *Child Development*, 1978, *49*(2), 466–478.

Dunn, J., & Kendrick, C. Interaction between young siblings in the context of family relationships. In M. Lewis & L. Rosenblum (Eds.), *The child and its family: The genesis of behavior* (Vol. 2). New York: Plenum, 1979.

Dunn, J., & Kendrick, C. The arrival of a sibling: Changes in patterns of interaction between mother and first-born child. *Journal of Child Psychology and Psychiatry*, 1980, *21*(2), 119–132.

Dunn, J., Kendrick, C., & MacNamee, R. The reaction of first-born children to the birth of a sibling: Mothers' reports. *Journal of Child Psychology and Psychiatry*, 1981, *22*, 1–18.

Eiduson, B. T. *The dynamics of the one-child family: Socialization implications.* Paper presented at a symposium on The Only Child at the meeting of the American Psychological Association, Washington, D.C., September 1976.

Falbo, T. The only child: A review. *Journal of Individual Psychology*, 1977, *33*(1), 47–61.

Falbo, T. Reasons for having an only child. *Journal of Population*, 1978, *1*(2), 181–184. (a)

Falbo, T. Only children and interpersonal behavior: An experimental and survey study. *Journal of Applied Social Psychology*, 1978, *8*(3), 244–253. (b)

Falbo, T. Only children, stereotypes, and research. In M. Lewis & L. Rosenblum (Eds.), *The child and its family: Genesis of behavior* (Vol. 2). New York: Plenum, 1979.

Falbo, T. *Only children, achievement and interpersonal orientation.* Paper presented at the meeting of the American Psychological Association, Montreal, September 1980.

Feiring, C., & Lewis, M. Temperament: Sex differences and stability in vigor, activity, and persistence in the first three years of life. *Journal of Genetic Psychology*, 1980, *136*, 65–75.

Galton, F. *English men of science: Their nature and nurture.* London: Macmillan, 1874.

Gewirtz, J. L., & Gewirtz, H. B. Stimulus conditions, infant behaviors, and social learning in four Israeli child-rearing environments: A preliminary report illustrating differences in environment and behavior between "only" and "youngest" child. In B. M. Foss (Eds.), *Determinants of infant behavior* (Vol. 3). New York: Wiley, 1965.

Greenberg, M. S. Role playing: An alternative to deception? *Journal of Personality and Social Psychology*, 1967, 7(2), 152–157.

Harper, L. V. The scope of offspring effects: From caregiver to culture. *Psychological Bulletin*, 1975, *82*, 784–801.

Hartup, W. W. Perspectives on child and family interaction: Past, present, and future. In R. M. Lerner & G. B. Spanier (Eds.), *Child influences on marital and family interaction: A life-span perspective.* New York: Academic Press, 1978.

Hawke, S., & Knox, D. The one-child family: A new life style. *Family Coordinator*, 1978, *27*(3), 215–219.

Hilton, I. Differences in the behavior of mothers toward first and later birth children. *Journal of Personality and Social Psychology*, 1967, 7, 282–290.

Hoyt, M. P., & Raven, B. H. Birth order and the 1971 Los Angeles earthquake. *Journal of Personality and Social Psychology*, 1973, *28*(1), 123–128.

Jaskir, J., & Lewis, M. *A factor analytic study of mother–infant interaction at 3, 12, and 24 months.* Paper presented at the meeting of the Eastern Psychological Association, New York, April 1981.

Jacobs, B. S., & Moss, H. A. Birth order and sex of sibling as determinants of mother–infant interaction. *Child Development*, 1976, *47*, 315–322.

Kagan, J. *Change and continuity in infancy.* New York: Wiley, 1971.

Lamb, M. E. (Ed.). *The role of the father in child development.* New York: Wiley, 1976.

Lewis, M. State as an infant–environment interaction: An analysis of mother–infant interaction as a function of sex. *Merrill-Palmer Quarterly*, 1972, *18*, 95–121.

Lewis, M. (Ed.). *The origins of intelligence: Infancy and early childhood.* New York: Plenum, 1976.

Lewis, M. *The effect of birth order on the mother–child relationship.* Final report to Population Research Bureau, NICHD, 1978.

Lewis, M., Feiring, C., & Kotsonis, M. The social network of 3 year olds: A developmental perspective. In M. Lewis (Ed.), *Beyond the dyad: The genesis of behavior*, (Vol. 4). New York: Plenum, in press.

Lewis, M., & Goldberg, S. Perceptual-cognitive development in infancy: A generalized expectancy model as a function of the mother–infant interaction. *Merrill-Palmer Quarterly*, 1969, *12*(1), 81–100.

Lewis, M., & Kreitzberg, V. The effects of birth order and spacing on mother–infant interactions. *Developmental Psychology*, 1979, *15*(6), 617–625.

Lewis, M., & Lee-Painter, S. An interactional approach to the mother–infant dyad. In M. Lewis & L. Rosenblum (Eds.), *The effect of the infant on its caregiver: The origins of behavior* (Vol. 1). New York: Wiley, 1974.

Lewis, M., & Rosenblum, L. (Eds.). *The effect of the infant on its caregiver: The origins of behavior* (Vol. 1). New York: Wiley, 1974.

Lewis, M., & Rosenblum, L. (Eds.). *The child and its family: The genesis of behavior* (Vol. 2). New York: Plenum, 1979.

Lewis, M., & Starr, M. Developmental continuity. In J. Osofsky (Ed.), *Handbook of infant development.* New York: Wiley, 1979.

Miley, C. H. Birth order research 1963–1967: Bibliography and index. *Journal of Individual Psychology*, 1969, *25*, 64–70.

Parke, R. D., & Sawin, D. B. *Infant characteristics and behavior as elicitors of maternal and paternal responsivity in the newborn period.* Paper presented to the Society for Research in Child Development, Denver, April 1975.

Pattison, M. A psychosocial kinship model for family therapy. *American Journal of Psychiatry*, 1975, *132*, 1246–1251.

Pinner, B., & Thompson, V. D. *The taboo against the one-child family.* Unpublished manuscript, University of North Carolina at Chapel Hill, 1974.

Polit, D. F. Stereotypes relating to family-size status. *Journal of Marriage and the Family*, 1978, *40*(1), 105–114.

Rosenberg, B. G., & Sutton-Smith, B. Sibling age spacing: Effects upon cognition. *Developmental Psychology*, 1969, *1*(6), 661–668.

Schachter, S. *The psychology of affiliation.* Stanford, Calif.: Stanford University Press, 1959.

Tatsuoka, M. M. *Discriminant analysis: The study of group differences.* Champaign, Ill.: Institute for Personality and Ability Testing, 1970.

Taylor, M. K., & Kogan, K. L. Effects of birth of a sibling on mother–child interactions. *Child Psychiatry and Human Development*, 1973, *4*(1), 53–58.

Thompson, V. D. Family size: Implicit policies and assumed psychological outcomes. *Journal of Social Issues*, 1974, *30*(4), 93–124.

Toman, W., & Toman, E. Sibling positions of a sample of distinguished persons. *Perceptual and Motor Skills*, 1970, *31*(3), 825–826.

Van den Berg, B. J., & Oechsli, F. W. *Studies on the one-child family*. Final report, NICHD contract NO1-HD-82851, 1980.

Warren, J. R. Birth order and social behavior. *Psychological Bulletin*, 1966, *65*, 38–49.

White, B. Critical influences in the origins of competence. *Merrill-Palmer Quarterly*, 1975, *21*, 243–266.

·3·

SEX-ROLE DEVELOPMENT AND THE ONE-CHILD FAMILY

PHYLLIS A. KATZ
SALLY L. BOSWELL

INTRODUCTION

Dramatic changes in family planning strategies have occurred over the past decade and a half. In contrast to the idealized portrayals of large families in the mass media of the 1950s (cf. Friedan, 1963), the goal of having many children is becoming increasingly rare (Thompson & Appelbaum, 1971), the birth rate has been decreasing accordingly (Taffel, 1977), and the ideal contemporary family size appears to be approaching two children. The reasons underlying these birth-rate changes have been widely discussed in both the scientific and popular literature. Some of these factors include better and more widespread birth-control technology, higher vocational aspirations among women, increased concern with the environment and quality of life, and the widely publicized negative effects of overpopulation. There has also been considerable governmental and institutional support for smaller families (e.g., Commission on Population Growth and the American Future, 1972).

In spite of the avowed goal of reducing family size, however, most individuals strongly resist the idea of having fewer than two children. Findings of recent studies suggest that people of child-bearing age perceive childlessness and having a single child as equally undesirable alternatives to large numbers of children (e.g., Blake, 1974, 1981). Thus, people hold strong opinions against both childless and one-child families. As a choice between these two alternatives,

Phyllis A. Katz and Sally L. Boswell. Institute for Research on Social Problems, Boulder, Colorado.

college students actually prefer childlessness (by a 6 : 1 ratio) to having only one child (Thompson & Appelbaum, 1971). Since there will always be those who prefer or have more than two children, an average of two cannot be a reality unless some wish to have fewer than two. The goal of decreasing overpopulation cannot be achieved, therefore, until normative pressures to have at least two children are removed (Thompson, 1974).

At least part of the pressure to have two children is attributable to the negative stereotypes people hold about those without siblings. Indeed, the very term "only child" carries the connotation that children without siblings are in some way deprived. Research conducted over the past 80 years demonstrates that only children are typically viewed as spoiled, maladjusted, self-centered, dependent on others, and socially inadequate (Bohannon, 1898; Fenton, 1928; Gough, 1952; Pinner & Thompson, 1974; Thompson, 1974). In contrast, however, the overwhelming majority of studies of only children have failed to provide any confirmation of these stereotypes (Adler, 1931; Campbell, 1934; Dyer, 1945; Falbo, 1976, 1977; Guilford & Worcester, 1930; Stuart, 1926; Thurstone & Thurstone, 1930). Interestingly, as Falbo (1977), has noted, when differences are found between only borns and others, they often reveal positive attributes associated with being only born. Only children, for example, score higher on IQ tests than later borns (Zajonc, 1976), exhibit higher academic achievement (Altus, 1965), attend college with greater frequency (Warren, 1967), comprise a disproportionately large number of eminent individuals (Belmont & Marolla, 1973; Breland, 1974), do better on multiple-choice tests (Wagner, Schubert & Schubert, 1979), and may even be more musical (Raychaudhuri, 1965). Although the evidence with regard to differences in personality and social behavior is less clear cut, only borns, like first borns, may be more affiliative (Schachter, 1959), more autonomous (Falbo, 1978), and have higher self-esteem (Rosenberg, 1965).

Thus the paradox: Despite the fact that research offers no support for the stereotype that only children are maladjusted, self-centered, and deviant and that there may indeed be more advantages than disadvantages associated with being born an only child (Blake, 1981; Falbo, 1982), the majority of individuals still hold strong negative attitudes about the one-child family that preclude their considering this alternative as a family planning option.

Genuine freedom in making family planning decisions cannot be experienced until we achieve a better understanding of (1) why people continue to hold strong negative stereotypes about only children, and (2) what processes are involved in overcoming such beliefs.

A clearer understanding of negative attitudes toward only children must begin with an analysis of why most people desire more than one child. Although relevant evidence and theory are generally lacking in this area, it appears that there are at least three major factors that support the maintenance of a two-child family ideal. These are: (1) fear of "putting all one's eggs in one basket," (2) a belief that children without siblings are deprived, and (3) a desire to experience gender diversity in parenting.

The first reason speaks for itself. Given the considerable emotional investment most parents make in their children, if something were to go wrong with a child (e.g., retardation, serious illness, death), the effect would be much more catastrophic on parents of an only child than on parents of more than one child.

With regard to the second factor, many people believe that it is selfish to deprive a child of the experience of having siblings. As noted earlier, research has not supported the view that absence of siblings leads to harmful outcomes. Nevertheless, it is often anticipated that an only child will not have as many people to interact with during childhood and will not have significant family members to rely upon during adulthood after the parents have died.

The third factor, wanting to raise both a son and a daughter, may be the most complex of the three but may also be the one most susceptible to modification. Obviously, a voluntary choice to have a single child implies abandoning the experience of having children of both sexes. The study discussed in this chapter focuses upon this factor in two ways: first, by assessing whether gender diversity needs are related to particular family constellations; second, by exploring the consequences of this factor for childhood sex-role socialization.

Two issues appear particularly germane to parental needs for gender diversity in their offspring. One is why this need appears to be so strong in couples contemplating childbearing decisions. Even when parents have two children, they express a greater desire to have more children if the two are of the same sex than if they are of the opposite sexes (Westoff, Potter, & Sagi, 1963). A second issue is whether such a need remains valid in the light of the considerable social changes that are occurring in the definition and development of sex roles.

The core of the gender diversity ideal is illustrated by the song "Tea for Two," the lyrics of which state "We will raise a family,/A boy for you, a girl for me." The folk wisdom embodied in these words suggests that it is important for the mother to interact in feminine ways with a daughter, whereas the father desires a son to interact with in masculine activities. On one level, this desire for children of both sexes may reflect the wish of each parent for self-replacement. It also reflects the fact that parents have traditionally associated different future aspirations for each sex: professional success and achievement from their sons and interpersonal rewards and grandchildren from their daughters.

There is evidence that some of these sex-role stereotypes may be changing. A number of investigators (Bem, 1974; Spence, Helmreich, & Stapp, 1975) have persuasively argued that masculinity and femininity should be conceptualized and measured separately. Subsequent research employing such measures shows that a number of individuals have strong personality traits in both areas, a pattern that has been labeled "androgynous." Research suggests that androgynous sex-role patterns are becoming more frequent and that there may be psychological advantages (such as better adjustment and greater creativity) associated with this less stereotyped personality (Bem & Lenney, 1976; Flake-Hobson, Skeen, & Robinson, 1980). Some societal changes in this area have been documented, namely, that some women are expressing higher career aspirations (Boswell, 1979; Hoffman, 1974) and some males are beginning to recognize the value of areas that were previously designated as feminine, including greater emotional expressiveness and nurturance behavior (Pleck, 1981; Tresemer & Pleck, 1973).

These changing gender-role patterns may have future ramifications for family planning in general and the one-child family in particular. If the need for gender diversity in children is becoming less salient by virtue of changes in adult behavior, having one child may become a more popular alternative. Looking backwards, it may also be the case that only children are less gender-role stereotyped and more androgynous than those with siblings, either because their parents had a weaker need for gender diversity or placed less importance on maintaining stringent sex typing in their socialization practices. Exploration of these various expectations constituted a basic purpose of our study.

It is of interest that earlier literature relevant to the sex-role orientations of only children suggests that they may indeed be less sex typed, although the findings have often been interpreted with the previously mentioned negative bias toward only borns. If a difference exists, it has usually been interpreted as a disadvantage for onlys. Sutton-Smith and Rosenberg (1970), for example, conclude that "the most striking data on only children have to do with sex-role differences between male and female only children," but they interpret these differences in terms of greater deviation from sex-role norms (i.e., only-born males are more feminine and only-born females are more masculine). Cited as support for this position are studies by Gundlach and Reiss (1967), Heilbrun and Frome (1965), Hooker (1931), and Rosenberg and Sutton-Smith (1964). Inspection of most of these studies reveals sufficient methodological problems to invalidate their conclusions. Although the study by Rosenberg & Sutton-Smith (1964) is methodologically sound, it is the view of the present writers that these investigators may have misinterpreted their data in the light of prevailing cultural mores. An interest in cross-sex toys is not necessarily a sign of deviance. In view of the fact that the only children included in their study played with toys "appropriate" for their sex as much as nononly children, they might have been demonstrating greater flexibility, perhaps a little ahead of their time.

To summarize, gender role may be importantly related to family planning, both as antecedent and consequent. If children are generally becoming more flexible, and if children without siblings are less stereotyped than others, then the need for having children of both sexes may become less important. In effect, it may be possible to replace the need for gender diversity with the actuality of gender-role diversity. The perceived desire for children of both sexes may be satisfied by a single child combining the positive role characteristics of both sexes. It is certainly arguable, for example, that the professionally successful daughter or the emotionally nurturant son could sufficiently satisfy the needs of both parents in a way that might reduce the need for gender diversity. If this type of androgynous development is indeed becoming more prevalent, then perhaps one of the motivations for multiple childbearing will be lessened.

What this reasoning suggests is that it is important to study sex-role development in only children, as well as its parental antecedents. This comprised the major objective of our research program.

RATIONALE, DESIGN, AND HYPOTHESES

Based upon the above reasoning, we sought to obtain information pertinent to the question of how couples' decisions to have one or more than one child related to their need for gender diversity on the one hand and their children's sex-role development on the other. Data were collected on several major issues: (1) the factors involved in decisions to have one or more children, (2) whether only children are more flexible than those with siblings, and (3) if so, when such differences occurred developmentally.

To obtain information relevant to these issues, two interrelated studies were conducted. The first focused on preschool and grade school children and compared the development of gender-role identity of only children with that of both first- and last-born children of comparable ages. The second study compared parents of only children with parents of two children along a number of dimensions, including sex-role attitudes, degree of sex typing, perceptions about their child's sex-role orientation, and factors related to their decisions about family size. Finally, relationships between children and their parents were studied.

The Child Study

How might the gender-role development of only borns differ from that of children with siblings? Before considering this, it is useful to consider the general processes involved in this development. A number of theoretical descriptions of sex-role acquisition have been offered, and these have emphasized such factors as reinforcement, modeling, cognition, and affective bonding (see Katz, 1979b; Maccoby & Jacklin, 1974; Worell, 1981, for reviews). Katz (1979a) has recently elaborated an integrative life span developmental view of gender-role acquisition, and this model constitutes the basic theoretical framework of our investigations.

In contrast to several earlier views, the Katz model assumes that gender-role development continues throughout the life cycle. It posits three major age-related levels of sex-role development. These include: (1) learning what is deemed appropriate behavior for a male or female child; (2) acquiring concepts about male and female adult behavior, and (3) behaving and developing as a male or female adult. Each level is divided into substages, each with its own cognitive and emotional tasks to be acquired and its own crises to be solved. Most important for purposes of the present study, each level is associated with various sources of social influence, and it is these patterns that may best differentiate persons with and without siblings.

Several general expectations about differential patterns of socialization associated with the one-child family have been discussed in the literature. The most prominently mentioned expectation is that only children receive more parental attention than others (e.g., Adams, 1972), which is supposed to lead to a stronger adult orientation than other children have. Even in early infancy, children without siblings apparently receive more social stimulation than others and consequently are more responsive (Lewis & Kreitzberg, 1979). This monopoly of parental attention during the early years may make the only child similar to the first born during this developmental period. The absence of a dethronement experience in later childhood, however, might have the opposite effect of making the only child more like the last-born child during this subsequent developmental period. This suggests that understanding the consequences of being an only child necessitates a developmental study.

The degree of available adult attention has been quantitatively treated in a recent confluence model linking family size and intellectual development (Zajonc & Markus, 1975). Within this model, a child's intellectual environment is determined by assigning numerical values to each family member in terms of age and potential contribution to stimulation. Briefly, the model suggests that a newborn in an all-adult environment will be intellectually superior to one in a social environment with many young children. Zajonc and Markus suggest that their confluence model may be applicable to areas of development other than intelligence. Extrapolating from this to the cognitive components of gender-role learning (such as the learning of sex-role stereotypes), it might be anticipated that this learning would develop earlier in children without siblings. A countervailing tendency, however, is that parents of an only child may be less rigid in their sex-role expectations, as discussed above, and consequently may reinforce nonstereotyped behavior. Thus predictions cannot be advanced unambiguously. Since parents of sons, however, are generally less flexible in sex typing than parents of daughters (Katz & Boswell, 1982), boys without siblings may exhibit a more clear-cut cognitive gender-role precocity than boys with siblings.

These various considerations suggest that there are a variety of ways in which the absence of siblings can affect the content, development, and orientation of gender roles. The first possibility is that parents who elect to have an only child (in the face of negative stereotypes) are different in personality and belief structures from other parents. At the very least, the choice of having one child means abandoning the possibility of having a child of the opposite sex as well. A second possibility is that only children may be socialized differently from nononly children. In order for only children to satisfy parental needs for gender diversity, they may learn to behave in both masculine *and* feminine ways. A third manner in which gender-role acquisition processes may differ for only borns, extrapolating from the Zajonc-Markus model, is in more rapid development. Finally, only borns may have a different, perhaps more emotionally intense relationship with their parents, which may also lead to greater precocity. These various possibilities are not necessarily mutually exclusive and may interact in complex ways.

Some additional, more specific ways in which the sex-role socialization of only and nononly children may differ are summarized in Table 3.1, which also delineates developmental trends. In accordance with the Katz model, it is assumed that parents are the primary influences during the preschool period, whereas peers and siblings are more significant during grade school.

Based on the above reasoning, the following hypotheses were tested in our study:

1. Preschool only children should be more advanced in sex-role development (because of greater parental availability and greater parental reinforcement). This should reflect itself in (a) earlier acquisition of gender constancy, and (b) greater knowledge about sex-role content. This trend should be more clear-cut in boys.
2. Only children at both age levels should exhibit more flexibility in gender-role orientations than nononly children.
3. Grade school children with a sibling (particularly an older

Table 3.1. Possible Differences in Gender-Role Socialization for Only and Non-only Children

SEX-ROLE TASKS TO BE ACQUIRED*	MAJOR SOURCES OF INFLUENCE		POSSIBLE DIFFERENCES
	PRESCHOOL LEVEL		
Acquisition of gender constancy	Parents:	Availability	Greater for onlies
		Sex-role atttitudes	More liberal for onlies
		Degree of sextyping	Less stringent for onlies
Starting to learn content of male and female child sex roles	Siblings		No clear-cut differences at this age level
	Media		Possible greater influence for onlies
	GRADE SCHOOL LEVEL		
Completion of sex-role content learning with regard to children	Peers		Important for both; may become more important for onlies
	Siblings		More models available for those with older and/or cross-sexed siblings. More teaching experience for those with younger siblings. Onlies must seek out models outside home and do not have tutoring opportunities as available
Beginning of learning about potential adult roles	Parents:	Availability	Greater for onlies, but less important than previously
		Sex-role attitudes	More liberal for onlies
		Degree of sextyping	Less stringent for onlies
	Media		Perhaps of greater influence for onlies; important for all at this age level.

*From Katz (1979a).

sibling) should be more knowledgeable about culturally designated sex-role content than other groups.

4. Peers and media are significant socialization sources for all grade school children (Katz & Boswell, 1982; Hartup, 1976) and should be related to their sex-role orientations. These socialization sources may play an even more important role for only children and thus should correlate more highly for this group.

5. Only children should most resemble first borns at the pre-

school level; at the grade school level there should be more similarity between onlys and last borns.

6. There should be a positive relationship between parental sex-role attitudes and their children's sex-role orientations.

The Parent Portion

There are virtually no studies of parents of only children, other than the documentation of the existence of negative attitudes towards such individuals (e.g., Rainwater, 1965). Although data have recently been collected on the motivations and consequences of childlessness (e.g., Feldman, 1974; Silka & Kiesler, 1977; Veevers, 1973), there is no evidence that those who elect to have a single child are similar to those who do not want children. In fact, it is arguable that the decision to have a single child is more similar to the decision to have more than one child than to the decision to have no children. Our study, therefore, focused upon attitudes unique to parents who have voluntarily chosen to have only one child, with a particular emphasis on how such individuals have dealt with some of the emotionally compelling reasons others have used to justify a multiple-child ideal.

Given the absence of theory in this area, predictions must be stated with some caution. Nevertheless, based upon the preceding considerations, it was expected that the following patterns would be obtained:

1. Parents who voluntarily decided to have a single child would place much less emphasis on gender diversity than parents of more than one child.
2. Parents who voluntarily decided to have only one child would exhibit a greater need to justify their decision than parents with two children.
3. Parents of only children would generally be more liberal in their attitudes toward sex roles and less stereotyped in sex typing their children than parents of more than one child.

SAMPLE

Our sample consisted of three groups: preschool children, grade school children, and parents. The preschool sample consisted of 170 children, 93 boys and 77 girls, with an average age of 5 years,

3 months ($SD = 10$ months). They were drawn from 21 nursery schools and kindergartens in the Boulder–Denver area. For many analyses the preschool sample was further divided into two age groups: a younger one ($n = 61$) with a mean age of 4 years, 4 months, and an older one ($n = 109$) with a mean age of 5 years, 9 months. The grade school sample was made up of 149 children, 72 boys and 77 girls, average age 9 years, 5 months ($SD = 8$ months). Subjects were drawn from 14 of the schools from which the preschool sample was drawn.

Children selected for participation were drawn from five different birth-order positions: (1) only children; children of two-child families in which the target child was (2) an older child with a same-sex sibling, (3) an older child with an opposite-sex sibling, (4) a younger child with a same-sex sibling, or (5) a younger child with an opposite-sex sibling. Because the study focused primarily upon only children, we oversampled this cell ($n = 96$). Sample size ranged from 47 to 68 in each of the other cells. The sample of two-child families was limited to those in which siblings differed in age by no more than three years.

In addition to the child samples, interviews about sex-role attitudes, childrearing and gender socialization practices, and family planning issues were conducted with 137 mothers and 90 fathers of preschoolers and 127 mothers and 67 fathers of grade-school-aged children. For 90 of the preschool children and 66 grade school children both parents were interviewed.

On the basis of biographical information, the parent sample may be described as follows: fathers' ages averaged 35.4, mothers' 33.7 years ($SD = 4.9$ and 4.2, respectively); 87% were married at the time of testing. The educational level of the mothers was somewhat lower than the educational level of the fathers.

CHILDREN'S STUDY

Preschool Measures

Based on the model of sex-role development described above, preschool-aged children were expected to be engaged in two primary gender-role tasks: the development of gender constancy (i.e., understanding that gender remains stable over time and across situations) and the learning of sex-role content. Consequently, the children were assessed along these dimensions. Gender-role orientation was measured in order to assess the other predictions concerning the only child's greater flexibility. Finally, the child's perceptions about how his or her friends, siblings, and parents would behave with regard to cross-sex toys was included to explore the possibility that the social environment as perceived by the child might vary as a function of family constellation. Each area was assessed by means of a multiscale battery. The specific tests employed are summarized in Table 3.2 and are described in greater detail in Katz and Boswell (1982).[1]

Grade School Measures

In accordance with our developmental model, we expected that grade school children would exhibit a continued elaboration of child sex-role content (revolving generally around activities and toys) and the beginning acquisition of knowledge of adult sex-role traits and behaviors (revolving mainly around personality traits, occupational choices, and domestic activities). A revised questionnaire adapted from an earlier study (Katz, 1979a) was used; it assessed three major areas: (1) knowledge of sex-role stereotypes, (2) the child's perception of important socialization agents (including friends, siblings, parents, and media), and (3) the flexibility or traditionality of the child's gender-role orientation. In addition, children's attitudes and beliefs about only children versus those with brothers and sisters were assessed. A summary of the various tests included in the battery is presented in Table 3.3. A more detailed description of the scales and their psychometric properties can be found in Katz and Boswell (1982).

Results of Children's Study

The Preschool Sample

As stated earlier, the preschool measure assessed four major areas: (1) gender constancy, (2) knowledge of gender-role content, (3) per-

1. More detailed information about all measures can be obtained by contacting the authors at the Institute for Research on Social Problems, 520 Pearl Street, Boulder, Colorado 80302.

Table 3.2. Summary of Measures and Results: Preschool Sample

AREA MEASURED	TEST	SHORT DESCRIPTION	SCORES OBTAINED	SIGNIFICANT DIFFERENCES OBTAINED
Gender constancy	Gender Constancy Scale (Slaby & Frey, 1975)	6 items, 3 subscales	Gender identity (0–2)	None
			Gender stability (0–2)	Age: older higher
			Gender constancy (0–2)	None
			Total gender constancy (0–6)	Family constellation difference: highest in children with opposite-sex siblings
Knowledge of gender-role content	Activity rating scale (Katz & Boswell, 1982)	8 photos of masculine and femine activities	Knowledge of masculine activity stereotypes (0–4)	Sex: boys higher Age: older higher
			Knowledge of feminine activity stereotypes (0–4)	Sex: girls higher Age: older higher
	Toy rating scale (Katz & Boswell, 1982)	14 photos of masculine, feminine, and neutral activities	Knowledge of masculine toy stereotypes (0–5)	Sex: boys higher Age: older higher Family constellation: onlies lowest
			Knowledge of feminine toy stereotypes (0–5)	Sex: girls higher Age: older higher Family constellation: Girls with older sisters highest, boys with older brothers lowest
	Personality Trait Stereotypes (Simms, Davis, Foushee, Holahan, Spence, & Helmreich, 1978)	5 feminine and 5 masculine adjectives	Knowledge of masculine adjectives (0–5)	Sex: boys higher
			Knowledge of feminine adjectives (0–5)	Sex: girls higher Age: older higher Family constellation: only boys higher

(*continued*)

Table 3.2. (*Continued*)

AREA MEASURED	TEST	SHORT DESCRIPTION	SCORES OBTAINED	SIGNIFICANT DIFFERENCES OBTAINED
			Combined knowledge of stereotypes (3 scales)	Sex: each sex more aware of same gender Age: older higher Family constellation: only males higher on female stereotypes
Perception of socialization influences	Expected peer reactions to cross-sex toys (Katz & Boswell, 1982)	10 photos of traditional, cross-sex, and neutral toys	Number of cross-sex items reacted to positively (0–5)	Age: lower scores in older subjects Family constellation for boys: only boys see friends as least flexible; boys with sisters see friends as most flexible
	Expected sibling reactions to cross-sex toys (Katz & Boswell, 1982)	10 photos (as above)	Number of cross-sex toys reacted to positively (0–5)	Children with sisters: girls view older sisters as less flexible than younger sisters; boys see reverse Children with brothers: older children viewed brothers as less flexible than younger children
	Expected parental reactions to cross-sex toys	10 photos (as above)	Number of cross-sex toys reacted to positively (0–5)	Age: older children see parents as less flexible Family constellation for girls: girls with brothers see parents as more permissive than only children or girls with sisters do

Gender-role flexibility	Toy preference (Katz, 1979a)	14 photos of masculine, feminine, and non-sex-typed toys	Number of masculine choices (0–5)	Sex: boys higher Age: younger higher Sex × age: girls decline with age, boys do not Family constellation: only girls higher (marginal)
			Number of feminine choices (0–5)	Sex: boys higher Age: younger higher Sex × age: boys decline with age, girls do not
			Number of neutral choices (0–4)	Neutral + masculine: only girls higher than other girls
	Personal Attributes Questionnaire (Simms, Davis, Foushee, Holahan, Spence, & Helmreich, 1978)	5 masculine and 5 feminine adjectives	Number of masculine adjectives chosen for self-description (0–5)	No significant differences
			Number of feminine adjectives chosen for self-description (0–5)	No significant differences
	Tolerance for flexibility in others	10 picture choices of traditional versus non-traditional activities, 5 of women 5 of men	Number of nontraditional choices for men (0–5)	Sex: girls prefer more Family constellation: first borns with opposite-sex sibling had lowest scores Age × sex: boys decline in tolerance, girls increase
			Number of nontraditional choices for women (0–5)	Sex: boys prefer more

Table 3.3. Summary of Measures and Results: Grade School Sample

AREA MEASURED	TEST	SHORT DESCRIPTION	SCORES OBTAINED	SIGNIFICANT DIFFERENCES OBTAINED
Knowledge of sex-role stereotypes	Vocations	Asked who usually does this; 5-point rating scale, 14 items, 5 feminine, 5 masculine, 4 neutral	Score for masculine items (0–20)	Sex: girls stereotype less
			Score for feminine items (0–20)	No significant difference
	Household	Same question as above; 14 items, 5 feminine, 5 masculine, 4 neutral	Score for masculine items (0–20)	No significant difference
			Score for feminine items (0–20)	No significant difference
	Toys and activities	Same question as above; 7 feminine, 7 masculine, 6 neutral items	Score for masculine items (0–28)	No significant difference
			Score for feminine items (0–28)	No significant difference
	Personality traits: Personal Attributes Questionnaire (Spence, Helmreich, & Stapp, 1974)	Same question as above; 5 feminine and 5 masculine items	Score for feminine items (0–5)	Girls more accurate
			Score for masculine items (0–5)	No significant difference
Perceptions of socialization influence	Expectations regarding peer ratings of cross-sex toys	10 same-sex, cross-sex, and neutral toys (same as preschool)	Number of cross-sex toys rated positively (0–5)	Sex: girls saw friends as more flexible and tolerant
	Expectations regarding sibling ratings	Same as above	Number of cross-sex toys rated positively (0–5)	No differences in perception of sisters, girls perceived brothers as more flexible than boys

Expectations regarding parent reactions to cross-sex toy play	Same as above	Number of cross-sex toys rated positively (0–5)	No significant difference
Traditionality of friends	Ratings of similarity to same sex	General same-sex similarity (0–4)	Sex: boys' friends higher
	Ratings of similarity to opposite sex	General opposite-sex similarity (0–4)	Sex: girls' friends higher Family constellation (marginal): only borns and first borns with opposite-sex siblings see friends as most flexible Sex × family constellation: above trend more pronounced in girls
Traditionality of siblings	Ratings of similarity to same sex	General same-sex similarity (0–5)	Sex: brothers more similar to males
	Ratings of similarity to opposite sex	General opposite-sex similarity (0–5)	Sex: sisters more similar to females
Traditionality of parents	Similarity to other men	Mothers' similarity to females (0–5); to males (0–5)	Sex: mothers more similar to females
	Similarity to other women	Fathers' similarity to females (0–5); to males (0–5)	Sex: fathers more similar to males
Domestic role models	Who does chores in child's household? 5 masculine, 5 feminine, 4 neutral items	Number of masculine chores done by males (0–10)	No significant difference
		By females (0–10)	No significant difference
		Number of feminine chores done by males (0–10)	No significant difference

(*continued*)

Table 3.3. (*Continued*)

AREA MEASURED	TEST	SHORT DESCRIPTION	SCORES OBTAINED	SIGNIFICANT DIFFERENCES OBTAINED
			By females (0–10)	No significant difference
	Occupational role models	Ratings of parental occupations in terms of how many males and females do it	Masculinity of mother's job (0–5)	No significant difference
			Feminity of mother's job (0–5)	No significant difference
			Masculinity of father's job (0–5)	No significant difference
			Femininity of father's job (0–5)	No significant difference
	Expected parental response to child's choice of nontraditional occupations	List of 14 traditional and nontraditional occupations	Number of nontraditional items responded to positively (0–5)	No significant difference
	Media preferences	Child's favorite characters in TV, movies, and books	Number of opposite-sex characters (0–3 in each medium)	Sex: boys choose more same-sex characters
			Desire to be like character (0–15)	Family constellation: only borns show stronger identification
	General role models	Who most like; who most want to be like	Similarity to parents, siblings, friends, and teachers	Family constellation: only borns more adult, less peer-oriented
General sex-role flexibility	Toy preferences	14-item list of masculine, feminine and neutral toys	Number of masculine items preferred (0–5)	Sex: boys higher
			Number of feminine items preferred (0–5)	Sex: girls higher

		Number of neutral items preferred (0–4)	Sex: girls higher
Personality Attributes Questionnaire (Spence, Helmreich, & Stapp, 1974)	10 adjectives and 5-point self-rating scale	Masculine adjectives used for self-description (0–25)	Sex: boys higher Family constellation: only girls use more
		Feminine adjectives used for self-description (0–25)	Sex: girls higher Family constellation: only boys use more
Future domestic aspirations	14-item list of masculine, feminine, and neutral household chores	Number of masculine items preferred (0–5)	Sex: boys higher
		Number of feminine items preferred (0–5)	Sex: girls higher
Future vocational expectations	14-item list of 5 feminine, 5 masculine	Number of masculine items preferred (0–5)	Sex: boys higher
		Number of feminine items preferred (0–5)	Sex: girls higher
Combined preference and self-descriptions		Present activities	Family constellation: onlys more flexible
		Future activities	No significant difference
Tolerance for flexibility in children	Two 10-item lists 10 cross-sex toys	Number of cross-sex toys approved for boys	No significant difference
		Number of cross-sex toys approved for girls	More tolerance than for boys
Preference for atraditionality	8 pairs of pictures, 4 for each sex	Number of atraditional activities chosen for boys (0–4)	No significant difference
		Number of atraditional activities chosen for girls (0–4)	No significant difference

(continued)

Table 3.3. (*Continued*)

AREA MEASURED	TEST	SHORT DESCRIPTION	SCORES OBTAINED	SIGNIFICANT DIFFERENCES OBTAINED
	Tolerance for cross-sex jobs	Two 14-item lists: "Should a woman be ___?" and "Should a man be ___?"	Number of cross-sex jobs approved for women (0–5)	No significant difference
			Number of cross-sex jobs approved for men (0–5)	No significant difference
	Preference for atraditional adult activities (Schwager, 1977)	10 pairs of drawings showing traditional and nontraditional pictures, 5 for each sex	Number of atraditional activities chosen for men (0–5)	No significant difference
			Number of atraditional activities chosen for women (0–5)	No significant difference
Attitudes and beliefs about sibling status	Preference for siblings	Choice elicited, plus advantages and disadvantages (open-ended)	Number of advantages/disadvantages associated with no siblings/siblings	Both advantages and disadvantages of only borns perceived
	Attitudes about only children	10-item questionnaire	Comparisons of attitudes of onlies and children with siblings	Onlies more positive less negative than those with siblings
	Knowledge of stereotypes about only children	8 true–false statements	Degree of stereotypy (0–8)	Onlies and nononlies hold stereotypes

ception of socialization agents, and (4) sex-role orientation. The statistically significant results obtained in each of these areas are discussed below, with emphasis on findings relevant to family constellation variables. A summary of specific results for each scale can be found in Table 3.2.

Gender Constancy. The gender constancy measure contained three subscales: gender identity, gender stability, and gender constancy. The results from the gender identity items revealed that almost all the preschool children in our sample were able to accurately label themselves. Age differences were obtained on the gender stability measure, which indicated that older preschool children showed greater gender stability than younger preschool children. The results of analyses of variance conducted on the data from the total scores (three subscales combined) indicated that responses differed depending on sibling constellation, but not in the predicted direction. Children with opposite-sex siblings or younger same-sex siblings had higher total gender constancy scores than children in the other groups.

Knowledge of Gender-Role Content. The results from the three scales employed to assess knowledge of gender-role content indicated that the age and sex of the child affects scores on these measures, often to a greater degree than sibling constellation. On all three scales, boys showed greater awareness of masculine stereotypes, whereas girls obtained higher scores on feminine ones. Generally speaking, toy stereotypes were best known, activity stereotypes were intermediate, and trait stereotypes were least known. On most scales, age differences were obtained in the expected direction. On the male toy stereotype scales, only children had lower scores, contrary to prediction. Girls with older sisters were most knowledgeable about female toy stereotypes, whereas boys with older brothers were least knowledgeable.

Some support for the prediction was obtained when the three subscales were combined. A significant sibling category effect was found for boys on the total female stereotypes, indicating that male children without siblings exhibited higher scores than children in the other groups.

It would appear from these findings that early sex-role acquisition is affected by sibling status to some extent, as well as by the child's developmental level and gender. Same-sex content appears to be learned earlier than content associated with the opposite sex. This "gendocentric" trend is consistent with the findings reported by others (e.g., Perry & Bussey, 1979; Slaby & Frey, 1975).

Perception of Socialization Agents. Children were asked their perceptions of how their siblings, friends, and parents would respond to a set of toys traditionally associated with the opposite sex. Perceptions about peers varied with age. Both boys and girls at the 3- to 4-year-old range viewed their friends as liking to play with cross-sex toys. This perception clearly changes in the 5- to 6-year-old group, where friends are seen as much less likely to play with such toys. Although this age difference was significant for both girls and boys, it was more pronounced for the boys. Male only children perceived their friends as being much less flexible than other boys did, whereas boys with sisters viewed their friends as most flexible.

Perceptions about parents revealed similar age trends. Older preschool children saw their parents as being somewhat more restrictive than younger ones did. Differences were also associated with sibling constellation for the female sample. Girls with brothers viewed their parents as most permissive, only children were intermediate, and girls with sisters saw their parents as least permissive. This trend may reflect the fact that girls with brothers are more likely to have masculine sex-typed toys in the household, and that parents with children of both sexes may be more permissive of toy sharing.

Findings with regard to siblings were analyzed separately for sex of sibling. Analogous to the peer findings, 5- and 6-year-old girls saw their sisters as less flexible than did 3- and 4-year-old girls. Girls also distinguished clearly between what an older versus a younger sister might wish to play with and viewed an older sister as considerably less flexible than a younger one. Boys were much less clear about this, however. At age 5 they showed a similar trend, but at the younger level they viewed an *older* sister as more likely to play with masculine toys than a *younger* sister. For children with brothers the only differences were associated with age. The older the children (of either sex), the more likely they were to see their brothers as relatively inflexible with regard to playing with feminine sex-typed toys.

To summarize, it appears that between the ages of 3 and 6 children become increasingly sensitive to other people's conceptions about sex roles. Friends are viewed as increasingly less interested in cross-sex play (particularly by only male children), as are siblings. Parents are viewed as less tolerant by older than by younger children. Girls with brothers view their parents as most tolerant of nontraditional play, a finding that may be related to greater accessibility of cross-sex toys.

Sex-Role Orientation. Findings about masculine toy preferences revealed significant differences associated with age and sex and a significant sex × age interaction. As expected, boys preferred masculine toys more than girls did. The age effect resulted in stronger preferences among the younger children. The sex × age interaction, however, revealed that this decline with age occurred only for the girls.

The data about feminine toys was similar to those about the masculine toys. There were stronger preferences by girls and younger children for feminine toys than for masculine toys. A significant age × sex interaction indicated that the age decline reflected diminished interest in female toys on the part of older boys (not girls). When responses to both cross-sex and neutral toys were analyzed, a difference emerged between only-born girls and other girls. As predicted, the only borns were more flexible.

No differences were found on the children's form of the Personality Attributes Questionnaire, suggesting that this scale is not one that discriminates for preschool children.

Boys preferred more nontraditional activities for women than girls did, whereas girls preferred more nontraditional activities for men than boys did. With regard to the male figures depicted, however there was a significant main effect of family constellation and a significant age × sex interaction. The age × sex interaction suggests that boys and girls show little difference in tolerance levels at 3 and 4 years of age. At 5 and 6 years, however, boys become markedly less tolerant of nontraditional behavior on the part of male adults, whereas older girls become more tolerant. The family constellation effect indicates that the highest preference for nontraditionality occurred in those with an older same-sex sibling, whereas the lowest preference occurred in first borns with an opposite-sex sibling. This latter group also obtained the highest gender constancy scores, suggesting that acquisition of gender constancy and level of tolerance for atraditionality may be influenced by similar factors.

The Grade School Sample

Grade school findings will be discussed in the following areas: knowledge and endorsement of sex-role stereotypes, descriptions of socialization agents in the environment, degree of gender-role flexibility or traditionality, and feelings and beliefs about only children. Specific results are summarized in Table 3.3.

Knowledge of Sex-Role Stereotypes. The child's knowledge of sex-role stereotypes was assessed with regard to toys and activities, domestic chores, occupational expectations, and personality traits. Results indicated that grade school children are quite aware of all these types of stereotypes. No differences were obtained that related to family constellation. Girls were more accurate than boys in identifying expressive traits as feminine. They also stereotyped masculine jobs less than boys did.

Perceptions of Socialization Agents. 1. Media choices—Children were asked questions about their favorite characters in the various media (television, books, movies) and asked to rate their value as an identification figure (i.e., how much they wanted to be like the character and how much other boys and girls wanted to be like the character). The results indicated that the type of medium has little effect on the sex of character boys selected as favorites, since males are invariably chosen. The few boys who did select females came from two-child families. The type of medium plays a significant role, however, in whether a girl will select a male or female character as a favorite, and girls chose the most same-sex characters in books. Both male and female only borns exhibited significantly stronger identification with media characters than did children with siblings. Only children also tended to show stronger preferences for adults over child characters.

2. Perception of parents—Children were asked a number of questions about their parents, including their perceptions of parental tolerance for toys and occupations traditionally associated with the opposite sex, the allocation of household chores, and their parents' personalities. The results obtained suggest that grade school children generally view their parents in a traditional manner. They see them as differentiating their children's toy and occupational choices along sex-typed lines. These perceptions did not differ depending on the sex or sibling constellation of the child.

3. Perception of peers—Children generally perceived their friends as not wanting to play with toys strongly associated with the opposite sex. Girls reported it to be unlikely that their friends would play with a race car set, a toy airplane, or a model boat, whereas boys were equally certain that their friends would almost never select a tea party set, a doll, or a play house. Girls viewed their friends as more flexible than boys did. No sibling category effect emerged for girls. A significant sibling effect for boys was that those with an older sister saw their friends as most traditional, whereas those with a younger sister viewed their friends as most flexible.

When asked whether their friends would like them to play with certain toys, the boys were equally adamant about their friend's wishes with regard to dolls, tea sets, and playing house. Girls, on the other hand, expected their peers to be somewhat more tolerant of toys traditionally associated with males. Thus the girls tended to perceive their peers as more tolerant than the boys did.

Open-ended ratings of their best friends in terms of same-sex similarity revealed that boys perceived their friends as very similar to most other boys, whereas girls perceived their friends as somewhat less similar to other girls (means of 3.51 vs. 3.03 out of a possible 4). Ratings of opposite-sex similarity revealed differences attributable to sex, a marginal family constellation effect ($p < .08$), and an interaction of sex × sibling category. The sex difference indicates that boys perceived greater opposite-sex dissimilarity in their friends than girls did. The sibling category indicates that only children and those with younger opposite-sex siblings perceive their friends as more androgynous than other groups do. An inspection of the sex × sibling interaction indicates that the above pattern is particularly characteristic of girls.

To summarize, peers are perceived as behaving in accordance with sex-typed norms, although girls perceive their peer group as being somewhat more flexible than boys do. Girls also perceive their friends as more nontraditional, a trend particularly pronounced in only children or girls with brothers.

4. Perceptions of siblings—Boys and girls were asked to anticipate their siblings' responses to various toys. There were no differences in girls' and boys' perceptions of their sisters. Girls, however, perceived their brothers as being more flexible than boys did. Both girls and boys perceived their siblings to be much less sex typed than their friends. For example, 84% of the girls and 68% of the boys said that their brothers would play with a doll. Both of these figures contrast sharply with the 8% of boys who thought their *friends* would play with a doll. Perhaps these differences have something to do with the availability of cross-sex toys when male and female children are both present in the household or with the stringent sex-role normative function projected upon friends.

5. General role models—Children were asked a number of questions about who in their social environment they would turn to for various needs, as well as who they most wanted to be like. The most interesting finding on this scale was that a greater proportion of only borns identified with and wanted to be like their parents, whereas those with siblings (particularly boys) were much more peer oriented in this realm. This finding is in accordance with media results demonstrating that only borns prefer more adult characters than do those with siblings. Female only children identify more with their fathers than other girls do.

Flexibility of Self-Described Gender-Role Behavior. Sex differences were fairly pronounced on all self-descriptive tasks. Boys preferred masculine sex-typed toys (e.g., race cars and water pistols), whereas girls preferred feminine ones (e.g., jump ropes and dolls). Boys exhibited preferences for male sex-typed jobs (e.g., truck driver, baseball player), whereas girls chose female sex-typed ones (e.g., teacher, nurse). The same trend was obtained for household chores and adjectives employed for self-description. Boys used more instrumental adjectives, whereas girls used more expressive ones.

Although most children showed strong evidence of sex typing, girls were less extreme than boys. They avoided cross-sex toys less and chose more cross-sex occupations than boys did.

No differences attributable to family constellation were obtained on chores, jobs, or toys (when considered as separate scales). Girls with brothers expected other boys to like their favorite leisure-time activity more than other girls did. With regard to personality characteristics, sibling category differences were found in the predicted direction. Only children more readily attributed opposite-sex adjectives to themselves than did children with siblings, although the only children did not differ from other groups on same-sex trait attributions, suggesting more androgynous orientations.

A final analysis was conducted on the combined self-descriptive tasks. The tasks were categorized with those that involved current or present-oriented tasks (e.g., toys, activities, current personality descriptions) and those that dealt with future adult tasks (e.g., job choices and anticipated domestic chores). This conceptualization is in accordance with the previously described theoretical model and is in keeping with factor analytic results obtained by Katz and Boswell (1982). Analysis of future-oriented nontraditionality yielded no significant differences. Analysis of present tasks, however, revealed a family constellation effect in the expected direction. Only borns were significantly more flexible than children with siblings.

Preference and Tolerance for Atraditionality in Others. Scales assessing preference for sex-role atraditional behavior revealed no differences attributable to the family constellation variable. Grade school children showed greater tolerance for girls playing with masculine toys than for boys playing with feminine ones. Girls were marginally more tolerant than boys.

Children were generally not tolerant of men and women working in nontraditional jobs, although girls were more tolerant than boys toward adult males engaging in female sex-typed occupations (e.g., nurses, models, ballet dancers). No differences were found in tolerance for adult females engaging in masculine sex-typed occupations. No differences attributable to family constellation were obtained on any of the tolerance tasks.

Future Family Aspirations. Children were asked about their future expectations of marriage, children, and the ideal composition of their future family. Several interesting trends emerged from this data. First, fewer boys than girls expressed a wish to marry (82% vs. 92%) or to have children (85% vs. 94%). Second, boys and girls did not differ in terms of the average number of children desired (two), but a much higher proportion indicated a desire for a single child than adult populations do. Third, the number of children desired was significantly related to the child's family constellation. Only children desired smaller future families than others. With regard to the desired gender composition of the projected family, each sex wants to reproduce itself. Girls want more daughters, and boys want more sons.

Attitudes toward Children without Siblings. Feelings and beliefs about sibling status were assessed on two scales. There were both similarities and differences in the perceptions of children with and without siblings. Differences as a function of family constellation were evident in the first question, which asked whether the child wanted to be an only child or have siblings. Those with brothers and sisters strongly preferred to have siblings (88%), whereas only children were about equally divided on the issue. Although almost half of the only borns liked their state, the fact that so many of them wanted siblings merits some discussion. One possible explanation is that only borns are less happy, either because they miss the experience of having siblings or believe they are deprived in some way. Another possibility, however, is that there may be many children with siblings who wish they were only borns but are restrained from saying this because of strong social pressures and socialization against expressions of hostility toward siblings. Both groups agreed upon some advantages of being an only child, such as living in a quieter house, with less fighting and fewer rules. On the other hand, the only child was also perceived to be lonelier and to be bossed more by friends. On the first scale, children had a choice of three responses (i.e., only child, those with siblings, or no difference). Table 3.4 presents the percentages of both groups for positive and negative items. As can be seen, those with siblings perceived only borns less positively and more negatively than did those without siblings.

The stereotype scale had a forced-choice format and did not give a "no difference" alternative. Items stated in a positive way included only borns having more friends, getting along better with others, being happier, and getting upset less. Negative items included being lonelier, spoiled, selfish, and shy. As can be seen from Table 3.4, only borns viewed themselves more positively than those with siblings viewed them. More than half of the only borns, however, also attributed many negative characteristics to only borns, a percentage only somewhat lower than those with siblings (this difference was not significant).

This was somewhat surprising, since it might be expected that only children, like other minority groups, would defend their own status. Although they do so with regard to positive attributes, they also agree with the stereotypic negative aspects of being an only child, particularly with regard to being lonely and spoiled.

The degree to which young children apparently hold well-formed belief structures about only children is quite surprising. These beliefs are in accordance with those held by adults, although the specific means of transmission remain unclear.

Table 3.4. Responses to Negative and Positive Items

TYPE OF ITEMS	RESPONSE CHOICE	GROUP	
		ONLY BORNS	THOSE WITH SIBLINGS
ATTITUDES TOWARD ONLY BORNS SCALE			
Positive	Only child	60%	44%
	Child with siblings	9%	15%
	No difference	31%	41%
Negative	Only child	22%	33%
	Child with siblings	36%	36%
	No difference	42%	31%
STEREOTYPES ABOUT ONLY BORNS SCALE			
Positive	True	51%	38%
	False	49%	62%
Negative	True	53%	56%
	False	47%	44%

Developmental Comparisons

Wherever possible, comparable measures were employed with the preschool and grade school samples so that developmental differences might be ascertained. This section presents the significant results obtained with the measures used for both age groups.

Stereotypes

Knowledge and endorsement of stereotypes about toys and personality traits were assessed at both age levels. Responses to masculine and feminine toys and personality traits yielded similar findings: an age difference in the expected direction (older children had higher scores) and a gendocentric sex difference (each sex endorsed own-sex stereotypes more). Age $\times$ sex interactions on all scales revealed that children catch up on knowledge of opposite-sex stereotypes by the time they reach the third grade. It is of interest to note that although grade school children clearly had more knowledge about stereotypes than preschoolers, such knowledge (or endorsement) correlated *negatively* with age in the grade school group. Only children (particularly females) endorsed fewer masculine and feminine toy stereotypes than other groups; only males endorsed more female toy stereotypes than others. A significant sex × age × sibling category obtained on the combined female-stereotype scores suggests that family constellation makes more of a difference for preschool boys than for other children. Both only-born boys and boys with an older sister were more knowledgeable about female stereotypes than were other boys.

Perception of Significant Others

Questions were asked about parents, peers, and siblings at both age levels to ascertain perceived flexibility toward cross-sex toy play. Older girls viewed their parents as less permissive than younger ones did. Boys' perceptions varied as a function of both age and family constellation. Older only-born boys perceived their parents as more stringent than younger ones did; boys with sisters, however, viewed their parents as more tolerant as they got older.

Grade school boys perceived their friends as much less flexible than younger boys did. They rarely expected their friends to play with cross-sex toys. Girls showed a similar age trend, but it was not as pronounced. A significant sibling category effect revealed that boys with younger sisters saw their friends as most flexible, whereas only children and boys with older sisters saw their peers as more traditional.

Girls perceived their brothers as more flexible than boys did. Perceptions about sisters did not vary systematically with sex of target child. They did, however, vary significantly as a joint function of age level and sibling category. Preschool children viewed their older sisters as less flexible than their younger sisters, whereas grade school children viewed their older sisters as more flexible than their younger ones.

It appears from these findings that the social environment perceived by older children is much less tolerant and flexible than that perceived by younger children.

Preference and Tolerance for Atraditional Behavior

All scales that assessed preference for atraditionality yielded quite similar patterns. There were gendocentric sex differences, in that nontraditionality was preferred in the opposite sex. Analogous to the results obtained from the perception scales, preference for traditionality is stronger at the grade school than at the preschool level. Only-born girls and girls with brothers showed the highest preference for nontraditional behavior.

Self-Descriptions of Flexibility

The two scales used with both age groups assessed toy preferences and use of self-descriptive adjectives. Sex differences in the expected direction were found in preferences for masculine and feminine sex-typed toys. These sex differences were significantly greater at the grade school level than at the preschool level. An analysis of the combined male and female items selected (which can be conceptualized as a type of androgyny score) revealed that girls preferred more of both kinds of items and that grade school children were less androgynous than preschool children. The sex difference occurred only at the younger age levels.

On the self-description scale, boys used more masculine adjectives than girls did. Girls used more feminine adjectives than boys but only at the older ages.

One prediction initially advanced was that preschool only children would most closely resemble first borns in terms of gender-role learning and orientation, whereas grade school only borns would most closely resemble last borns. A comparison of the means obtained on the various scales corroborated this expectation. For the preschool sample, only children's means were closer to first borns' 9 out of 14 times; in contrast, grade school only borns were closer to first borns in only 5 out of 16 instances (i.e., 11 out of 16 were more similar to second borns). This trend was statistically significant ($p < .01$).

An additional prediction was made regarding sex differences within the various sibling constellations. Because of the anticipated differences in androgyny, it was expected that boys and girls who had no siblings would differ less than those who did. This expectation was corroborated with the older children and the combined sample. Of a possible 32 comparisons, 22 yielded sex differences that were smaller for the onlies. Inspection of the preschool children's scores, however, revealed an opposite trend: Only children exhibited more pronounced sex differences (of marginal significance) than children with siblings, particularly on the masculine content scales. This suggests that the absence of siblings may accentuate sex differences during the preschool period but attenuate them later on.

PARENT PORTION

Measures

The interviews conducted with parents yielded data on general sex-role orientations and attitudes, sex-role socialization techniques, and family planning decisions. Demographic information was also obtained, including age, education, religious and ethnic background, marital status and employment, and composition of parental family of origin. The scales used to assess each of these areas are described fully in Katz and Boswell (1982).

General information and attitudes relevant to sex roles assessed included attitudes toward women working, mothers' commitment to work, comfort with nontraditional activities (Helmreich, Spence & Holahan, 1979), division of household chores, and a political liberalism–conservatism scale. In addition, each parent was asked to describe himself or herself in terms of instrumental and expressive adjectives on the Personal Attributes Questionnaire (Spence *et al.*, 1975).

Child-rearing techniques relevant to sex typing were examined along a number of dimensions, including parental permissiveness (Spence, Helmreich, & Davis, 1980), tolerance for gender-role flexibility in play, and parents' present and future aspirations for their child (e.g., in access to media, occupational choice, and household chores).

A final portion of the questionnaire dealt with family planning issues, including family background and composition, ideal family preferences before having children, and factors that contributed to decisions about family size. Parents were also asked about their attitudes and beliefs concerning sibling status, including the stereotypes they held regarding only children. Additionally, parents of only borns were asked about pressures they had experienced to increase their family size.

Results

Sex-Role Attitudes and Orientations

The overwhelming majority of parents (98.2%) felt that it would be permissible for mothers to work *at some time* during their child's development. When and how much, however, varied somewhat as a function of the age and sex of the child. Parents of grade school children favored the child being older when the mother worked than parents of preschoolers. Most parents felt that the mother's decision to work while a child was young was more justified when financial need existed. Husbands were in favor of wives working part-time rather than full-time. There were no differences between parents of one and two children in these beliefs.

In terms of actual work experience, the majority of mothers indicated that they worked during their first pregnancy (no differences between mothers of one and two children). After the birth of their first or only child, 62% of the mothers returned to work within three years. Significantly more mothers of only children worked for pay some time after the birth of their child than mothers of two children.

Questions concerning division of labor within the household revealed that mothers cared for their child or children approximately 70% of the time on an average weekday, compared to 30% for the fathers. These figures were unrelated to either mothers' work status or number of children in the household. Patterns of household labor were quite traditional. Mothers reported doing 84% of house-cleaning chores to fathers' 16%. The comparable figure for working mothers was 78%, with mothers of sons performing more chores than mothers of daughters. Fathers contributed approximately 82% of the income (97% when wives were not employed, and 73% when wives were employed). Mothers who viewed their employment as a "career" rather than a "job" contributed a greater percentage to the total household income (32% vs. 19%). None of these trends differed by family constellation or age of the child, nor did the degree of comfort parents expressed with nontraditional activities. Thus, at least in terms of what is immediately observable, children are being exposed to fairly traditional parental role models. Although household behavior did not differentiate parents on the basis of number of children, parents of one child had higher scores on the political liberalism scale than parents of two children.

We were interested in ascertaining whether parents of only children also described themselves in more androgynous terms on the Personal Attributes Questionnaire (PAQ). This questionnaire is composed of three subscales: an F scale (comprised of female-valued items), an M scale (male-valued items), which is orthogonal to the F scale, and an MF scale, a bipolar masculinity scale. Some controversy exists about the designation of androgyny on the PAQ (see Spence, 1982). Although androgyny was originally conceptualized by Bem (1975) as a balance between the M and F scales, many researchers currently define an androgynous individual as one who obtains relatively high scores (above the median) on *both* the masculinity and femininity scales when utilizing the fourfold classification scheme described by Spence and Helmreich (1978). Because of the controversy, we analyzed the data in a number of ways, including individual subscale analysis and combinations.

Not surprisingly, fathers obtained significantly higher scores on the M scale than mothers, and mothers obtained higher F-scale scores than fathers. Fathers of grade school only borns had higher M scores than fathers of grade school children with siblings, although fathers of preschool onlies and nononlies did not differ. Masculinity scores were highest for fathers of only-born sons. Scores on the femininity scale did not differentiate either mothers or fathers on the basis of the number of children they had. Analysis of the MF scale revealed higher scores for fathers than mothers. A significant sibling-category main effect of family constellation was obtained: MF scores were higher for parents of one child than of two children.

Use of the fourfold classification for the M and F scales yielded no significant difference between parents of one child and parents of two children. Androgyny defined as an M × F interaction term also yielded no significant differences. Thus, parents of one versus two children did not differ in androgyny level.

Sex-Role Socialization Techniques

Parental Permissiveness. The Child-Rearing Practices Questionnaire (Spence, Helmreich, & Davis, 1980) contained two subscales: rule making (e.g., "I [always . . . never] stick to the rules I make) and independence granting (e.g., "I [always . . . never] allow my child to disagree with my ideas"). Results revealed that mothers both impose more rules on their children and grant them more independence than fathers do. Mothers of an only female child and mothers of a male child with a sibling make more rules than other mothers. Parents of girls report granting more independence to their children than parents of boys, a reverse of other findings reported in the literature.

Tolerance for Flexibility. Parents were asked how they would feel if someone gave their son or daughter each toy on a list of traditionally masculine and feminine toys. As expected, boys' parents felt more positive about masculine items than were girls' parents. Parents of one child felt more positive about masculine toys than those with two children, although an interaction made it clear that family constellation made a difference only for girls. Parents of an only daughter were much more tolerant about their child's receiving masculine toys than parents of daughters with a sibling.

The results on the feminine-toys scale indicated that girls' parents felt more positive about feminine toys than boys' parents and that those with younger chlidren were most positive. Although mothers and fathers did not differ with regard to feminine toy choices for their daughters, they did differ with regard to their sons: Boys' fathers were much less tolerant of cross-sex play than mothers were. It is of interest to note that only-born males and females are responded to differently in terms of tolerance for cross-sex toy play. Parents of only daughters are *most* tolerant, whereas parents of only sons are *least* tolerant.

Parental Preferences and Future Expectations. Parents were asked to name the main characters from the books, television shows, and movies they preferred for their children. Very few female characters were mentioned on any of the media items. Out of a maximum score of 3 on each, an average of .49 female book characters, .26 female television characters, and .56 female movie characters were mentioned. This preponderance of preferred male models may reflect either the availability or memorability of the characters or parents' greater valuing of masculine characteristics in adult models. Generally, mothers mentioned more female characters than fathers did, although not overwhelmingly so. Significantly more female characters were also mentioned by parents of daughters, particularly those at the grade school level. Mothers of grade school daughters without siblings preferred more female book models than other mothers. Mothers of only children mentioned more female movie characters than mothers of two children. When scores of both parents were combined, parents of one-child families mentioned significantly more male movie characters than those of two-child families. When these latter two results are considered together, they suggest that parents of only children may want them to emulate both feminine and masculine characteristics.

With regard to future expectations, most parents held high educational goals for their children: 62% wanted their children to complete college. The highest educational aspirations were held by mothers of only sons.

Tolerance for nontraditional occupations was assessed by responses to six hypothetical situations, three describing sons going into occupations traditionally performed by women (e.g., secretary, home economics professor) and three describing daughters entering occupations traditionally performed by men (e.g., truck driver, engineering professor). Parents of daughters were more enthusiastic about these atypical careers for their hypothetical sons than were actual parents of sons. Parents of a preschool only daughter were most tolerant, whereas parents of a grade school son with siblings were least enthusiastic about the idea of a male selecting a traditionally female occupation. Mothers were more positive than fathers about hypothetical daughters choosing masculine occupations, and parents of daughters showed more enthusiasm than parents of sons. The most tolerant parents were those with an only daughter.

Family Planning and Attitudes toward Only Borns

Subjects were asked to recall their feelings about ideal family composition before they became parents. Almost all had had some ideas about this issue. A large majority of the parents (81%) spontaneously mentioned the number of children they had wanted. Gender of the children was not mentioned as frequently as number in the earlier, hypothetical family, although fathers mentioned gender more frequently than mothers did. In accordance with prediction, parents of two children mentioned gender more than parents of only children. This finding was particularly pronounced at the preschool level. Thus, as expected, gender seems to be less salient as a family planning consideration for parents of only children.

Some differences in ideal families were reported as a function of existing family composition. For example, parents of boys reported wanting more boys originally than did parents of girls. Parents of only girls said they originally wanted fewer sons than others, while parents of only boys had wanted more sons.

In response to questions concerning factors influencing family size, most parents responded that their reasons for not having additional children were voluntary, and parents of two children did not differ significantly from parents of an only child on this. As anticipated, parents of one child gave more open-ended responses justifying their decision than others. There were both similarities and differences in the content of responses given by the different groups. The most frequent first response given by both the one-child and two-child parents related to financial considerations. Differences between the two groups appeared on the second most frequent response. Parents of one child frequently mentioned "parental freedom" as a factor influencing their decision to have only one child. On the other hand, parents of two children said that the "child's best interest" was an important influence in their family size.

In discussing the relative advantages and disadvantages of the one-child family, positive personality characteristics, financial privileges, convenience, and ease of travel were prominently mentioned. Only 28% of only-child parents mentioned any disadvantages at all. Significantly more advantages were mentioned by one- than by two-child parents. This suggests either that the former are more pleased or that they feel in greater need to justify their choice.

Advantages mentioned by parents of two children included better social interaction skills, closeness, companionship, financial privileges, and parental ease and convenience. More parents of two children than of only borns mentioned disadvantages (65%), and these included sibling rivalry, reduced parental attention, financial difficulty, and noise.

When asked to describe a "typical" only child, most parents mentioned one or two characteristics. In the majority of cases the first response mentioned was negative (e.g., spoiled, self-centered, selfish, lonely, or materialistic). More parents of two children (66%) mentioned negative characteristics than did parents who actually had one child (37%), and fathers reported more negative characteristics than mothers. Twice as many parents of one child mentioned positive social attributes (e.g., "more mature," "more self-reliant") than did parents of two children (36% vs. 17%). More two-child parents indicated that being an only child is a disadvantage than did only-child parents (63% and 14%, respectively). Thus, parents of more than one child appear more willing to endorse stereotypes about only-borns, both on open-ended and agree–disagree formats.

There were significant differences between parents of only borns and others on almost all attitude questions. Parents of only borns believed that they had closer relationships with their child, that onlies are less likely to be spoiled, that mothers of only borns are more likely to pursue a career, that raising two children is harder and more expensive, that parenting one child is just as satisfying, and that having one child is not a selfish decision. Thus, it appears that one's actual family experiences influence belief structures in this area considerably.

RELATIONS BETWEEN CHILDREN AND PARENTS

A number of correlations were obtained between children's gender-role flexibility scores and parental educational, personality, and socialization practices as a function of both age and sex of the child. Of greatest interest was the finding that the particular parent whose influence is most prominent varies with each group. These trends are summarized in Table 3.5, which presents the number of significant correlations obtained between each child–parent dyad.

It is clear that at the grade school level the preponderance of correlations occur between same-sex dyads (i.e., sons and fathers, daughters and mothers). For girls this appears to represent a strong departure from the preschool period, during which fathers appear to have the greatest influence. In younger boys both parents were equally represented, although the socialization practices of the mother correlated more highly with the boys' flexibility scores. To summarize, it appears that the parent of the opposite sex may be more influential at early age levels (particularly for girls), whereas the same-sex parent may play a more significant role during middle childhood.

Table 3.5. Number of Significant Parent–Child Correlations

	AGE OF CHILD			
	PRESCHOOL		GRADE SCHOOL	
PARENTS	SONS	DAUGHTERS	SONS	DAUGHTERS
Mother	9	1	11	29
Father	7	10	19	14
Total	16	11	30	43

At the preschool level parent–child correlations were higher for only children than for others, suggesting that parental influence is stronger in those without siblings.

In order to determine which parent variables maximally distinguished between children with and without siblings, several discriminant function analyses were conducted. Table 3.6 presents the discriminant functions obtained for boys and girls separately. As can be seen, both mothers' and fathers' scores play a predictive role, but these do not always function in the same directions. For the sample of boys (preschool and grade school combined), the most differentiating variables were the degree to which mothers endorsed traditional jobs (higher for nononlys), father's masculinity score (higher for onlys), father's tolerance for cross-sex play (lower for onlys), and mother's tolerance for cross-sex jobs (higher for onlys). This analysis correctly classified boys' sibling categories 66% of the time. An interesting aspect of this pattern is that the mothers and fathers of boys with no siblings appear to present conflicting models and socialization practices. Fathers of only boys were more masculine sex typed themselves and less tolerant of cross-sex play than were fathers of boys with siblings. In contrast, mothers of only children were more tolerant of cross-sex play in their only sons and less apt to endorse strongly sex-typed occupational goals for them than were mothers of sons with siblings. Therefore mothers of only boys may be more desirous of instilling gender-flexible patterns; fathers, on the other hand, may encourage their only sons to be traditionally masculine. Since fathers' scores correlated more than mothers' with those of their grade school sons, the paternal influence might well prevail in the case of conflicting information.

Table 3.6. Standardized Canonical Discriminant Function Coefficients of Parental Scores for Only Children versus Those with Siblings

PREDICTORS	FUNCTION 1*
BOYS	
Mother's endorsement of same-sex occupations	−3.57
Father's tolerance of cross-sex occupations	.81
Mother's femininity score on PAQ	.63
Father's masculinity score on PAQ	2.31
Mother's MF score on PAQ	.07
Father's tolerance of cross-sex play	−2.16
Mother's tolerance of cross-sex occupations	1.77
GIRLS	
Mother's tolerance of cross-sex play	.53
Mother's femininity score on PAQ	−.61
Mother's MF score on PAQ	.04
Father's MF score on PAQ	.31
Father's endorsement of same-sex occupations	.14
Mother's enforcement of rules	.78
Mother's tolerance of cross-sex occupations	.51
Mother's permissiveness	−.52
Mother's endorsement of same-sex occupations	−.54

*This function correctly classifies 66% of the boys and 80% of the girls into only and nononly groups.

The pattern obtained for girls was more consistent and also yielded more accurate family constellation classifications. The discriminant function analysis accurately classified only and nononly girls (at both age levels) 80% of the time. Mothers of only daughters were more tolerant of cross-sex play, more tolerant of nontraditional occupational choices, less endorsing of sex-typical jobs, and less self-descriptively feminine than mothers of daughters who have siblings. Mothers of only girls were also more likely to make more rules but to grant more independence. Fathers' scores for the most part were not as predictive for classifying girls according to sibling status. Fathers of only girls, however, were more androgynous than fathers of those with siblings, thus perhaps providing a more flexible personality model. In any event, there does not seem to be the same inconsistency between parents for only daughters as for sons.

Several discriminant and regression analyses were conducted using the entire set of variables (both parent and child) in order to assess the combination of variables that best differentiated only children from those with siblings. These analyses were performed only on the grade school sample, since more information about socialization correlates was available for this age group. Because of the consistent sex differences obtained, separate analyses were carried out for boys and girls, resulting in a relatively small number of subjects for whom data on both mothers and fathers were available. Wherever possible, combination scores were used to assess the broad parameters. Because of the relatively small number of subjects, these findings should be regarded as exploratory.

The following variables were entered into the analysis: (1) a combined gender-role flexibility score (toy preferences, domestic and occupational expectations, and CPAQ scores, the children's version of the PAQ); (2) a combined peer-perception score (anticipated friend's play activities, reactions to cross-sex play, and masculinity-femininity ratings of best friend); (3) self-ratings of masculinity and femininity; (4) knowledge of stereotypes in four areas (toys, jobs, chores, and personality traits); (5) mother's sex-role socialization practices (tolerance for nontraditional play, jobs, and domestic activities); (6) father's sex-role socialization practices (same criteria as mother's); (7) mother's education; (8) father's education; (9) mother's androgyny score on the PAQ (computed as the difference between same-sex and opposite-sex adjectives); (10) father's androgyny score (computed same as mother's); and (11) media preferences (number of opposite-sex favorite characters selected in television, books, and movies).

Based upon these scores, the most predictive standardized canonical discriminant function obtained for girls is presented in Table 3.7. This function correctly categorized only girls and girls with siblings 70% of the time. Briefly summarized, female only children describe both themselves and their friends as more flexible than do girls with siblings, they choose more opposite-sex media characters as favorites, and their parents exhibit greater flexibility in sex-role socialization practices. A comparable discriminant function conducted with the boys yielded the best discriminant function coefficients as presented in Table 3.7. This function correctly categorized only boys

Table 3.7. Discriminant Coefficients of Flexibility Scores for Girls and Boys

PREDICTOR	FUNCTION 1
Girls' flexibility score	−.34
Parental cross-sex tolerance	−.48
Peer perceptions	−.79
Media choices	−.27
Boys' flexibility scores	.91
Fathers' practices	.27
Peer perceptions	−.93
Media choices	.18

and boys with siblings 76% of the time. This function indicates that the flexibility score differentiates boys in the two family constellations, and that only boys see themselves as less flexible than others. Only borns choose fewer opposite-sex favorite media characters, and their fathers are more traditional in their socialization practices. Interestingly, however, friends of only children are perceived as being more flexible, although it should be noted that peers are generally seen as inflexible.

It appears from these findings that the effects of sibling absence on gender orientations are quite different for grade school boys and girls. In accordance with the hypotheses initially advanced, girls without siblings are more flexible than only-born boys, as is their social environment. In contrast, however, boys who are only children appear to be more traditional in some areas than their counterparts with brothers and sisters.

DISCUSSION

The results of this study partially substantiate the initial expectations, although the patterns were more complex than originally anticipated. In general, the presence or absence of siblings did make a difference in children's sex-role content and development, but the effect was often contingent upon both the age and gender of the child.

It should be recalled that we made five specific predictions regarding only children. The first was that preschool only children, particularly boys, would be more advanced in terms of gender constancy and knowledge of gender-role stereotypes. Results of gender constancy measures did not support this expectation, but some corroboration was obtained on stereotype knowledge for only boys (not for girls). A second prediction was that peers and media would be more significant socialization agents for only borns than for other children. Only children did identify more strongly with media characters; there was no difference, however, in peer influence, which was strong for all children. Parents were stronger influences for preschool only children than for preschooler children with siblings.

A third prediction was that grade school children with siblings would be more advanced in stereotype information than onlys. This was not corroborated. Instead, all grade school children had high knowledge of gender-role stereotypes and few differences between groups emerged. A fourth expectation was that only preschool children would be more like first borns on all sex-role measures, whereas grade school onlys would most resemble last borns. This trend was obtained. Finally, it was initially advanced that only children would be more flexible with regard to gender roles. There were a number of instances in which this was true. In general, however, this trend was much clearer for girls than for boys. Girls without siblings preferred more cross-sex and neutral play and perceived their parents as most tolerant of atraditionality. This suggests that although a need for gender diversity may indeed be a determinant of parental behavior, the preference for males and masculine behavior noted by other investigators (e.g., Cushna, 1966; Hoffman, 1975) may also be operative. A recent article in *The New York Times* by Christopher Wren (1982) noted that the strong desire for sons in China was the greatest obstacle for achieving the official policy of permitting only one-child families. Despite government measures to increase the status of only daughters, much discrimination against them (and their mothers) still persists.

The absence of support for the expectation that only children would be more cognitively advanced in sex-role development warrants some discussion. The relative absence of differences in gender constancy still leaves open the possibility that such differences might be found at earlier developmental levels. As originally predicted, preschool only boys were more cognitively advanced on stereotyping tasks than those with siblings, but only girls had lower scores than nononly girls and thus appeared to be less cognitively advanced.

Several other findings in the study, however, suggest that knowledge of stereotypes may not be a "pure" cognitive measure but may itself reflect a child's gender-role orientation. For the sample as a whole, knowledge of opposite-sex stereotypes was negatively related to gender-role flexibility and parental educational level; at the grade school level it was negatively related to age. This latter finding was also obtained by Emmerich, Goldman, Kirsh, and Sharabany (1977) and Plumb and Cowan (in press). Thus, it may be that past a certain developmental period, measures of *knowledge* of stereotypes may actually be tapping *endorsement* of stereotypes. If this is the case, then another interpretation of our results is that only girls endorse stereotypes less than other girls, whereas only boys endorse them more than other boys. This latter interpretation is also in keeping with other more traditional trends exhibited by the younger only-born boys, who, for example, perceived their friends as least flexible and tolerant in this area.

There was some evidence that families with both sons and daughters may have socialization patterns that are distinct from those of two-child families in which the children are of the same sex. At the preschool level, children with opposite-sex siblings exhibited higher gender stability scores and expressed the lowest preference for non-traditionality in others. Thus, the presence of an opposite-sex sibling may make early sex roles more clear-cut. On the other hand, boys with sisters perceived their friends as less traditional than other boys, whereas girls with brothers viewed their parents as quite permissive. This suggests greater flexibility when opposite-sex siblings are present, a finding obtained also with adolescents by Grotevant (1978) and with younger children by others (Brim, 1958; Koch, 1955, 1956; Sutton-Smith, 1982). At earlier age levels, the presence of an opposite-sex sibling increases the availability of cross-sex toys. Under these circumstances, parents may indeed be more permissive than children without opposite-sex siblings believe their parents would be. The greater availability of toys associated with the opposite sex also make peer responses more apparent and less caricatured.

Gender-role development generally appears to be active and intense between the ages of 3 and 5. It is affected not only by family constellation (as discussed above) but also by age, gender, and the child's social environment. Certain developmental trends emerged quite clearly in this study. At the preschool level there was a general "gendocentric" trend such that children learned stereotypes associated with their own gender earlier than they learned those associated with the opposite sex. Stereotypes about toys were learned first, activities next, and trait attributions still later. Preschool children, in fact, were not very knowledgeable about personality characteristics and sex typing. During the preschool period knowledge of stereotypes increased, and cross-sex play and preference for nontraditionality in others decreased. Preschool children also became increasingly sensitive to other people's conceptualizations of gender roles. Parents, for example, were viewed as less tolerant by 5-year-olds than by 4-year-olds, and this was reflected in the child's own tolerance levels as well. In summary, it appears that for preschool children, sex-role development and orientation are related to family practices, sibling constellation, gender, age, and peer influences.

At the grade school level many differences between only children and others emerged. Only children of both sexes displayed more gender-role flexibility on a combined score based on preferences, activity choices, and personality self-descriptions than children with siblings. This difference did not emerge, however, with regard to future sex-role expectations. Only children (particularly girls) described themselves and their friends as more androgynous and expected opposite-sex children to like what they did more than nononly children did.

Some additional differences associated with only children were found with regard to media and role-model choices. A preference for male media models was quite extensive for all children and adults, although more female only children and their mothers selected female characters. Only children of both sexes identified more with adult characters than other children did and identified more strongly with their favorite character. They also identified more frequently with actual adults in their environment rather than with peers. This suggests that the absence of siblings may serve to make other socialization agents relatively more significant. It is possible, for example, that books, television, parents, and teachers may play more important roles in the lives of only children than in the lives of children with siblings.

In contrast to our findings, previous studies have obtained somewhat contradictory results about the relation between sibling status and sex-role development. Brown and Weinraub (1982) reported no differences in toy preferences for 2- and 3-year-olds as a function of sibling status, and Vreogh (1971) found no relationship between sibling status and masculine or feminine interests for grade school and junior high school children. On the other hand, Bigner (1972), Sutton-Smith and Rosenberg (1970), and Sutton-Smith (1982) report that the presence of an older sibling is significant for the learning of sex roles and that last borns learn more quickly than onlys. MacDonald (1969), however, suggests that stronger sex typing is evident in first borns. Thus, no agreement exists about whether and how sibling constellation affects sex-role development. This suggests that it may be particularly important to use multiple measures when assessing sibling status variables, for it is clear that not all measures differentiate various family configurations. Our findings also demonstrate that sibling status has differential impact as a function of developmental level. This may help explain some of the contradictory findings that occur when age is not taken into account. At the very least, it underscores the need for further theoretical development in this area.

In both the present study and others, gender differences have been much more consistently obtained than family constellation differences. In our study, although children of both sexes preferred same-sex toys and activities and avoided cross-sex ones, this trend was much less marked for girls. Boys rated their friends as highly sex typed, whereas girls viewed their peers as more flexible and more tolerant. Boys rarely chose female media characters as favorites, whereas girls often chose male ones. Sisters were seen as more androgynous than brothers. There was greater tolerance toward female models engaged in cross-sex play than toward male models similarly engaged.

It should be noted that girls were not uniformly less stereotyped than boys; rather, each gender exhibited different areas of flexibility. Girls, for example, were more flexible about future job expectations and rated themselves as more similar to the opposite sex than boys did. Boys, on the other hand, were more flexible about future household chores and more frequently described themselves with cross-sex adjectives. Sex differences were more pronounced in preschool only children but less pronounced in grade school only children. This suggests that exaggerating sex differences may be an important factor in early sex-role learning.

The importance of peers on sex-role behavior has recently been demonstrated with children as young as 3 (Serbin, Connor, Burchardt, & Citron, 1979). Our results with children in the intermediate grades suggest that they are equally important at later ages. Sex-role flexibility was related to tolerance for atypical behavior in others and to permissiveness of significant others (most often friends). Peer influence may be stronger for boys than for girls. Boys, for example, choose their best friend as a role model significantly more frequently than girls do. Interestingly, siblings are perceived as more flexible than friends are. Boys believed that only 8% of their friends would ever play with a doll. On the other hand, girls report that over 60% of their brothers would play with a doll. Thus friends may play more of the stereotype-enforcer role than siblings do at this age level.

Attitudes toward only children were negative and pervasive in both children and their parents. Although onlys are perceived as having a few advantages, such as a quieter home and fewer rules (which, parenthetically, is not true, since parents of onlys make more rules), they are also perceived as lonelier, bossed by friends, spoiled, and socially maladjusted. It is clear that 8- and 9-year-old children are very much aware of the stereotypes associated with only children and believe them. These stereotypes are endorsed by children both with and without siblings. More research is needed to determine how this information gets transmitted.

By 8 years of age, children express the desire to replace both themselves and their family of origin. Thus only children desire significantly fewer offspring than those with siblings. Furthermore, girls want to have more daughters, whereas boys wish to have sons. How early the "girl for you, boy for me" begins! Since research shows that people of parenting age are more desirous of sons (Hoffman, 1975), there must be a developmental shift in girls' preferences in this area. It is not clear, however, when this occurs.

The parent sampling in the present study is quite unique. To our knowledge, it is the first in-depth investigation of parents of only children. The data from the parent sample indicated that parents of one child differ from parents of two children along a number of dimensions. It should be recalled that three predictions about parents of only children were initially advanced: First, it was expected that they would place less emphasis on gender diversity; second, that they would need to justify their family planning decision to a greater extent; and third, that they would be more liberal and less stereotyped. All of these expectations received some corroboration in the present study. Parents of one and more than one child did not differ in terms of androgyny, however.

When asked about what their "ideal family" was before their marriage, parents of only children mentioned gender of children significantly less often than parents of two children. When queried about factors involved in family planning decisions, parents of onlys gave significantly more reasons and mentioned more advantages associated with their choice (both suggestive of a need for justification). With regard to these reasons, parents of one child (both mothers and fathers) seemed to place more importance on their own time, their own careers, and parental freedom.

Our data show that parents of onlys are more permissive in their sex-role socialization practices, particularly with respect to their daughters. Differences did emerge on measures of tolerance of flexibility and occupational aspirations for their children. On these measures parents of one child showed more flexible attitudes, which in turn seem to have had an impact on their children. On a scale of general political attitudes, mothers of only borns were most liberal.

Parents of one child appeared quite aware of negative stereotypes concerning only children but were actually more positive about their family configuration than parents of two children. They more strongly believed, for example, that only children had closer relationships with their parents than do children with siblings, that raising two children was more difficult and expensive, and that raising a single child was not selfish. In accordance with earlier literature, parents of two children expressed many more negative sentiments about the one-child family.

Correlations were obtained between parental personality variables and socialization practices on the one hand and children's flexibility scores on the other, but differential patterns emerged at the two age levels. More correlations were obtained between the child and the cross-sex parent at the early age levels, whereas during middle childhood the preponderance of correlations occurred between the child and the same-sex parent. This pattern was not predicted. It is, however, in accordance with psychoanalytic conceptions of identification phenomena. It is also suggestive of results obtained by Kohlberg & Zigler (1967), who found that preschool children imitated cross-sex adults more but that older children switched to same-sex imitation.

The influence of various socialization agents differed for boys and girls without siblings. Only boys were exposed to a more inconsistent pattern. Their mothers were quite tolerant of cross-sex play, but their fathers had higher masculinity scores and showed less tolerance for cross-sex play than other fathers. Additionally, these boys perceived their friends as more flexible in personality but less tolerant toward atraditionality. This suggests that boys without siblings may experience considerably more conflict than girls do. For girls the picture was more consistent. Their fathers, mothers, and friends were more permissive and/or androgynous. Consequently, so were they.

In terms of the issues raised at the outset, our results suggest that there remains considerable resistance to the one-child family and that this resistance may begin in childhood. Negative stereotypes about only children were strongly held by parents who had more than one child and by both only and nononly children as young as age 8. Further research is warranted to investigate the developmental mechanisms involved in this prejudice. Part of the reason for this prejudice in adults does seem to be involved with a need for gender diversity, which was stronger in two-child than in one-child parents. When asked about future families, children expressed strong desires for having children of their own sex. Their desire for self-replacement appears strongly at an early age and may be the developmental forerunner of the typical desire for at least one child of each sex. Families who opt to have only one child do so for a variety of reasons, including medical, financial, and career. They do not seem to have the same need for gender diversity, and their sex-role socialization priorities (particularly of mothers) tend to be less stringent.

In accordance with prediction, only children do seem to be more gender-role flexible in a variety of areas. This was truer of girls than of boys. Part of the reason for this sex difference may lie in the less consistent socialization boys receive. Another possible explanation is that parents of only children may prefer masculine traits and activities in their children and that both only boys and girls consequently are raised to be masculine. The general preference parents express for male children (Hoffman, 1975) may be even more pronounced when one has only a single child (Cushna, 1966).

What emerges clearly from this study is that sibling status does have an effect on sex-role development and orientation, but it is clearly not a simple one. It varies with both gender and developmental level. Some of the hypotheses explored herein could quite fruitfully be explored with older groups in order to trace these patterns further.

ACKNOWLEDGMENTS

This research was supported by the National Institute of Child Health and Human Development (Contract No. NO1-HD-92820).

The authors would like to thank Diane Coulter for her help in the statistical analyses, Sara Rank and Carol Hathaway-Clark for their coordination efforts, and

Susie Gulbrandsen for her continued and invaluable aid in editing and typing. We would also like to express particular gratitude to Dr. Diane Proctor for helping us obtain our sample and to the cooperating principals of the many schools we sampled in Boulder and Jefferson counties.

REFERENCES

Adams, B. A. Birth order: A critical review. *Sociometry*, 1972, *35*, 411–439.

Adler, A. *What life should mean to you*. Boston: Little, Brown, 1931.

Altus, W. D. Birth order and academic primogeniture. *Journal of Personality and Social Psychology*, 1965, *21*, 872–876.

Belmont, L., & Marolla, F. A. Birth order, family size and intelligence. *Science*, 1973, *182*, 1096–1101.

Bem, S. L. The measurement of psychological androgyny. *Journal of Consulting and Clinical Psychology*, 1974, *42*, 155–162.

Bem, S. L. Sex-role adaptability: One consequence of psychological androgyny. *Journal of Personality and Social Psychology*, 1975, *21*, 634–643.

Bem, S. L., & Lenney, E. Sex-typing and the avoidance of cross-sex behavior. *Journal of Personality and Social Psychology*, 1976, *33*, 48–54.

Bigner, J. Sibling influence on sex-role preference of young children. *Journal of Genetic Psychology*, 1972, *121*, 271–282.

Blake, J. Can we believe recent data on birth expectation in the United States? *Demography*, 1974, *11*, 25–44.

Blake, J. The only child in America: Prejudice versus performance. *Population and Development Review*, 1981, 7, 43–54.

Bohannon, E. W. The only child in a family. *Pedagogical Seminary*, 1898, 5, 474–496.

Boswell, S. L. *Sex roles, attitudes and achievements in mathematics: A study of elementary school children and Ph.D.'s*. Paper presented at the meeting of the Society for Research on Child Development, San Francisco, March 1979.

Breland, H. M. Birth order, family configuration and verbal achievement. *Child Development*, 1974, *43*, 1011–1019.

Brim, O. G., Jr. Family structure and sex-role learning by children. *Sociometry*, 1958, *28*, 1–16.

Brown, L. M., & Weinraub, M. *Sibling status: Implications for sex-typed toy preferences and sex-role knowledge in 2- to 3-year-old children*. Paper presented at meeting of the Society for Research in Child Development, Boston, April 1981.

Campbell, A. A. The personality adjustments of only children. *Psychological Bulletin*, 1934, *31*, 193–203.

Commission on Population Growth and the American Future. *Population and the American future*. New York: Signet, 1972.

Cushna, B. *Agency and birth order differences in very early childhood*. Paper presented at the meeting of the American Psychological Association, New York, September 1966.

Dyer, D. T. Are only children different? *Journal of Educational Psychology*, 1945, *36*, 297–302.

Emmerich, W., Goldman, K. S., & Kirsh, B., & Sharabany, R. Evidence for a transitional phase in the development of gender constancy. *Child Development*, 1977, *48*, 930–936.

Falbo, T. Does the only child grow up miserable? *Psychology Today*, September 1976, 60–63.

Falbo, T. The only child: A review. *Journal of Individual Psychology*, 1977, *33*, 47–61.

Falbo, T. Only children and interpersonal behavior: An experimental and survey study. *Journal of Applied Social Psychology*, 1978, *8*(3), 244–253.

Falbo, T. Only children in America. In M. Lamb & B. Sutton-Smith (Eds.), *Sibling relationships: Their nature and significance across the lifespan*. Hillsdale, N.J.: Lawrence Erlbaum, 1982.

Feldman, H. Changes in marriage and parenthood: A methodological design. In E. Peck & J. Senderowitz (Eds.), *Pronatalism: The myth of mom and apple pie*. New York: Crowell, 1974.

Fenton, N. The only child. *Journal of Genetic Psychology*, 1928, *35*, 546–556.

Flake-Hobson, C., Skeen, P., & Robinson, B. E. Review of theories and research concerning sex-role development and androgyny with suggestions for teachers. *Family Relations*, 1980, *29*, 155–162.

Friedan, B. *The feminine mystique*. New York: Norton, 1963.

Gough, H. Identifying psychological femininity. *Educational and Psychological Measurement*, 1952, *12*, 427–439.

Grotevant, H. D. Sibling constellations and sex typing of interests in adolescents. *Child Development*, 1978, *49*, 540–542.

Guilford, R. B., & Worcester, D. A. A comparative study of the only and non-only child. *Journal of Genetic Psychology*, 1930, *38*, 411–426.

Gundlach, R. H., & Reiss, B. F. Birth order and sex of siblings in a sample of lesbians and non-lesbians. *Psychological Reports*, 1967, *20*, 61–62.

Hartup, W. W. Peer interaction and the behavioral development of the individual child. In E. Schopler & R. J. Reichler (Eds.), *Psychopathology and child development*. New York: Plenum, 1976.

Heilbrun, A. E., & Frome, D. K. Parental identification of late adolescence and level of adjustment: The importance of parental model attributes, ordinal position and sex of child. *Journal of Genetic Psychology*, 1965, *197*, 49–59.

Helmreich, R. L., & Spence, J. T., & Holahan, C. K. Psychological androgyny and sex-role flexibility: A test of two hypotheses. *Journal of Personality and Social Psychology*, 1979, *37*, 1631–1644.

Hoffman, L. W. Effects of maternal employment on the child—A review of the research. *Developmental Psychology*, 1974, *10*, 204–228.

Hoffman, L. W. The employment of women, education and fertility. In M. T. Mednick, S. S. Tangri, & L. W. Hoffman (Eds.), *Women and achievement*. Washington, D.C.: Hemisphere, 1975.

Hooker, H. F. The study of the only child at school. *Journal of Genetic Psychology*, 1931, *39*, 122–126.

Katz, P. A. *Determinants of sex-role flexibility in children*. Paper presented at the Society for Research on Child Development, San Francisco, March 1979. (a)

Katz, P. A. The development of female identity. In C. Kopp & M. Kirkpatrick (Eds.), *Growing up female*. New York: Plenum, 1979. (b)

Katz, P. A., & Boswell, S. L. *Flexibility and traditionality in children's gender roles*. Manuscript submitted for publication, 1982.

Koch, H. Some personality correlates of sex, sibling position and sex of sibling among five- and six-year-old children. *Genetic Psychology Monographs*, 1955, *52*, 3–50.

Koch, H. Sissiness and tomboyishness in relation to sibling characteristics. *Journal of Genetic Psychology*, 1956, *88*, 231–244.

Kohlberg, L., & Zigler, E. The impact of cognitive maturity on the development of sex-role attitudes in the years four to eight. *Genetic Psychology Monographs*, 1967, *75*, 89–165.

Lewis, M., & Kreitzberg, V. Effects of birth order and spacing on mother–infant interactions. *Developmental Psychology*, 1979, *5*, 617–625.

Maccoby, E. E., & Jacklin, E. E. *The psychology of sex differences*. Palo Alto, Calif.: Stanford University Press, 1974.

MacDonald, A. Manifestations of differential levels of socialization by birth order. *Developmental Psychology*, 1969, *3*, 485–492.

Perry, D. G., & Bussey, K. The social learning theory of sex difference: Imitation is alive and well. *Journal of Personality and Social Psychology*, 1979, *37*, 1699–1712.

Pinner, B., & Thompson, V. D. *The taboo against the one-child family*. Unpublished manuscript, University of North Carolina, Chapel Hill, 1974.

Pleck, J. H. *The myth of masculinity*. Cambridge, Mass.: MIT Press, 1981.

Plumb, P., & Cowan, G. A developmental study of destereotyping and androgynous activity preferences of tomboys, non-tomboys, and males. *Sex Roles*, in press.

Rainwater, L. *Family design: Marital asexuality, family size and contraception*. Chicago: Aldine, 1965.

Raychaudhuri, M. Differential socialization and musical creativity: A comparison of Indian and American musicians. *Indian Journal of Psychology*, 1965, *40*, 51–59.

Rosenberg, B. G., & Sutton-Smith, B. Ordinal position and sex-role identification. *Genetic Psychology Monographs*, 1964, *70*, 297–328.

Rosenberg, M. *Society and the adolescent self-image*. Princeton: Princeton University Press, 1965.

Schachter, S. *The psychology of affiliation*. Stanford, Calif.: Stanford University Press, 1959.

Schwager, J. *The effects of sex of model and sex-appropriateness of activity on the activity preferences of three- and five-year olds*. Unpublished manuscript, City University of New York, 1977.

Serbin, L. A., Connor, J. M., Burchardt, C. J., & Citron, C. C. Effects of peer presence on sex-typing of children's play behavior. *Journal of Experimental Child Psychology*, 1979, *27*, 303–309.

Silka, L., & Kiesler, S. Couples who choose to remain childless. *Family Planning Perspectives*, 1977, *9*, 16–25.

Simms, R. E., Davis, M. H., Foushee, H. C., Holahan, C. K., Spence, J. T., & Helmreich, R. L. *Psychological masculinity and femininity in children and their relationships to trait stereotypes and toy preference*. Paper presented at the annual meeting of the Southwestern Psychological Association, New Orleans, April 1978.

Slaby, R. G., & Frey, K. S. Development of gender constancy and selective attention to same-sex models. *Child Development*, 1975, *46*, 849–856.

Spence, J. T. Comments on Baumrind's "Are androgynous individuals more effective persons and parents?" *Child Development*, 1982, *53*, 76–80.

Spence, J. T., & Helmreich, R. L. *Masculinity and femininity: Their psychological dimensions, correlates and antecedents*. Austin, Texas: University of Texas Press, 1978.

Spence, J. T., Helmreich, R. L., & Davis, M. Personal communication. April 1980.

Spence, J. T., Helmreich, R. L., & Stapp, J. The Personal Attributes Questionnaire: A measure of sex-role stereotypes and masculinity–femininity. *JSAS: Catalogue of Selected Documents in Psychology*, 1974, *4*, 127.

Spence, J. T., Helmreich, R. L., & Stapp, J. Ratings of self and peers on sex-role attributes and their relation to self-esteem and conceptions of masculinity and femininity. *Journal of Personality and Social Psychology*, 1975, *32*, 29–39.

Stuart, J. C. Data on the alleged psychopathology of the only child. *Journal of Abnormal and Social Psychology*, 1926, *20*, 441.

Sutton-Smith, B. Birth order and sibling status effects. In M. Lamb & B. Sutton-Smith (Eds.), *Sibling relationships: Their nature and significance across the lifespan*. Hillsdale, N.J.: Lawrence Erlbaum, 1982.

Sutton-Smith, B., & Rosenberg, B. G. *The sibling*. New York: Holt, Rinehart & Winston, 1970.

Taffel, S. Trends in fertility in the United States. *Vital and health statistics Series 21, Number 28*. Washington, D.C.: U.S. Government Printing Office, 1977.

Thompson, V. D. Family size: Implicit policies and assumed psychological outcomes. *Journal of Social Issues*, 1974, *30*, 93–121.

Thompson, V. D., & Appelbaum, M. I. *Social psychological approaches to studies of population issues*. Paper presented at the meeting of the American Psychological Association, Washington, D.C., 1971.

Thurstone, L. L., & Thurstone, T. G. A neurotic inventory. *Journal of Social Psychology*, 1930, *1*, 3–29.

Tresemer, D., & Pleck, J. Sex-role boundaries and resistance to sex-role change. *Women's Studies*, 1973, *1*, 1–18.

Veevers, J. E. Voluntarily childless wives: An exploratory study. *Sociology and Social Research*, 1973, *57*, 356–366.

Vreogh, K. The relationship of birth order and sex of siblings to gender role identity. *Developmental Psychology*, 1971, *4*, 407–411.

Wagner, M. E., Schubert, H. J. P., & Schubert, D. S. P. Sibship-constellation effects on psychosocial development, creativity, and health. *Advances in Child Development and Behavior*, 1979, *14*, 57–148.

Warren, J. R. Birth order and social behavior. *Psychological Bulletin*, 1967, *65*, 38–49.

Westoff, C. F., Potter, R. G., Jr., & Sagi, P. C. *The third child: A study in the prediction of fertility*. Princeton, N.J.: Princeton University Press, 1963.

Worell, J. Life-span sex roles: Development, continuity and change. In R. Lerner & N. Busch-Rossnagel (Eds.), *Individuals as producers of their development*. New York: Academic Press, 1981.

Wren, C. S. Old nemesis haunts China on birth plan. *The New York Times*, August 1, 1982.

Zajonc, R. B. Family configuration and intelligence. *Science*, 1976, *192*, 227–236.
Zajonc, R. B., & Markus, G. B. Birth order and intellectual development. *Psychological Review*, 1975, *82*, 74–88.

·4·

PREDICTING ADOLESCENT ROLE TAKING AND IDENTITY EXPLORATION FROM FAMILY COMMUNICATION PATTERNS: A COMPARISON OF ONE- AND TWO-CHILD FAMILIES

CATHERINE R. COOPER
HAROLD D. GROTEVANT
MARY SUE MOORE
SHERRI M. CONDON

For a variety of social, psychological, and economic reasons, American couples are now choosing to have fewer children than in the past. As this trend has emerged, both couples and social scientists have been concerned with the consequences to a child of growing up with few or no siblings. In the absence of substantial psychological evidence about the consequences of being an only child, many couples have been guided by popular negative stereotypes of both only children (e.g., Thompson, 1974) and their parents (e.g., Polit, 1978).

In an effort to counteract these negative stereotypes and to develop an objective data base concerning this issue, several large-

Catherine R. Cooper and Harold D. Grotevant. Department of Psychology and Division of Child Development and Family Relationships, Department of Home Economics, The University of Texas, Austin, Texas.

Mary Sue Moore. Learning Disabilities Center, The University of Texas, Austin, Texas.

Sherri M. Condon. Department of Linguistics, The University of Texas, Austin, Texas.

scale investigations have focused on a variety of consequences of being raised an only child (e.g., Claudy, Farrell, & Dayton, 1979; Doby, Levin, & Mitra, 1980; Falbo, 1981; Groat, Wicks, & Neal, 1980; Van den Berg & Oechsli, 1980). These projects attempted to predict a variety of dependent variables (including intelligence, academic achievement, health status, family formation, labor force participation) from sibling status for children of various ages. The overriding conclusion of these studies was that sibling status had relatively little predictive power for these dependent variables; furthermore, when differences based on sibling status were found, only children were usually not at a disadvantage when compared with children who had siblings.

Although some research has demonstrated that the intensive, uninterrupted parental contact characteristic of one-child families may be beneficial for domains such as intellectual development, this close parent–child relationship may present possible vulnerabilities in other domains. "Only children develop an early pattern of accommodation to the adult world, which may be manifested in precocious development. At the same time, they may manifest difficulty in the development of autonomy and the ability to share, cooperate, and compete with others" (Minuchin, 1974, p. 59).

In order to assess the validity of such claims, we have investigated the relation between family structure and process and two developmental outcomes particularly important in adolescence. The first concerns constructing a sense of identity, which includes formulating a cohesive set of personal values and beliefs, not simply by making a commitment, but as a result of exploring alternatives (Erikson, 1968). The second is mature role-taking skill, which involves the ability to differentiate and coordinate multiple points of view (Feffer & Gourevitch, 1960; Flavell, 1974). These two developmental tasks of adolescence are pertinent not only to the clarification of individual values, such as vocational choice, but also to a variety of interpersonal behaviors, including communication effectiveness, altruism, and popularity (Shantz, 1975).

Both identity formation and mature role-taking ability require that the adolescent possess a viewpoint, be aware of the views of others, and be able to integrate those views yet differentiate his or her own views from them. In identity, these skills may be seen in the identification and active exploration of alternatives for the future and in the integration of these possibilities into a coherent, consistent sense of self. In role taking, these skills may be seen in the ability to identify other perspectives and to coordinate them into an interpersonally viable mode of relating to others.

The purpose of this chapter is to investigate the relation between family characteristics and the two adolescent developmental outcomes of identity exploration and role taking skill. Two approaches are used: prediction from *status* and *process* variables. The more traditional status approach involves determining whether there are group differences in these adolescent developmental outcomes as a function of sibling status. In this chapter we will first use this status approach by contrasting a group of adolescent only children with groups made up of adolescents who are the first born or second born of two children in the family.

In general, one might expect only children as a group to exhibit lower identity exploration than children with a sibling or siblings for two reasons. First, the intense exposure of an only child to his or her parents may limit the range of possible options for the future to which the child may be exposed, especially in a homogeneous family environment (e.g., Grotevant, 1979). Second, only children lack contact with a sibling who can serve as a target for deidentification (e.g., Schachter, Shore, Feldman-Rotman, Marquis, & Campbell, 1976). Such a process may help children define a sense of themselves in terms of who they are not as well as who they are.

We also test the traditional prediction that only children as a group are less skilled at role taking than are children with siblings. With less opportunity for interaction with peers, the only child might be expected to have had fewer opportunities than children with siblings for taking the point of view of another child, especially in resolving conflicts and arguments (Piaget, 1932; Toman, 1969).

Although such group differences may emerge, they tell only a part of the story. In order to understand the processes that mediate any such differences, our second approach, in which we have more confidence, is to examine family process predictors of identity and role taking directly. This approach enables us to understand the considerable heterogeneity we expect to find within each sibling status group of only, first-born, or second-born children. In this chapter, we report the results of intensive case studies of seven one-child and seven two-child families. With this intensive exploratory study, we have attempted to identify important variables for systematic study in future investigations employing larger samples.

To understand variation within the status groups of one- and two-child families, family systems theory was used to characterize differences in the quality of family process and to develop predictions concerning the relationship of qualities of family interaction to the two adolescent developmental measures of identity exploration and role taking. (Detailed treatments of family systems theory may be found in the following sources: Aldous, 1978; Broderick & Smith, 1979; Buckley, 1967; Hill, 1971; Lewis, Beavers, Gossett, & Phillips, 1976; and Rausch, Greif, & Nugent, 1979.)

In family systems theory, family structure is viewed as a network of interdependent individuals and relationships in which the behaviors of each member regulate those of others. The child is seen as one element in this network of developing individuals. Thus, constructs from systems theory facilitate the conceptualization of complex directions of effects impinging on the developing child.

Most family systems are organized hierarchically into subsystems. Subsystems may emerge because goals or purposes are shared by certain parts of the system but not by others. These subsystems often form along the lines of age, sex, function, or interests, and may be altered or dissolved as the ages or interests of family members change (Minuchin, 1974). The functioning of key family subsystems is related to family effectiveness. For example, clinicians (Haley, 1980; Minuchin, 1974; Napier & Whitaker, 1978) have documented the way in which a weak marital subsystem can negatively affect the development of autonomy in an adolescent. In our work, the functioning of the marital, parent–child, and sibling subsystems were related to differences in adolescent development. Family systems theory has provided the basis for linking family communication patterns, both within the family as a whole and within these subsystems, to adolescent development (Grotevant & Cooper, 1983).

A CONCEPTUAL MODEL: INDIVIDUALITY AND CONNECTEDNESS IN RELATIONSHIPS

In this chapter we consider how a model of relationships based on family systems theory can account for individual differences in adolescent identity exploration and role-taking skill. Our conceptual model focuses on patterns of individuality and connectedness in family relationships that can be observed in patterns of communication (Grotevant & Cooper, 1983; Lewis *et al.*, 1976; Olson, Sprenkle, & Russell, 1979). In general, we predicted that identity exploration and role-taking development would be facilitated most when adolescents have the opportunity to observe interactions in which differences of opinion are expressed and to participate in interactions that both sharpen a sense of self as separate from others (by means of communication behaviors such as self-assertion or disagreement) and facilitate a sense of self as connected to others (by means of communication behaviors such as acknowledgment, agreement, and requests for information). Thus, when each family member is free to express a point of view, show responsiveness and respect of others' views, yet distinguish those views from his or her own, then an adolescent's ability to formulate a distinctive point of view, essential for both identity formation and role taking, may be enhanced.

Within the marital relationship, the expression of both individuality and connectedness can offer clear leadership for the family and can provide an opportunity for the child to observe a model of an effective relationship (Bandura, 1977; Lewis *et al.*, 1976; Minuchin, 1974; Olson *et al.*, 1979). Within the parent–child subsystem, freedom to state a viewpoint and disagree with a parent while giving and receiving validation can enable the adolescent to participate in problem-solving interaction and ultimately to separate from the family of origin (Haley, 1980). Likewise, the experience within an individuated sibling subsystem, especially with a sibling of similar age, can offer the adolescent the give and take that Piaget (1926) associated with the reduction of egocentrism. With an actively engaged sibling, the adolescent may be required to negotiate more frequently and extensively than an only child, who may experience more matter-of-fact explanations, demands, or even permissive behavior from parents.

Four Patterns of Marital Relationships

We adapted models of individuality and connectedness suggested by clinicians such as Minuchin (Minuchin, 1974; Minuchin, Rosman, & Baker, 1978) and Olson *et al.* (1979) in order to make predictions concerning patterns of marital interactions and their relation to adolescent identity exploration and role-taking development. Figure 4.1 represents four patterns of marital relationships determined by levels of individuality and connectedness.

The Individuated Marriage

The individuated marital subsystem is characterized by active involvement of both spouses, the co-occurrence of communication patterns indicating both individuality and connectedness of the marital partners, and consequently a low parental need for the child to play a mediating role between the marital partners. The adolescent comes to view his or her parents as separate individuals who are free to express their individuality (by stating their own preferences, disagreeing, etc.) but who also respond to and acknowledge their partner's point of view. Such individuated marital relationships do not require the child to serve as a bridge or mediator between the parents. Consequently, when it is time for the adolescent to become more autonomous, he or she is free to "leave home" (Haley, 1980; Minuchin, 1974).

The Disengaged Marriage

When the marital relationship is disengaged (low sense of connectedness between the spouses and few disagreements between them), the

Figure 4.1. Four patterns of marital relationships.

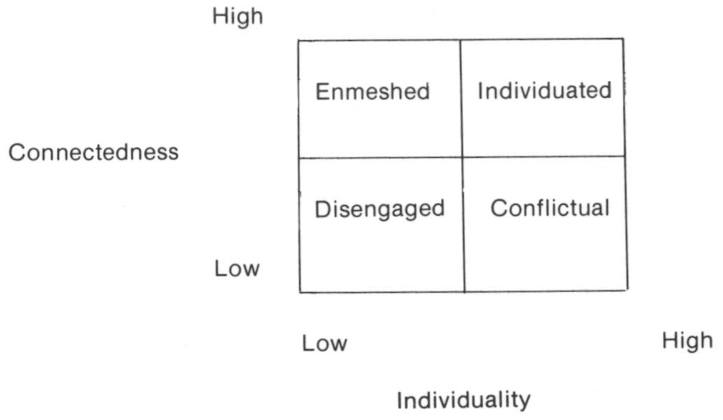

adolescent is denied access to differing points of view and to the opportunity to learn procedures for reconciling them. Since the development of role taking requires exposure to conflict as well as its resolution, it was predicted that adolescents from families with a disengaged marital subsystem would score low on the role-taking measure. In terms of identity exploration, adolescents from these families may withdraw or become apathetic in response to the marital disengagement, or they may disengage from their parents and establish identity on their own, free of parental influence. If one or both parents turns to the adolescent for responsiveness, he or she may explore only those options consistent with parental needs or goals.

The Enmeshed Marriage

An enmeshed relationship is characterized by a high degree of connectedness and infrequent disagreements in the marital subsystem. In such families, closeness may be defined as thinking and feeling alike (Beavers, 1977), and consequently the achievement of a separate identity is not promoted. Individual family members may express a point of view to the degree that it conforms to the family's point of view. However, the adolescent is prevented from hearing differences of opinion and from experiencing the freedom to develop his or her own distinctive viewpoint. Therefore, we predicted that identity exploration of such adolescents would be limited to options approved by the family. In addition, because different points of view are not expressed in such a family, the adolescent is denied the opportunity to observe or participate in processes such as negotiation and compromise that might sharpen his or her role-taking skills.

The Conflictual Marriage

Marriages that are characterized by high individuality but low connectedness of the spouses may present a special risk for the adolescent's psychosocial development. With encouragement from one or both spouses, the adolescent may be drawn into a mediator role, thus compensating for the lack of connectedness between the spouses (Miller, 1981; Satir, 1967; Turner, 1970). Maintaining such a role may reduce the adolescent's opportunities to clarify his or her own point of view, express these views directly, and receive feedback. Because the mediating child is not free to clarify his or her own distinctive feelings without viewing them vis-à-vis the family, he or she may be less free to engage in varied identity exploration. However, because being a mediator requires the adolescent to identify and coordinate the viewpoints of each parent, role-taking skill may be enhanced. Similarily, from a psychoanalytic perspective, Miller (1981) has posited that when the marital relationship does not meet the unconscious needs of one or both parents for unqualified acceptance and love, children may be pulled into an intensified relationship with the unsatisfied parent or parents and into an overly responsive role. These children may develop skills related to meeting others' needs, but at the expense of understanding or fulfilling their own needs.

In sum, theorists from diverse perspectives, including social learning (Bandura, 1977), cognitive developmental (Piaget, 1926, 1932); psychoanalytic (Miller, 1981); and family systems (Haley, 1980; Minuchin, 1974) converge on the prediction that the child's opportunity to observe and participate in active exchanges of ideas, characterized by the expression of individual points of view and responsiveness to the viewpoints of others, will facilitate the development of identity and role taking. The present chapter assesses these dimensions of family communication empirically using a family systems perspective.

METHOD

Subjects

The subjects in this study were 90 families drawn from a larger sample of 121 white, middle-class, two-parent families, each including an adolescent who was a high school senior. For purposes of the status variable analyses, subjects included 7 one-child families, 59 families in which the adolescent was the first-born of two children, and 24 families in which the adolescent was the second-born of two children. The process variable analyses focused on 14 families: the 7 with one child (3 with male and 4 with female adolescents) and 7 with two (with first borns of the same age and sex as the only children) that were drawn at random from possible subjects in the larger sample. In this chapter, the families are designated by the number of children and sex of the adolescent (e.g., 101F refers to data from the family of a female only child, 201M to that of a first-born male in a two-child family). With one exception, all parents of these children indicated that they would either probably ($n = 11$) or definitely ($n = 16$) have no additional children, and, with one exception that their decision to have no more children had been voluntary. The sample was restricted to white families to avoid confounding of social class and cultural patterns in attitudes toward family size and cooperative versus competitive behavior (e.g., Bradshaw & Bean, 1972). Families were recruited through newspaper articles and advertisements, by enlisting the cooperation of high schools and churches, and by referrals from other participating families.

Procedures

Each family participated in two data-collection sessions. The first session involved both parents and the target adolescent and took place in the family's home. Measures administered to the family during this session included the Family Interaction Task (to the whole family), the Parent Questionnaire (individually to each parent), the Extended Range Vocabulary Test, and the Ego Identity Interview (to the adolescent). After the home visit, the adolescent was brought to a university laboratory for a second group of activities, which included the Role Taking Task.

Measures and Scoring

Family Interaction Task

In the Family Interaction Task (FIT), the family was seated at their kitchen table and asked to make plans together for a 2-week vacation for which they had unlimited funds. Their task was to plan the day-by-day itinerary, listing both the location and activities planned for each day. The research assistant gave them 20 minutes to reach their decision, turned on an audiotape recorder, and left the room. The FIT was designed to elicit active participation from all family members in a task in which the adolescent's interest and expertise might contribute to the family's decisions.

This particular task was designed to maximize the degree of family individuation that might be observed in several ways. First, the participation of the adolescents was facilitated by providing a topic about which they might have some expertise to contribute; thus the difficulty of the task was easy or moderate for all family members. Second, we chose a plan-something-together task rather than a revealed or unrevealed-differences task because such tasks maximize the opportunity for conflict to arise. In these latter tasks, in which family members make individual decisions before discussion begins, they may feel an investment in trying to have their decision adopted by the others in the family. Tasks structured so as not to focus the family on their differences should allow "power sharing" (non-zero-sum interactions) rather than "power wielding" (zero-sum interactions) to predominate (Olson, Cromwell, & Klein, 1975). Third, we allowed unlimited funds for the hypothetical vacation so as not to activate preestablished family roles and parental coalitions concerning the allocation of money, such as those that might be observed in the actual purchase of a car. Finally, in order to optimize participation of all family members, the task required multiple decisions rather than a single decision.

On the basis of time-sampling evidence that key family interaction patterns stabilize on this task within the first 300 utterances, verbatim transcripts of the FIT were made from audiotapes (Cooper, Grotevant, & Condon, 1982). The units of analysis were utterances, which correspond roughly to sentences (independent clauses were separated whenever possible but never from clauses connected to them by subordinating conjunctions). Responsive particles such as "yes," "no," and "uh huh" were considered as separate units because of the salience of their interactional (as opposed to propositional) content.

Coders designated each utterance with one of six move categories (including a category for "no clear move function") as well as one of eight response categories (including a category for "no clear response function"). Organizing the code in this manner acknowledges the fact that some utterances appear to both direct or "move" the conversation while they also respond to previous utterances by other participants. The frequencies can be considered separately or they can be combined into mutually exclusive and exhaustive move–response pairs. (Complete coding procedures are documented in Condon, Cooper, & Grotevant, 1983.)

For this analysis, the first 300 utterances made at each family session were coded for indexes of individuality and connectedness. Connectedness was indicated when one person acknowledged the statement of another family member ("Oh, I see what you mean"), agreed with another's idea ("Sure, let's do it"), or requested information from another person ("Do you remember how far Pisa is from Rome?"). Having a separate point of view was indicated when a person made a self-assertion by suggesting an activity ("I'd like to go to Japan") or disagreed with another's ideas ("I don't want to do that"; "That's too much for one day").

Interjudge reliabilities (percent agreement) for individual categories averaged .80. Each transcript was reviewed by the fourth author, a linguist, and discrepancies were resolved by consultation with a coding manual (Condon *et al.*, 1983).

Parent Questionnaire

The Parent Questionnaire (PQ), completed independently by each parent, provided basic demographic information about each family as well as information about the parents' childbearing histories and plans.

Vocabulary

The Extended Range Vocabulary Test (Ekstrom, French, Harman, & Derman, 1976) was administered to each family member. It consists of 48 words with 5 response options each, given in 2 timed 6-minute sections.

Ego Identity Interview

In the Ego Identity Interview (EII), each adolescent was interviewed by a research assistant of the same gender with an instrument that assessed the subject's degree of exploration of alternatives and commitment to decisions and personal values in the domains of occupation, religion, politics, friendships, dating, and sex roles (Grotevant & Cooper, 1981; Marcia, 1966). Tapes of the interviews were scored by two raters who were blind to the subject's sibling status and to the hypotheses of the study. Scoring disagreements were settled by a third rater. For each subject, an identity exploration rating was assigned in each of the six identity domains listed above. For each of the six areas, a score was assigned on a 1-to-4 point scale in which 1 = complete absence of exploration; 2 = weak or superficial exploration; 3 = moderate exploration, either with depth (exploring one option by several means) or with breadth (exploring several options); and 4 = strong exploration (both depth and breadth). Subjects' identity exploration ratings were summed across the six domains to derive a total identity exploration score (potentially ranging from 6 to 24 points).

Role Taking Task

Each adolescent was administered the Role Taking Task (RTT) (Feffer & Gourevitch, 1960), in which he or she was shown a stimulus picture of three individuals (facing away from the viewer) in a kitchen scene. The subject was first asked to make up a dramatic story about the actors in the picture and then to retell the story three times, once from the perspective of each person in the picture. Role-taking scores (with a possible range of 0 to 20 points) assessed the degree to which the adolescent could differentiate and coordinate multiple perspectives in the task.

An RTT protocol that lacks reciprocal perspective taking between characters can obtain a maximum score of 10. When reciprocal perspective taking is evidenced, scores can range from 11 to 20, depending on the quality and depth of the elaboration. For example, reciprocal perspective taking would be credited in related stories in which the child, in the story told from his perspective, states: "Mom is working too hard. I should have been helping her. I think I'll ask what I can do," and the mother, in the story told from her perspective, states: "I've been working all alone today on housework, and I'm tired. My son looks concerned, though. Maybe he'll offer to help me."

In addition, the projective content or themes and formal structure (Bellak, 1975) of each adolescent's RTT responses were examined by a clinical psychologist (the third author) in order to supplement other data regarding each adolescent's communication style and perceptions of family issues.

RESULTS AND DISCUSSION

Results will be presented in three sections. First, individual scores and group means will be presented on adolescent developmental measures for the one- and two-child families. Second, the relation between family process and levels of adolescent role taking and identity exploration will be examined. Finally, distinctive patterns of connectedness and individuality in the marital, parent–child, and sibling subsystems that are exemplified in individual families in the sample will be discussed.

Group Differences in Adolescent Developmental Measures: The Status Approach

Group means and standard deviations for identity exploration ratings, role-taking scores, and vocabulary scores are presented in Table 4.1. In each case, *F* ratios from one-way analyses of variance were non-significant. Pearson correlations among the three measures (in the full sample of adolescents) indicated moderate degrees of relatedness: EII-RTT: $r = .31$, $p < .01$; RTT-VOC: $r = .27$, $p < .01$; EII-VOC: $r = .04$, ns.

Table 4.1. Mean Performance and *F* Ratios for Identity Exploration, Role Taking, and Vocabulary Scores of Only, First-Born, and Second-Born Adolescents

MEASURE	ONLY CHILDREN	FIRST BORNS OF TWO	SECOND BORNS OF TWO	*F*
Identity exploration				
$\bar{x}$	15.86	14.75	15.83	1.90 (ns)
(*SD*)	(2.19)	(2.29)	(3.13)	
n	7	59	24	
Role taking				
$\bar{x}$	11.14	11.06	10.68	.06 (ns)
(*SD*)	(2.91)	(4.70)	(4.57)	
n	7	54	22	
Vocabulary				
$\bar{x}$	17.10	20.04	17.49	.96 (ns)
(*SD*)	(4.00)	(9.55)	(6.10)	
n	6	59	24	

Patterns of Individuality and Connectedness: Case Studies

By examining the patterns of separateness and connectedness within individual families, the interrelationships of the marital, parent–child, and (where present) sibling subsystems can be examined. The frequencies of measures of separateness and connectedness are presented for the individual families with only and first-born adolescents in Tables 4.2 and 4.3. For this section, we have selected families from among the 14 discussed in this chapter to illustrate the patterns we have identified.

Individuated Patterns

The opportunity for expressions of both individuality and connectedness in the individuated marital relationship provides a context in which the adolescent's development can take different directions; possible developmental outcomes are not limited as they are when the marital subsystem is either disengaged or enmeshed. The adolescents in families 101F (Carol, an only child) and 201M (Henry, a first born of two) are examples of this diversity.

Each family's interaction in the Family Interaction Task (FIT) was characterized by active involvement of both spouses. Carol's mother and father made 22 and 33 self-assertions, respectively; Henry's parents made 33 and 9, respectively. Most importantly, the husbands and wives in these families displayed evidence of both individuality by their willingness to disagree with one another and connectedness by their mutual responsiveness. For example, in the FIT:

> *Henry's mother:* I want to go to Hawaii.
> *Father:* Well, we'll get you there.

But later:

> *Mother:* I've got Paris up here. You want to go to Paris the next day?
> *Father:* You can't do Rome and Paris the same day, honey.
> *Mother:* O.K.

Table 4.2. Measures of Individuality and Connectedness in Families: Only Children

MEASURE	FAMILY						
	101F	102F	103M	104M	105M	106F	107F
Adolescent measures							
Role taking	15	14	12	12	9	9	7
Identity exploration	18	13	18	16	14	14	18
Vocabulary	22.0	22.0	12.8	15.8	*	13.8	16.2
Self-assertions							
Father (F)	22	24	34	14	21	38	9
Mother (M)	33	5	32	23	7	45	13
Adolescent (A)	29	43	20	19	20	5	27
Marital subsystem							
F-to-M disagree	2	2	8	5	3	6	0
M-to-F disagree	5	1	5	3	1	2	0
F-to-M connectedness†	9	9	16	23	8	23	4
M-to-F connectedness	16	9	12	19	10	23	6
Marital–child interaction							
M/F-to-A disagree	8	13	5	3	10	2	8
A-to-M/F disagree	4	4	3	3	9	4	9
M/F-to-A connectedness	9	19	12	24	18	18	46
A-to-M/F connectedness	41	47	30	13	19	8	39
Parent–child subsystems							
A-to-F disagree	1	4	0	2	7	4	4
F-to-A disagree	4	11	2	1	7	2	1
A-to-F connectedness	17	44	19	10	17	2	12
F-to-A connectedness	5	18	7	11	18	3	9
A-to-M disagree	3	0	3	1	2	0	5
M-to-A disagree	4	2	3	2	3	0	7
A-to-M connectedness	24	3	11	3	2	6	27
M-to-A connectedness	4	1	5	13	0	15	37

*Missing data.

†Connectedness = agreements + acknowledgments + requests for information.

Some insight into Carol's perception of her parents' relationship can be gained from her Role Taking Task (RTT). In one story she related the mother's special activities with the child when the father was away, suggesting that the "normal" family interaction was characterized by a joint parenting style. In a second story, the father was depicted as expressing compassion and concern for his wife and the parents as spending time together at a special dinner while the child, who felt happy that Dad was cheering Mom up, stayed home.

Table 4.3. Measures of Individuality and Connectedness in Families: First-Born Children

	FAMILY						
MEASURE	201M	202F	203M	204F	205F	206F	207M
Adolescent measures							
Role taking	16	14	14	12	9	9	6
Identity exploration	18	15	15	18	13	14	14
Vocabulary	25.6	15.0	3.8	*	36.6	22.0	13.2
Self-assertions							
Father (F)	33	24	26	12	29	20	26
Mother (M)	9	9	22	30	5	15	16
Adolescent (A)	23	10	18	51	13	26	19
Sibling (S)	9	17	23	18	21	14	7
Marital subsystem							
F-to-M disagree	2	1	1	0	0	0	2
M-to-F disagree	7	4	5	2	1	3	5
F-to-M connectedness†	8	19	7	2	19	4	14
M-to-F connectedness	18	18	20	4	8	16	11
Marital–child interaction							
M/F-to-A disagree	3	2	2	3	6	8	3
A-to-M/F disagree	8	4	0	4	1	7	2
M/F-to-A connectedness	21	28	13	11	34	25	11
A-to-M/F connectedness	32	11	19	24	13	18	19
Parent–child subsystems							
A-to-F disagree	4	4	0	2	1	6	1
F-to-A disagree	1	1	1	0	0	4	2
A-to-F connectedness	24	10	12	3	29	8	11
F-to-A connectedness	6	17	10	6	10	11	10
A-to-M disagree	4	0	0	2	0	1	1
M-to-A disagree	2	1	1	3	0	4	1
A-to-M connectedness	8	1	7	21	5	10	8
M-to-A connectedness	15	11	3	5	3	14	1
Sibling subsystem							
A-to-S disagree	0	0	0	6	1	0	0
S-to-A disagree	1	0	0	6	0	2	0
A-to-S connectedness	2	6	4	6	10	1	1
S-to-A connectedness	2	4	4	4	9	10	2

*Missing data.

†Connectedness = agreements + acknowledgments + requests for information.

These excerpts reflected a perception of the child's parents as a caring couple as well as caring parents.

This engagement in the marital subsystem provided the opportunity for Carol and Henry each to observe an effective marital relationship; engagement of the parents with one another also meant that the adolescents were not required to serve as a bridge or a mediator between the parents. In her identity interview, Carol described her family's decision-making style: "I have a say, but not a deciding vote in family decisions."

In addition to having the opportunity to observe individuated marriages, Carol and Henry themselves also participated in individuated relationships with each of their parents. For example, Henry showed a willingness to disagree with both parents, but he was also responsive to them. Both parents were in turn responsive to him. Carol's father reflected this quality in his first statement on the FIT:

> I think probably what we all ought to do is decide the things that we want to do. Each one of us individually. And then, maybe we'll be able to reconcile from that point. . . . Let's go ahead and take a few minutes to decide where we'd like to go and what we would like to do. And maybe we'll be able to work everything everybody wants to do in these 14 days. O.K.?

As predicted, both Carol and Henry achieved high role-taking scores (15 and 16, respectively), showing high levels of understanding of reciprocal perspectives, by coordinating the perspectives of characters in their stories and elaborating both their external behavior and emotional experiences. In addition, Carol and Henry each scored 18 on the identity exploration scale, reflecting active exploration of issues related to identity formation. For example, on the identity interview, Carol discussed her close relationship with two friends who were very different from each other. She maintained her relationship with one of these friends because she felt it was an important one despite the disapproval of her mother. Her discussion illustrated ways in which she had learned about herself as she tried to maintain these two friendships. Henry's choice of a career in medicine thoughtfully integrated consideration of his own values (financial security, helping people, status), his achievement in science courses, and his observations of doctors at work.

Disengaged Patterns

In contrast to these individuated patterns, families with disengaged marital subsystems offer the adolescent little opportunity to see either individuality or connectedness modeled in the relationship. This pattern is illustrated in families 107F (that of Evelyn, an only child) and 204F (that of Isadora, a first born of two).

As may be seen in Table 4.2, Evelyn's parents never disagreed with one another during the FIT; their frequencies of mutual responsiveness were also quite low relative to other marriages. Likewise, Isadora's mother expressed only two disagreements to her husband (who never disagreed with her), while both demonstrated very low levels of mutual responsiveness. For example:

> *Mother:* I'd like to spend about 4 days in England.
> *Father:* Well, let's see now. We've got . . . we've got Paris . . .

Although the patterns of marital interaction in both of these families may be described as disengaged, the overall family patterns were different. The content of her family's interaction suggested that Evelyn had been given license to criticize her parents, disagree with them, and organize their actions. For example:

> *Evelyn:* (to Mother) I don't care. I don't care. I want to ride the train.

Evelyn's high identity exploration seemed related to her parents' goals for her. Several sources of data from Evelyn's family indicated a strong parental awareness of the family's socioeconomic status and a desire for their only daughter to do better than they had. For example, as a high school senior she had already obtained a more prestigious salaried position than either of her parents had held. On the identity interview, she commented that her parents influenced her career plans in that they "helped her to see that she wanted to be upper middle class" (which her parents were not.) She noted that her entire family was "thrilled" when she considered studying medicine and was disappointed when she changed her mind.

Evelyn's high degree of identity exploration showed a pattern of depth of exploration of one particular option within each identity domain, but not investigation of a variety of options. In fact, she noted that her mother became "scared" when she considered changing religion. She had had few disagreements with her parents about friends, dates, or ideas about sex roles. Thus, Evelyn's family illustrates encouragement of identity exploration only to the degree that it is approved by the adolescent's parents.

Role-taking scores of both young women were low. However, Isadora's score of 12 is at the lowest level of reciprocity, qualitatively higher than Evelyn's score of 7, which indicates no mastery of the coordination of reciprocal but different viewpoints. One key difference between these families was that Isadora appeared to be involved in an individuated relationship with her younger sister; these siblings expressed both disagreement and responsiveness to each other. In contrast, Evelyn, as an only child, did not have this subsystem available to her. For example:

> *Younger sister:* I wouldn't mind going to Africa.
> *Isadora:* Yeah, see the elephants in the wild game preserves!

And later:

> *Younger sister:* One day in each.
> *Isadora:* But one day won't be enough in each place! Like in Paris, we're gonna have to have three days to do all that.

Also:

> *Isadora:* We'll start out with California . . . no but it it . . . no, no, California isn't that important. Which one of these is important?
> *Younger sister:* Grand Canyon.
> *Isadora:* Okay, we'll go to the Grand Canyon.

The disengaged marriages in both Evelyn's and Isadora's families did not prevent each of the subjects from being actively engaged with at least one of her parents. This family pattern of disengagement in the marital subsystem and engagement with at least one parent, and the potential of engagement with a sibling, raises the question of to what degree the adolescent's engagement in other relationships may compensate for developmental benefits lost because of disengagement in his or her parents' marriage. Engagement with one parent or with a sibling may make the difference between an adolescent who withdraws, unwilling to explore identity options, and an adolescent who has the self-confidence to pursue his or her own interests.

Minuchin (1974) has suggested that children from disengaged families "may function autonomously but have a skewed sense of independence" (p. 55). Consistent with this view, both Evelyn and Isadora showed evidence of exploring identity issues in all six domains. However, in Evelyn's case, exploration was sanctioned to the degree that it was consistent with her parents' goals for her to hold a prestigious career. Isadora felt that her career choice was her own: "My parents have backed up what I wanted to do and not what they wanted." However, she was planning to be a teacher, just like her mother and her aunt.

Enmeshed Patterns

A family in which the marital subsystem reflects an enmeshed interactive style (few disagreements, self-assertions that largely coincide with the family's point of view, and frequent expressions of connectedness) was seen most clearly in family 205F (that of Janet, a first born of two children). The marital agreement/disagreement ratio in the FIT for Janet's parents was 16.00, the highest among the 14 families.

Janet also appeared to participate in an enmeshed relationship with her father (she disagreed with him only once, and he never disagreed with her, whereas she was responsive to him 29 times, and he was responsive to her 10 times.) Enmeshment in this family's interaction was illustrated in the first five utterances on the FIT for Janet's family.

> *Mother:* Where shall we go?
> *Father:* Back to Spain.
> *Mother:* Back to Spain.
> *Janet:* Back to Spain.
> *Sister:* Back to Spain.

When Janet's father later asked for more suggestions, she said, "And then, I don't . . . I mean, you go on, Dad, 'cause I don't know . . . what else."

Janet's low role-taking score of 9 reflected a lack of ability to express both separate and reciprocal points of view. While telling her story, Janet commented, "I don't know what the others are thinking, because I'm thinking of it only as if I'm the girl." She later said, "The other two characters [here Janet breaks off the story to say she doesn't know what they're thinking] will act like they belong there." In each case, the enmeshed relationship between the adolescent and one parent was also reflected on the RTT. The formal structure and content of the stories included run-on sentences with unclear beginnings and endings, as well as themes reflecting difficulty in decision making: "At this point she has no idea what the outcome will be. She can't figure out what's going on at all." "She's totally confused."

Janet's identity exploration rating of 13 was also low, possibly reflecting a lack of exploration of issues outside the consensual family beliefs. The necessity for agreement and connectedness among family members in enmeshed families and the family members' excessive involvement in each other's identity appears to hinder the adolescent's development of individual (and at times different) ideas regarding careers, dating, and so forth. With regard to career choice, Janet commented, "I'm having a hard time deciding what to do. It would be easier if they would *tell* me what to do—but of course, I don't want that." Thus, the enmeshed family communication patterns that Janet observed in her parents' relationship and participated in with her father appeared to inhibit her ability both to coordinate different perspectives and to engage in identity exploration.

Conflictual Patterns

Interaction patterns in conflictual marriages were characterized by frequent expressions of individuality and few expressions of connectedness. We did not expect to find, and did not find, extreme cases of conflictual marriages in our study, for three reasons. First, since our Family Interaction Task required that multiple decisions be made, less conflict was elicited than might have been the case if we asked the families to name only one location for their trip. Second, we assume the operation of a strong selection bias of nonconflictual marriages into our volunteer sample, since members of conflictual families may be unwilling to present themselves for study. Finally, the social desirability constraints against the open expression of conflict in the presence of a tape recorder are presumably strong.

SUMMARY AND IMPLICATIONS

This chapter has reported an investigation of the relationship between status and process predictors of adolescent identity and role-taking skills. In such areas, only children as a group have conventionally been seen as disadvantaged. It was anticipated that individual differences in adolescent competence could be predicted more effectively from *process* variables, especially those reflecting qualities of family individuality and connectedness, than from the *status* variables of being an only child or being a first born.

Several key findings have emerged from this investigation. First, our findings corroborate those of many others (e.g., Claudy *et al.*, 1979; Doby *et al.*, 1980; Falbo, 1981; Groat *et al.*, 1980; Van den Berg & Oechsli, 1980) in showing that sibling status has relatively little predictive power for the variables under investigation. Second, as predicted, qualities of family interaction, especially within the marital subsystem, were significantly associated with adolescent role taking and identity development. Three distinctive patterns of individuality and connectedness in marital interaction were related to developmental outcomes in adolescents. In *individuated* marital relationships, the free expression of separate points of view and responsiveness to the partner seemed to offer an opportunity for the adolescent to observe effective problem solving between the parents without being required to mediate their conflicts. These adolescents experienced support for expressing their own point of view yet were also exposed to other viewpoints. In such families, adolescents could develop reciprocal role-taking skills and engage in identity exploration that went beyond the fulfillment of parental needs. In enmeshed marital relationships, since communication in the marital relationship lacked expressions of individuality and working out of different points of view, adolescents were less likely to be able to observe these behaviors. Participation by the adolescent in such a family climate seems hesitant, as though impeded by attempts at guessing the correct consensual view held by other family members. In such families, then, both role taking and identity exploration seem impaired. In *disengaged* marital relationships, in which spouses express low levels of individuality and connectedness, the adolescent may lack the opportunity to observe distinctive points of view either being expressed or integrated with those of the other parent. However, in two families who exemplified this disengaged marital style, greater individuation was apparent in other subsystems: in one case the parent–child subsystem, in the other the sibling. In the family with the stronger parent–child subsystem, the adolescent showed higher identity exploration, although role-taking skill was low. Within the other family, where the parent–child and sibling subsystems both seemed individuated, the adolescent showed evidence of high levels of identity exploration as well as moderate role-taking skill.

Thus, although parent–child and sibling subsystems appear to complement the marital relationship and possibly compensate for it when it does not offer positive models, the marital subsystem, at least as it was reflected in our family interaction task, seems especially important to the adolescent's development. The adolescent's participation in reciprocal interaction seems beneficial within an active parent–child relationship but inappropriate when the child is substituting for one parent with the other.

In family systems theory, the significance of co-occurring periods of developmental transition for children and their parents are emphasized (e.g., Appleton, 1981; Hill, 1958). For example, adults in their fifties may experience diminished self-esteem as they begin to perceive declines in their physical fitness, health, career potential, or marital satisfaction (Turner, 1970). These issues may be heightened by parents' growing awareness that their adolescent children are entering a period of expanded potential in these areas. With stress in the marital system, the consequence for children of assuming, even temporarily, a role that constrains development may be long lasting. A key implication of our work is that the adolescent child may be vulnerable to being cast in a central role when family conflict or strong parental needs occur. If the marriage becomes disengaged, enmeshed, or conflictual, the child drawn into such a role experiences limitations in the range of possible choices he or she feels free to consider in developing a system of personal beliefs. The development of mature role-taking skill may also suffer when the child cannot observe or participate in free exchanges of different points of view. Although such patterns can occur in families with any number of children, the only child, simply by being the only child available, and because he or she has fewer compensatory subsystems available in the family, may be at higher risk of being cast in such sensitive roles amidst marital and family stress.

ACKNOWLEDGMENTS

This work was supported in part by the Institute of Human Development and Family Studies and the University Research Institute, both at The University of Texas at Austin; the Hogg Foundation for Mental Health; and a National Institute of Child Health and Human Development Contract (No. NO1-HD-92819) to the two senior authors.

We appreciate the helpful contributions of the following persons in the preparation of this chapter: Susan Ayers-Lopez, Michael Brody, Deborah Edward, Timothy Gregg, Patricia Griffin-Heilburn, Thomas Hoeffner, Linda Lamb, Sandra Rice, and Daniel Tousley.

REFERENCES

Aldous, J. *Family careers: Developmental change in families*. New York: Wiley, 1978.

Appleton, W. S. *Fathers and daughters*. New York: Doubleday, 1981.

Bandura, A. *Social learning theory*. Englewood Cliffs, N.J.: Prentice-Hall, 1977.

Beavers, W. R. *Psychotherapy and growth: A family systems perspective*. New York: Brunner/Mazel, 1977.

Bellak, L. *The T.A.T., C.A.T., and S.A.T. in clinical use*. New York: Grune & Stratton, 1975.

Bradshaw, B. S., & Bean, F. D. *Some aspects of the fertility of Mexican Americans: Demographic and social aspects of population growth*. Report of the Commission on Population Growth and the American Future. Research Papers, Vol. 1. Washington: U.S. Government Printing Office, 1972.

Broderick, C. J., & Smith, J. The general system approach to the family. In W. R. Burr, R. Hill, F. I. Nye, & I. Reiss (Eds.), *Contemporary theories about the family* (Vol. 2). New York: Free Press, 1979.

Buckley, W. *Sociology and modern systems theory*. Englewood Cliffs, N.J.: Prentice-Hall, 1967.

Claudy, J. G., Farrell, W. S., & Dayton, C. W. *The consequences of being an only child: An analysis of Project TALENT data*. Final report to the National Institute of Child Health and Human Development, 1979.

Condon, S. L., Cooper, C. R., & Grotevant, H. D. *A manual for the analysis of family discourse*. Manuscript submitted for publication, 1983.

Cooper, C. R., Grotevant, H. D., & Condon, S. M. Methodological challenges of selectivity in family interaction: Addressing temporal patterns of individuation. *Journal of Marriage and the Family*, 1982, *44*, 749–754.

Doby, J. T., Levin, M. L., & Mitra, S. *An empirical investigation into the intellectual, physical, psychological, and social consequences of being reared an only child.* Final report to the National Institute of Child Health and Human Development, 1980.

Ekstrom, R. B., French, J. W., Harman, H. H., & Derman, D. *Manual for kit of factor-referenced cognitive tests.* Princeton, N.J.: Educational Testing Service, 1976.

Erikson, E. *Identity: Youth and crisis.* New York: Norton, 1968.

Falbo, T. *The consequences of being and having an only child, on intelligence, interpersonal orientation, attitudes, and time use.* Final report to the National Institute of Child Health and Human Development, 1981.

Feffer, M. H., & Gourevitch, V. Cognitive aspects of roletaking. *Journal of Personality*, 1960, *28*, 383–396.

Flavell, J. H. The development of inferences about others. In T. Mischel (Ed.), *Understanding other persons.* Oxford, England: Blackwell, Banl, & Mott, 1974.

Groat, H. T., Wicks, J. W., & Neal, A. G. *Differential consequences of having an only versus a sibling child.* Final report to the National Institute of Child Health and Human Development, 1980.

Grotevant, H. D. Environmental influences on vocational interest development in adolescents from adoptive and biological families. *Child Development*, 1979, *50*, 854–860.

Grotevant, H. D., & Cooper, C. R. Assessing adolescent identity in the areas of occupation, religion, politics, friendship, dating, and sex roles: Manual for administration and coding of the interview. JSAS *Catalog of Selected Documents in Psychology*, 1981, *11*, 52. (Ms. No. 2295)

Grotevant, H. D., & Cooper, C. R. *Individuation in family relationships: Its role in the development of identity and role taking skill in adolescence.* Manuscript submitted for publication, 1983.

Haley, J. *Leaving Home.* New York: McGraw-Hill, 1980.

Hill, R. Social stresses on the family: Generic features of families under stress. *Social Casework*, 1958, *39*, 139–150.

Hill, R. Modern systems theory and the family: A confrontation. *Social Science Information*, 1971, *10*(5), 7–26.

Lewis, J. M., Beavers, W. R., Gossett, J. T., & Phillips, V. A. *No single thread: Psychological health in family systems.* New York: Brunner/Mazel, 1976.

Marcia, J. E. Development and validation of ego identity status. *Journal of Personality and Social Psychology*, 1966, *3*, 551–558.

Miller, A. *Prisoners of childhood.* New York: Basic Books, 1981.

Minuchin, S. *Families and family therapy.* Cambridge, Mass.: Harvard University Press, 1974.

Minuchin, S., Rosman, B. L., & Baker, L. *Psychosomatic families.* Cambridge, Mass.: Harvard University Press, 1978.

Napier, A. Y., & Whitaker, C. A. *The family crucible.* New York: Harper & Row, 1978.

Olson, D. H., Cromwell, R. E., & Klein, D. M. Beyond family power. In R. E.

Cromwell & D. H. Olson (Eds.), *Power in families*. New York: Halsted Press, 1975.

Olson, D. H., Sprenkle, D. H., & Russell, C. S. Circumplex model of marital and family systems: I. Cohesion and adaptability dimensions, family types, and clinical applications. *Family Process*, 1979, *18*, 3–28.

Piaget, J. *The language and thought of the child*. New York: Harcourt Brace, 1926.

Piaget, J. *The moral judgment of the child*. London: Kegan Paul, 1932.

Polit, D. F. Stereotypes relating to family size status. *Journal of Marriage and the Family*, 1978, *40*, 105–116.

Rausch, H. L., Grief, A. C., & Nugent, J. Communication in couples and families. In W. R. Burr, R. Hill, I. Nye, & I. L. Reiss (Eds.), *Contemporary theories about the family* (Vol. 1). New York: Free Press, 1979.

Satir, V. *Conjoint family therapy*. Palo Alto, Calif.: Science and Behavior Books, 1967.

Schachter, F. F., Shore, E., Feldman-Rotman, S., Marquis, R. E., & Campbell, S. Sibling deidentification. *Developmental Psychology*, 1976, *12*, 418–427.

Shantz, C. U. The development of social cognition. In E. M. Hetherington (Ed.), *Review of child development research* (Vol. 5). Chicago: University of Chicago Press, 1975.

Thompson, V. D. Family size: Implicit policies and assumed psychological outcomes. *Journal of Social Issues*, 1974, *30*, 93–124.

Toman, W. *Family constellation: Its effects on personality and social behavior*. New York: Springer, 1969.

Turner, R. H. *Family interaction*. New York: Wiley, 1970.

Van den Berg, B. J., & Oechsli, F. W. *Studies on the one-child family*. Final report to the National Institute of Child Health and Human Development, 1980.

·5·

EXPERIMENTAL TESTS OF THE SIBLING TUTORING FACTOR

TONI FALBO
WILLIAM E. SNELL, JR.

This chapter examines the sibling tutoring component of the confluence model. The confluence model (Zajonc & Markus, 1975) provides an explanation for the frequently observed relationships between several family configuration factors and intelligence. This popular (Zajonc, 1975) and award-winning ("Zajonc Defuses IQ Debate," 1976) model consists of two components. The first component reflects the intellectual environment of the family by combining the intellectual levels of all family members. The relationship between this component and intellectual development was stated to be positive. That is, families with higher intellectual environment scores were expected to produce young adults with higher mental ages than families with lower intellectual environment scores. To date, this part of the confluence model has received the most attention and generated the most controversy (e.g., Galbraith, 1982; Berbaum, Markus, & Zajonc, 1982).

The second component was called the "sibling tutoring factor." This factor was created to account for the two discontinuities found in the otherwise linear relationship between the intellectual environment component and intelligence. Briefly, Zajonc and Markus stated that only borns and last borns scored lower than expected on intelligence measures because they did not have a younger sibling to tutor. Tutoring a younger sibling was thought to make a significant contribution to a child's intellectual development. With the addition of this component, Zajonc and Markus (1975) reported that the regres-

Toni Falbo and William E. Snell, Jr. Department of Educational Psychology, The University of Texas, Austin, Texas.

sion equation expressing the confluence model accounted for 97% of the variance associated with the Raven Progressive Matrices scores of 400,000 Dutch men.

More recently, Zajonc, Markus, and Markus (1979) refined the sibling tutoring factor so that it reflected the gains and losses associated with having a younger sibling. That is, before younger siblings became tutorable, their presence was considered to have a negative effect on intellectual development. However, over time, the model stated that the positive effects of tutoring the younger siblings accumulated and eventually outweighed the negative effects of having siblings. In particular, Zajonc *et al.* (1979) demonstrated that during early childhood, only children scored better on intelligence tests than children from two-child families. This situation gradually reversed during adolescence, so that by young adulthood only children scored lower than first borns from two-child families. In addition, last borns from two-child families were portrayed as surpassing only borns by young adulthood. Although Zajonc *et al.* did not explain why this happened, one can guess that the tutoring received by these younger siblings boosted their intellectual development so that they too surpassed the levels achieved by the untutoring and untutored only children.

To summarize, the underlying justification for the sibling tutoring factor in the confluence model came from three sources: (1) plausibility, (2) parsimony (one explanation served both only and last borns), and (3) empirical support from the overall tests of the confluence model. However, while there is some evidence to document the occurrence of sibling tutoring in families (Pepler, 1981; Pepler, Abramovitch, & Corter, 1981), there is no strong evidence that tutoring someone younger leads to a gain in intelligence that surpasses the gain that results from being tutored.

Indeed, there is some evidence that cross-age tutoring has beneficial effects on the tutor's achievement. But achievement is not intelligence, and the evidence here is more equivocal than Zajonc *et al.* have suggested. They cite five studies (Devin-Sheehan, Feldman, & Allen, 1976; Duff, 1974; Morgan & Toy, 1970; Richer, 1973; Wu, 1974) as support of the notion that teaching someone younger leads to intelligence gains. Four of the five were reports of individual studies; the fifth was a review of the tutoring literature. None of the four studies used an accepted measure of intelligence as a dependent variable. Instead, a variety of standardized achievement, personality, and behavioral assessments were made. Furthermore, the review article (Devin-Sheehan *et al.*, 1976) gave little support to the notion that tutoring someone younger leads to consistent gains in intelligence or that tutors benefit more than tutees. On the contrary, this review concluded that "several different kinds of tutoring programs can effectively improve academic performance of tutees and, in some cases, that of tutors as well" (p. 363).

A complete review of the literature on cross-age tutoring would conclude that no consistent results favoring tutors or tutees have been found. Some cross-age tutoring studies report comparable gains in academic performance for both tutor and tutee (e.g., Crenshaw Community Youth Study Association, 1968; Morita, 1972); some report greater gains for tutees than for tutors (e.g., Boyd, 1969; Ellis, 1971; Rogers, 1970; Snapp, Oakland, & Williams, 1972; Werth, 1968); whereas some do report greater gains for tutors than for tutees (Allen & Feldman, 1973; Cloward, 1967; Morgan & Toy, 1970).

Unfortunately, the three studies that are most frequently cited to demonstrate the advantage of the tutor have many methodological weaknesses. The first such report (Cloward, 1967) contained separate studies to evaluate the impact of being tutored and the impact of tutoring on reading achievement and on a variety of attitudinal and personality variables. Compared to control subjects who had no special training, both tutees and tutors gained in their reading achievement. Cloward translated the raw gains into grade equivalents and reported that the tutees with the longest tutoring sessions gained 6 months in reading achievement whereas the no-treatment controls showed only 3½ months improvement. In contrast, the tutors experienced a mean growth of 3.4 years as compared to 1.7 years for control subjects. No direct comparison was made of the reading gains of tutees and tutors, probably because different measures of reading achievement were taken of tutors and tutees. Also, the "control" group received less instructional time than either tutors or tutees.

The second study (Morgan & Toy, 1970) frequently cited as demonstrating greater tutor than tutee benefits also failed to compare directly the gains of the study's 10 tutors with the gains of the 13 tutees. The achievement scores for tutors were analyzed separately from the scores for tutees, and the gains of both were compared to the pretest–posttest gains made by comparable students who were kept in study hall. Compared to these control subjects, tutors experienced a significant gain on the reading subtest, but nonsignificant gains on the spelling and arithmetic subtests. The comparisons between tutees and their age mate controls failed to produce any significant differences. Thus, although this study has been cited by Zajonc *et al.* as support for the sibling tutoring hypothesis, the facts that (1) achievement and not intellectual ability was the dependent variable, (2) few subjects were involved, (3) the gains of tutors were not directly compared to the gains of tutees, and (4) only one in three achievement tests indicated a gain over that obtained by control subjects suggest that the support this study provides for the sibling tutoring factor is limited.

The third study (Allen & Feldman, 1973) frequently cited as demonstrating the benefits of tutors attempted to improve upon the methodology of the previous studies by having elementary-school-aged subjects serve as their own controls. For 10 days, the seven tutors of this study alternated between tutoring one day and studying the same material on their own the next day. Similarly, the seven tutees alternated between being taught and studying alone. In addition, tutors were given 10 extra minutes to prepare for the 20-minute tutoring session. The lessons studied consisted of both science and language topics, and the dependent measure of this study consisted of scores generated from tests of the specific content in these lessons. The data were analyzed separately for tutors and tutees, and it was reported that by the last two tutoring trials the older subjects performed significantly better after they had tutored than after they had studied alone. For the younger subjects, no differences in performance were found between being tutored and studying alone. Consequently, when the gains of tutors were compared with those of tutees, tutors demonstrated a significant improvement relative to tutees.

The basic problems with this study concern the small number of subjects, the extra instructional time given to tutors, and the fact that the order of the study-alone and tutoring session was never considered as a variable in the analyses. Consequently, some tutors had the sequence of studying alone (20 minutes), tutor preparation (10 minutes), and then tutoring (20 minutes) on the same lesson, while other tutors had only tutor preparation before tutoring and then studying alone. One would guess that the more exposure to the material before tutoring, the better the performance as a tutor and the greater the benefits to the tutor. Although Allen and Feldman reported they had counterbalanced the order of tutoring and studying alone, since only seven tutoring pairs completed the study, it is inevitable that an imbalance of this ordering factor occurred.

Despite the successes of the three studies, none supports the essential elements of the sibling tutoring factor. That is, there is still no evidence that tutoring someone younger leads to gains in intellectual abilities, primarily because cross-age tutoring studies have not selected intellectual abilities as dependent measures. Instead, such variables as content or skill acquisition, self-esteem, or liking for school are the most likely outcomes assessed. Secondarily, these studies have failed to provide the desired support because the control groups used have been inadequate. In making the subjects serve as their own controls, Allen and Feldman (1973) confounded the treatment effect by failing to control for the variance associated with the order of tutoring and studying alone. In the Cloward (1967) and Morgan and Toy (1970) studies, the control subjects were simply left in study hall or given no other training, while the tutoring subjects had additional instructional time plus the special attention associated with being part of an experimental manipulation. The issue of what constitutes an appropriate control group is essential in evaluating the effects of tutoring. Clearly, in order to evaluate tutoring adequately, one must have a control group that is as identical to the tutoring manipulation as possible. In particular, those in the control group should receive equivalent instructional time and have equal motivations to perform.

In fact, the major reason that schools engage in cross-age tutoring programs is that tutoring programs provide the extra instruction needed for low-achieving students while at the same time providing the student-tutors with additional status. This enhancement of status is expected to improve the tutors' performance in school. Note that all three studies cited above involved low-achieving students either as tutors (Cloward, 1967; Allen & Feldman, 1973) or tutees (Morgan & Toy, 1970). It seems likely that greater gains in academic performance can be obtained from low achievers than from students achieving at grade level. Therefore, by selecting low achievers as subjects, these studies increased the likelihood that significant gains would be found as a result of participation in the tutoring program.

The two studies presented here were conducted to determine if tutoring someone younger leads to greater gains in intellectual abilities than being taught by someone older. If the sibling tutoring hypothesis is correct, then tutoring should lead to greater gains in intellectual abilities than being tutored. Further, although the confluence model does not directly say so, it is expected that engaging in tutoring, either as tutor or tutee, will have greater benefits for intellectual abilities than studying the same material alone. This hypothesis is based on the data Zajonc *et al.* (1979) presented during their comparison of the one- and two-child families. According to their results, last borns from two-child families outperform only children, although no explanation is given for this finding, a point that has been noted elsewhere (Galbraith, 1982). The difficulty here lies in the fact that neither last nor only borns have a younger sibling to tutor. Therefore, last borns of a two-child family should perform similarly to only borns or somewhat worse, because last borns have another child's mental age in their family, which the only borns do not. However, last borns do have the opportunity to be tutored, which only borns lack. In the absence of an alternate explanation for this phenomenon, one is left with the supposition that being tutored also has positive effects on intellectual abilities relative to self-teaching. The following two experiments tested these hypotheses.

This chapter presents two experiments that attempted to provide the needed empirical support for the sibling tutoring factor and to improve upon the methodology used in previous research. Subjects were volunteers with no special achievement problems. Procedures were directed toward making the tutoring and control pairs as comparable as possible, especially in terms of overall instructional time and motivation to perform.

STUDY 1

Method

Subjects

The subjects were 110 teenagers (ranging in age from 12.9 to 18.1 years) who were paid $3 each for participating in a one-hour training session. The subjects were paired so that one member of each pair was at least one year older than the other and both members were of the same sex. None of the subjects knew their partners before the training sessions. The age difference was necessary in order to test the major sibling tutoring hypothesis that teaching someone younger leads to gains in intellectual abilities. The subjects in each pair were of the same sex in order to eliminate any possible effects of mixed-sex dyads on the dependent variables of this study. Although research comparing same sex versus mixed-sex pairings has met with mixed results (Devin-Sheehan *et al.*, 1976; Ehly & Larsen, 1980), it seemed likely that for adolescent subjects mixing the sexes might result in the addition of unwanted variance into the performance measures.

To reduce the influence of family size and birth order on the tutoring results, first, last, or only borns from one-, two-, or three-child families were selected. All pair combinations of first, last, and only borns by age status (nine possibilities) were represented in the sample. For example, one pair type was first-born older subject paired with last-born younger subject. Another pair type was first-born older subject with only-born younger subject.

The tutoring treatment was contrasted with a self-teaching control treatment. Self-teaching was selected as the alternate training type because it was analogous to the experience of only children. That is, if we believe the Zajonc *et al.* portrayal, only children are neither tutored nor do they tutor. Therefore, if instructional time is to be held constant, tutoring should be contrasted with the only instruction left for only borns to do: teach themselves. In fact, self-teaching has been used as a control treatment in previous research that has reported greater tutor than tutee benefits (Allen & Feldman, 1973; Morgan & Toy, 1970).

Pairs were randomly assigned to the tutoring or self-teaching condition on the ratio of five tutoring pairs to one self-teaching pair. While the precise ratio (5:1) was arbitrarily chosen, the decision to have many more tutoring than self-teaching pairs was based on two considerations. First, the purpose of including the self-teaching group was simply to have an alternate training or control group to test the second hypothesis. That is, the first goal of this study was to test the hypothesis that tutoring has a greater impact on intellectual abilities than being tutored. This could be tested by simply comparing the performance of tutors with that of tutees. The secondary goal of the study was to test the additional hypothesis implicit in the sibling tutoring factor that tutoring (regardless of role) is superior to self-teaching. Therefore, the purpose of the self-teaching pairs was to provide a comparison score for the tutoring condition, not to examine self-teaching *per se*.

The second reason why more tutoring than self-teaching pairs were run concerns the anticipated need to control the impact of birth order on the results. That is, if the confluence model is correct, first borns in general should have more experience at tutoring than either only or last borns. However, this experience would vary depending on the number of younger siblings and the age difference between the first born and his or her younger sibling. Because of these variations, more tutoring pairs were thought to be needed to produce a stable mean. In contrast, because no interaction occurred between members of a self-teaching pair, the impact of birth order on their performance was thought to be minimal to nonexistent. Consequently, the number of tutoring-condition subjects in each birth-order-pair-type ranged from four to nine, with approximately equal numbers of each pair type for each gender. In contrast, in the self-teaching condition, only one representative of each birth-order-pair-type was run. Therefore, the total number of birth-order pairs in the self-teaching condition was 9, whereas the total number of tutoring-condition pairs was 46.

Instrument

The instrument used was the Raven Progressive Matrices (RPM), sets A through E and Set II (Raven, 1960). The RPM was selected for two reasons: First, the original tests of the confluence model, including the sibling tutoring factor, was conducted with RPM scores. Second, the matrices are carefully devised to be incremental in difficulty. That is, Set B is harder than Set A, and so on. Furthermore, there is an advanced set (Set II) to be used for subjects with higher abilities.

In order to facilitate the assessment of the effect of training, the RPM Set E was selected as the task to be taught or studied. It was hoped that even though the experiment consisted of only one training session, measurable effects of the training on the subjects' subsequent Set II performance could be obtained, because the training task was highly similar to the instrument used to assess the effect.

Although RPM scores are frequently used to indicate intelligence (e.g., Belmont & Marolla, 1973; Zajonc & Markus, 1975), the authors of the RPM do not consider it to be a test of general intelligence, because it measures only geometric reasoning. Nonetheless Anastasi (1976) reports that "correlations with both verbal and performance tests of intelligence range between .40 and .75, tending to be higher with performance than with verbal tests" (p. 292). Test–retest reliability ranges between .70 and .90 among samples of older children and adults.

Procedure

Subjects were recruited from families that had participated in another study ($n = 95$) and by word of mouth ($n = 15$). Designation of the teenagers as potential subjects was determined by their fitting a needed sex, birth order, and age group. For subjects recruited from the previous study, the RPM sets A through E were administered as part of that study. Subjects who were specially recruited for this experiment were mailed the RPM sets A through E and completed them at their home before participating in the experiment. When the members of a pair arrived at the laboratory, both were taken into a room with a one-way mirror and seated at the same table. The older subjects in the tutoring condition were told to teach their younger partner how to do Set E of the RPM in 10 minutes. The tutors were told they could use any teaching technique they thought best. Both subjects were given a test booklet and an answer sheet. The tutoring session was videotaped from behind the one-way mirror. An inspection of these videotapes indicated that all tutors followed the instructions to teach, but that the strength of their teaching efforts varied.

Subjects in the self-teaching condition underwent the same procedure as the tutoring pairs except that the older subject was not told to teach the younger one. Instead, when the subjects arrived, they sat in the room together and were told to practice Set E of the RPM alone for 10 minutes.

After the 10 minutes of tutoring or self-teaching, the subjects were placed in separate rooms and told to do Set E as quickly as they could. Their performances were timed, and subjects were given a maximum of 10 minutes to complete the task. Then each subject was given the next most advanced series of the RPM, Set II. The experimenters told the subjects to do this as quickly as possible and timed the performance. The timing of Set E and Set II was incorporated into the procedure to facilitate the motivation to perform.

Data Analysis

In order to test both parts of the sibling tutoring hypothesis, a multivariate analysis of variance was conducted with age status (older, younger), teaching type (tutoring vs. self-teaching), and ability group (high vs. low) as the independent variables. Designation as either high or low in ability was based upon a median split of the number of correct matrices completed in the RPM sets A through E, which were taken before the experiment began. Ability level was included in the analysis because previous research has found that the degree of benefit students obtain in special peer-group learning activities depends upon their initial abilities (Peterson, Janicki, & Swing, 1980; Webb, 1980). The two dependent variables were the number of correct and incorrect Set II matrices completed after the tutoring or self-teaching sessions.

A series of preliminary analyses was conducted before the hypothesis-testing analyses in order to examine the potential impact of several possible confounding factors, including gender, birth order, and recruitment origin.

Results

Preliminary Analyses

Three separate three-way analyses of variance were conducted in order to determine whether the subject's gender, birth order, or recruitment origin was significantly associated with the two dependent variables used to assess the hypotheses. In each analysis, age status and teaching type were two of the three independent variables. The third independent variable was gender, birth order, or recruitment origin. None of these three analyses produced a significant main effect for gender, birth order, or recruitment origin or a significant interaction of any of these three variables with age status or teaching type. Therefore, the subjects' gender, birth order, and recruitment origin did not directly alter the results of this study.

In order to determine whether the unit of analysis used here should be the individual or the pair, correlations of the two Set II scores were conducted between one member of the pair and the other member of the pair. These three correlations between pair members were not significant. Therefore, the individual and not the pair was the unit of analysis used to test the hypothesis.

In addition, to confirm the initial equivalence of the two treatment groups, a two-way univariate analysis of variance was conducted with teaching type and age status as the independent variables and the number of correct matrices on the RPM sets A through E as the dependent variable. The results indicated that the two independent variables did not significantly interact and that there was no significant main effect for teaching type. However, age status produced a significant effect, indicating that older subjects scored higher than younger ones ($F\ (106) = 4.79$, $p < .03$). This finding enhances the analogy between this study and the sibling tutoring situations: Like older siblings, the older subjects in this study were performing at a higher intellectual level than their younger counterparts.

Hypothesis Testing

The hypothesis of the study was that tutors would score better on intellectual abilities than tutees and that subjects in the tutoring condition would score better than subjects in the self-teaching condition. Therefore, support for the hypothesis would be found if a significant interaction between age status and teaching type was found such that tutors scored significantly better than tutees. In addition, support for the second part of the sibling tutoring hypothesis would be found if a significant main effect for teaching type was found such that tutoring subjects scored better than self-teaching subjects.

The results of the three-way multivariate analysis of variance did not support the first part of the hypothesis. The interaction between age status and teaching type was not significant. With one exception, none of the interactions produced a significant *F*. This single significant interaction was between teaching type and ability level ($F\ (8{,}95) = 3.09$, $p < .004$). Subsequent univariate analyses indicated that this interaction was significant for both the number of correct matrices completed in Set II ($F\ (1{,}102) = 11.57$, $p < .001$) and the number of incorrect matrices completed ($F\ (1{,}102) = 7.49$, $p < .007$). Table 5.1 presents the means.

The performance of high-ability subjects was good regardless of whether the subject was in the tutoring or self-teaching condition (Table 5.1). In contrast, performance of low-ability subjects depended upon whether they engaged in the tutoring or self-teaching condition. Indeed, low-ability self-teaching subjects did significantly worse than any of the other three groups of subjects. Planned comparisons between low- and high-ability self-teaching subjects were significant for the number of matrices correctly ($F\ (1,17) = 16.11, p < .001$) and for the number incorrectly ($F\ (1,17) = 10.63, p < .005$) completed. Comparisons between self-teaching and tutoring low-ability subjects were significant for the number correct ($F\ (1,50) = 11.85, p < .001$) and the number incorrect ($F\ (1,50) = 6.78, p < .001$) matrices completed. Also, comparisons between low-ability self-teaching subjects and high-ability tutoring subjects were significant for the number correct ($F\ (1,56) = 25.85, p < .001$) and the number incorrect ($F\ (1,56) = 37.99, p < .001$) matrices completed. Since the three-way interaction was not significant, one can assume that age status was not related to this effect.

The second part of the hypothesis was supported by a significant multivariate main effect for teaching type ($F\ (8,95) = 3.03, p < .005$). As predicted, subjects in the tutoring condition did better than subjects in the self-teaching condition.

As the data presented in Table 5.1 suggest, there was a significant multivariate main effect for ability level ($F\ (8,95) = 14.56, p < .00001$), with high-ability subjects performing much better than low-ability subjects. This finding was found with both dependent variables. In addition, the multivariate analysis also yielded a significant main effect for age status ($F\ (8,95) = 5.49, p < .02$). Here, older

Table 5.1. Mean Number Correct/Incorrect by Teaching Type and Ability Level

	TEACHING TYPE	
ABILITY LEVEL	TUTORING	SELF-TEACHING
High	18.23/3.40	19.75/3.17
Low	15.86/7.40	10.20/14.63

subjects scored better than younger ones. This finding is consistent with the preliminary result that older subjects scored better on the RPM sets A through E at the outset of the study than younger subjects.

Discussion

This study failed to demonstrate a significant gain in intellectual abilities for tutors or tutees relative to self-teaching subjects. Despite the fact that aspects of the experiment were analogous to the sibling tutoring situation, tutors did not experience a significant improvement in intellectual abilities above that experienced by tutees. However, consistent with part of the sibling tutoring hypothesis, subjects who engaged in tutoring, either as tutor or tutee, scored better than those who taught themselves.

The significant interaction found between ability levels and teaching conditions is somewhat consistent with the results of previous research. Dividing elementary-aged students into three ability groups, Webb (1980) and Peterson *et al.* (1980) found that low-ability students performed achievement tests better after peer tutoring than after equivalent instruction in traditional classrooms. This is somewhat consistent with the present study's results in that low-ability subjects were found to perform better in the tutoring than self-teaching conditions. However, both Webb and Peterson *et al.* also found that the performance of high-ability students was improved more by peer tutoring treatment than by traditional classroom experience. Such a result was not obtained in the present study. This difference in results could be explained by the fact that the Webb and Peterson *et al.* treatments differed from the present study's treatments. That is, their peer teaching treatment consisted of small groups of children of mixed abilities, whereas their comparison groups received traditional classroom instruction. The results of the present study suggest that high-ability students do as well on their own as they do when they teach a younger person, whereas low-ability subjects perform better when they are tutored than when they are self-taught.

Two additional findings of the present study support the overall credibility of the results. In particular, older subjects scored higher on the initial and posttreatment ability assessments than younger subjects. This age difference result supports the analogy between the present study and sibling tutoring, in that the confluence model assumes that older siblings are more intelligent than younger ones.

Although our results do not support the sibling tutoring factor, one could argue that the treatments used in this experiment consisted of a single trial, whereas the confluence model states that sibling tutoring takes many years of practice before it begins to have a measurable effect on intellectual development. Therefore, a second experiment was done that involved repeated training trials.

This second study distinguishes between two types of abilities and corresponding tasks. Cattell (1971) grouped intellectual abilities into two broad categories, crystallized and fluid. "Crystallized" abilities are culturally specific and are acquired through experience within a culture. Verbal abilities, especially those represented by vocabulary tests, are examples. In contrast, "fluid" abilities are associated with neurological characteristics and have little to do with learning within a culture. Fluid abilities are exemplified by spatial abilities. On the basis of these definitions, one might expect crystallized abilities to be more easily affected by tutoring than spatial abilities would be. However, Zajonc and his colleagues have never differentiated between intellectual abilities in explaining the confluence model or sibling tutoring. Indeed, Zajonc *et al.* have used terms such as "intellectual environment," "intellectual level," "intellectual development," and even "IQ" rather than make any distinctions between types of intellectual abilities. The Raven Progressive Matrices used by Zajonc and Markus in their original presentation of the confluence model are generally regarded as measures of fluid (i.e., spatial) ability. However, Zajonc *et al.* have also used a variety of other measures in their empirical tests of their model, including more traditional intelligence measures as well as measures such as the National Merit Scholarship Qualifying Test (all subscales combined). Therefore, it appears that the authors of the confluence model assume that the sibling tutoring effect should occur regardless of the type of ability being tutored. The second experiment is designed to test this assumption.

In addition, the second experiment possessed many methodological improvements over the first. The number of subjects overall was increased so that the sample consisted of larger numbers of each birth-order-pair type and treatment type than Study 1. Furthermore, it was observed that tutors in the first study used a variety of teaching behaviors. Since the type of teaching behavior chosen by the tutor could influence the amount of benefit received from tutoring, the second experiment videotaped the tutoring sessions and assessed the types of teaching behaviors used by the tutors. In this way the types of teaching behavior selected could be considered in the analyses of the effects of the teaching on intellectual outcomes.

STUDY 2

Method

Subjects

Undergraduate women ($n = 426$) were recruited from advertisements in the student newspaper. All were from one- or two-child families. All but 26 of the volunteers were paired, and the pairing was randomly made within two constraints: (1) one member of the pair (a senior) was older than the other (a freshman), and (2) the older/younger distinction was completely crossed by birth order (only, first, last borns). Failure to be paired was caused by incompatible schedules or an overabundance of some birth orders. Table 5.2 presents the

Table 5.2. Distribution of Pairs by Birth Order and Teaching Type

BIRTH ORDER COMBINATION	TEACHING TYPE		
	TUTORING	SELF-TEACHING	TOTAL
First–last	10	10	20
First–only	10	7	17
First–first	10	8	18
Last–first	16	10	26
Last–only	8	2	10
Last–last	13	3	16
Only–first	10	8	18
Only–last	10	3	13
Only–only	10	4	14
	97	55	152

distribution of pairs by birth order and teaching type. Of the 200 pairs that began the study, 152 completed it.

Pairs were randomly assigned to teaching treatments on the basis of two tutoring pairs for one self-teaching pair. The tutors were allowed to vary their tutoring styles at will, whereas subjects in the self-teaching group could only self-teach. More tutoring pairs than self-teaching pairs were run so that a large enough sample of these varying tutoring styles could be videotaped and assessed.

Within teaching treatments, subjects were randomly assigned to one of two task types. Each task represented a distinct ability group. Crystallized abilities were measured by various vocabulary tests and trained through performance on a series of crossword puzzles. Fluid abilities were measured by various spatial ability tests and trained through the performance of a series of paperfolds. Later, 11 female undergraduates were selected to observe and evaluate the teaching behavior of the tutors from the videotapes. These 11 women were students from the same university as the subjects and they had been recruited by announcements on campus. They were within the same age range as the subjects, but did not know them.

Instruments

Five types of measures were used: an intake questionnaire, ability tests, skill assessments, postexperiment ratings, and teaching behavior evaluations.

Intake Questionnaire. This two-page questionnaire contained questions about the subject's birth order and family size, class standing, and other information, including an assessment of their familiarity with crossword puzzles and paperfolding. Subjects indicated their familiarity with these activities by checking one of the following options: once a day, once a week, once a month, once every other month, once every 6 months, once a year, once every few years, never.

Ability Tests. Nine timed ability tests were given to the subjects before, at the midpoint, and after the series of treatment trials. These consisted of four verbal and five spatial tests. The verbal tests were: Nelson–Denny (Brown, 1960), the Advanced Vocabulary Test (French, Ekstrom, & Price, 1963), the Controlled Associations Test (French *et al.*, 1963) and a vocabulary test consisting of 18 items from the crossword puzzles. The spatial ability tests all came from the *Kit of Reference Tests for Cognitive Factors* (French *et al.*, 1963). These five were: the Map Planning Test, the Hidden Pattern Test, the Identical Pictures Test, the Paper Folding Test, and the Surface Development Test. All ability tests were scored in terms of the number correct.

Seven of the nine ability tests consisted of two parts. Scores from both parts of each test were combined in order to produce individual ability test scores for these seven abilities. This procedure was justified by the fact that parts one and two of each ability test were strongly and significantly correlated.

Separate factor analyses were conducted for the spatial and verbal ability tests to determine if single spatial ability and verbal ability scores could be derived. Therefore, two principal component analyses were conducted with varimax rotations on the scores derived from the first administration of the five spatial and four verbal ability tests, respectively. The number of factors to be produced was allowed to vary. However, in both analyses, only a single factor was produced. For the spatial abilities, this factor had a eigenvalue of 2.08 and accounted for 100% of the variance. For verbal abilities, this factor had an eigenvalue of 2.54 and accounted for 100% of the variance. Because of these results, the five spatial scores were added together to produce one score for each of the three assessments. Likewise, the four verbal scores were combined for each administration to produce one verbal score for each of the assessments.

Because intellectual ability gain was the theoretical construct being assessed here, two gain scores were generated for use in the hypothesis-testing analyses. The combined spatial score obtained at the first administration was subtracted from the combined spatial score obtained from the third administration, thus yielding a spatial ability gain score. Similarly, the combined verbal score from the first administration was subtracted from the combined verbal score from the third administration to yield a verbal ability gain score.

Skill Rates. Two skill rates were used and both were based on an evaluation of the third, timed trial of the task performed each day. One skill rate, consisting of paperfolding performance, was scored in terms of a 3-point completion scale, with 1 point indicating minimum accomplishment, 2 points indicating more progress toward completion, and 3 points indicating successful completion of the paperfold. These assessments were made by two judges; interjudge agreement was 87%. These 3-point ratings were divided by the time needed to achieve the level of task completed, and these scores were then multiplied by 100. The crossword puzzle score was based on the number of correct words placed in the puzzle. This value was divided by the speed of performance and then multiplied by 100.

Both types of skill scores were summed across 10 days to produce a single skill score that represented either paperfolding or crossword puzzle performance. Because the skill scores for paperfolding were of a different magnitude from the skill scores for crossword puzzles, all skill scores were Z-scored so that the paperfolding and crossword puzzle skill scores were comparable.

Posttest Ratings. After the experiment was completed, subjects made several ratings, each on a 7-point scale. Three of these ratings are of interest to this study. First, each subject was asked to rate how well she liked her partner, ranging from liking her very well to liking her not at all. Second, subjects rated how much responsibility they felt they had for their own task performance, on a scale ranging from very much to very little. Third, subjects indicated the extent to which they were involved with teaching (or learning from) their partners, on a scale ranging from involved to uninvolved.

Teaching Behavior Evaluations. The behavior ratings were made by the 11 female undergraduates described above. These peer evaluators observed videotapes of selected portions of the tutoring sessions and rated the general frequency of each teaching behavior on a 5-point scale. Each of the three sessions videotaped was edited to reduce the length of the segments to be observed from 10 minutes to 3 minutes per segment. This editing consisted of randomly selecting a 3-minute segment from each session videotaped. Therefore, each peer evaluator observed three 3-minute portions of all the tutoring subjects' videotaped sessions (9 minutes per pair).

The behavior ratings made by the 11 peer evaluators consisted of five types of behaviors selected for assessment because they represented teaching/learning styles discussed in the tutoring literature (e.g., Peterson & Janicki, 1979) and because they occurred frequently during the videotaped sessions. These five behaviors are: instructing, directing, collaborating, working alone, and following. "Instructing" was defined as a teaching style characterized by giving explanation and feedback to the tutee. "Directing" was a teaching style characterized by giving the answer to the tutee or otherwise telling the tutee what to do without explaining why. "Collaborating" was defined as a simultaneous performance of the task by both members of the pair with continuous two-way communication. When subjects collaborated, both were alternatively taking the tutor and tutee roles. "Working alone" occurred when both subjects worked on the task alone, without communication. "Following" was defined as a receptive learning style characterized by paying attention to the tutor and behaviorally following the instruction or direction of the tutor.

The peer evaluators were trained to identify these five behaviors so that their level of agreement with a standard was .90 or better. The peers were also trained to use 5-point scales in making their ratings. These scales ranged from never to always with a midpoint of moderately. The behavior ratings used in the analyses were averaged twice. First, the behavior ratings were averaged across the three segments. Second, these scores were then averaged across the 11 peer evaluators.

Procedure

The subjects met once a day for 10 continuous weekdays (two 5-day weeks separated by a weekend). Pairs were scheduled to meet together every day for approximately 40 minutes. Each day, each member of a pair repeated the same task three times. Each repetition of the task began afresh. That is, the subjects did not simply start where they had left off.

Each day, the arrival of the members of each pair was staggered so that the older subject arrived 10 minutes before her younger partner to learn a specific crossword puzzle or paperfold. Then, after the young subject arrived, the older one in the tutoring condition was instructed to teach her younger partner how to do the task she had just learned. The instructions were repeated before each tutoring session:

> Now this is your [looking at older subject] opportunity to teach [name of younger subject] how to do the paperfold (or crossword puzzle). You should teach—the best way you can think of, as long as you stay in this room and at this table.

In the self-teaching condition, the older subjects simply repeated the same task a second time while the younger ones entered the room, sat at a separate table, and began learning the task for the first time. Otherwise, the experience of the subjects in the self-teaching and tutoring conditions were identical. After 10 minutes of tutoring or self-teaching, the members of each pair were separated and placed in their own rooms. At this time, the older one was instructed to do the same task (her third trial) as quickly as possible. The experimenter timed this third performance, which was terminated after 10 minutes if the subject had not finished the task. Simultaneously, the younger woman was given 10 minutes to practice the same task for her second time.

After her second trial, the younger subject began her third repetition of the same task. As with her older partner, the experimenter instructed her to do the task as quickly as possible, and she was timed. This attempt was terminated after 10 minutes if the task was not completed.

The tutoring sessions were videotaped on the first, sixth, and last (tenth) days. This was done to collect a sample of the behavior exhibited during the tutoring sessions.

The tasks were selected so that they became more difficult each day. At the beginning of each trial, subjects engaging in paperfolding were given the completed object as a model and one sheet of paper. During their practice trials, all self-teaching subjects and tutoring subjects were instructed to make an object identical to the model with their sheet of paper. They were told that they could disassemble the model in order to learn how to make the object.

Subjects engaging in crossword puzzles were given a blank puzzle and a crossword puzzle dictionary at the beginning of each trial. All self-teaching subjects and tutoring condition subjects were instructed to complete the puzzle and use the dictionary whenever needed during their practice trials.

After the last ability test on the last day of the 10-day training period, subjects made a series of ratings about their performance and their partner. Subjects were then debriefed and paid approximately $60.

After the videotapes were edited, the 11 peer evaluators viewed samples of the three videotapes made of each of the pairs to look for the incidence of five types of behavior. These women met in two groups for 4 hours a day for 10 consecutive days. The first 2 days were devoted to training the evaluators to recognize the five specific behaviors and to use the rating scales. The remaining 8 days were used for collecting the data. During training and afterwards, the peer evaluators gathered around a table, at the end of which was located a videotape monitor.

Once the peers were skilled enough to rate the five behaviors reliably, they were shown 3-minute segments of each of the three recorded sessions for each pair of subjects. After viewing each segment, the peer evaluators rated each member of each pair in terms of their impression of the incidence of the five behaviors. The peers alternated between evaluating the subject on the left of the screen first and evaluating the subject on the right of the screen first. The peers were paid for 40 hours of work. Because they varied in number of years of education attained (their class standing), their pay ranged from $139.20 to $172.80.

Results

Preliminary Analyses

Before the hypothesis-testing results are presented, several preliminary analyses will be described: an examination of the unit of analysis used in testing the hypotheses, a test of the initial equivalence of the groups, presentation of the reliabilities of the peer evaluators' ratings, and a description of the measures designed to check the teaching styles and perceptions of the older and younger members of each pair.

Unit of Analysis. To determine if the scores of the members of each pair were related, correlations within pairs were conducted for both ability and skill scores. The verbal and spatial ability and skill scores for one member of the pair were correlated with the same scores for the other member of the pair. None of the six ability correlations (2 types of ability test $\times$ 3 administrations) was significant. However, the skill correlation was significant ($r\,(167) = .66$, $p < .001$). Therefore, the unit of analysis best suited to the ability data is the individual, whereas the pair is preferable for the skill data. However, because the hypotheses are couched in terms of individuals, the unit of analysis used here is the individual.

Equivalence of Groups. The first nine ability tests given to subjects were analyzed to determine if there were any initial ability differences between the teaching-type, task-type (crossword puzzle or paperfolding), or birth-order groups. Two 3-way analyses of variance were conducted, one with spatial and the other with verbal abilities as the dependent variable. No significant main effects or interactions were produced in either analysis. Therefore, the groups were considered generally equivalent in ability at the outset of the study. In addition, the amount of liking for the subject's partner was considered as a potentially confounding variable in this experiment. Previous research on peer and cross-age tutoring has indicated that the outcome of tutoring often is affected by the extent of liking between tutor and tutee (Ehly & Larsen, 1980). Therefore, an additional 3-way analysis of variance (teaching type by task type by birth order) was conducted, with liking as the dependent variable. Again, no main effects or interactions were produced by this analysis. Therefore, these three variables appear not to have influenced the amount of liking generated for partners. Finally, two 3-way analyses of variance were conducted in order to determine if the groups differed in terms of their previous familiarity with crossword puzzles and paperfolding. No significant main effects or interactions were found. The average familiarity score for crossword puzzles ($\overline{x} = 3.9$) was greater than that for paperfolding ($\overline{x} = 1.3$), indicating that the subjects generally were more familiar with crossword puzzles than with paperfolding.

Reliabilities. The six behavior ratings were examined for reliability. In these analyses, the 11 peers were treated as 11 items and the six types of ratings were treated as separate scales. All α coefficients were above .90. Specifically, these α coefficients were: instructing, .92; directing, .96; collaborating, .96; working alone, .98; following, .96; socializing, .99. Given the strength of these reliabilities, the ratings made by all 11 peers for each subject were averaged to produce six scores for each subject.

Manipulation Checks. Three types of checks were made to determine whether the older/younger status variable and the distinction between tutoring and self-teaching were perceived and acted on by the subjects. In the first type, analyses were conducted to determine if older subjects engaged in more teaching than their younger counterparts and whether, in turn, the younger subjects engaged in more following than did their older counterparts. Three of the five behavior ratings, instructing, directing, and following, were analyzed to determine if the frequency of these behaviors varied as a function of the status difference. The results of these analyses indicated an association. In particular, older subjects instructed (F (1,186) = 32.76, $p < .001$) and directed more (F (1,186) = 51.02, $p < .001$) than their younger counterparts. Conversely, the younger subjects followed their partners' teaching (F (1,186) = 67.16, $p < .001$) more than did the older subjects. Therefore, the older subjects in the tutoring condition generally did take a tutoring role relative to their partners, and the younger partners generally took a tutee role.

In the second type of manipulation check, perceptions of responsibility were the dependent variable. Presumably, subjects assigned to the tutoring role would feel more responsible for their task performance than subjects assigned to the tutee role. Also, since they had no one else to attribute their performance to, self-teaching subjects would be expected to take more responsibility than tutoring-condition subjects. Therefore, an analysis of variance was conducted with two independent variables, teaching type and age status. The results indicated support for the validity of these two manipulations. That is, older subjects took more responsibility for their task performance than younger ones (F (1,330) = 12.94, $p < .001$), and subjects in the self-teaching condition took more responsibility for their performance than subjects in the tutoring condition (F (1,330) = 33.50, $p < .001$). In addition, status and teaching type interacted (F (1,330) = 6.73, $p < .01$). An examination of the means suggested that tutors and all self-teaching subjects felt more responsible for their task performance than did tutees. Overall, these results suggest that the distinctions between older and younger subjects were perceived by these subjects. Further, it appears that tutees felt less responsibility for their performance than other subjects did.

The third manipulation check concerned whether older subjects had higher abilities than younger ones. If this was true then the analogy between this experiment and sibling tutoring would be stronger. Unfortunately, only one initial ability measure yielded a significant age status main effect: Older subjects had higher combined verbal ability scores than younger subjects (F (1,155) = 3.93, $p < .05$).

Hypothesis Tests

The hypothesis was tested by two steps in the analysis process. In Step 1, the scores of self-teaching subjects were compared to those subjects in the tutoring condition. In Step 2, the teaching behaviors of subjects in the tutoring condition were added to the analysis in order to determine if one's choice of tutoring behavior affected the tutoring outcome.

Step 1. In order to test the sibling tutoring hypothesis of this study, two multivariate analyses of variance were conducted with teaching type, age status, and ability level as the independent variables. Separate analyses were conducted for paperfolding and crossword puzzle subjects, because the training experience for paperfolding subjects was considered to be different from that of crossword puzzle subjects. The independent variables were similar to those used in Study 1, with ability level here based on a median split of either the initial combined verbal abilities scores for crossword puzzle subjects, or the initial combined spatial abilities scores for paperfolding subjects.

The dependent variables in both analyses consisted of an ability gain score and a skill score. For crossword puzzle subjects, the ability gain score represented the third combined verbal ability score minus the first combined verbal ability score. The skill score represented a Z score of the number of correct crossword puzzle words accomplished divided by the amount of time taken, combined over 10 days. The dependent measures for paperfolding subjects were comparable, except that the ability gain scores were based on the spatial ability scores and the skill scores were based on a Z scoring of paperfolding rates.

Support for the sibling tutoring hypothesis would be found if age status interacted with teaching type such that tutors performed better than tutees and better than subjects in the self-teaching condition. For crossword puzzle subjects, this interaction was significant ($F(2,155) = 3.49, p < .03$). Subsequent univariate analyses conducted to aid in interpreting this significant multivariate effect indicated that only puzzle skill scores yielded a significant univariate interaction between age status and teaching type ($F(1,156) = 5.30, p < .02$). The means are presented in Table 5.3.

The means in Table 5.3 indicate that younger subjects did significantly better when tutored than when self-taught ($F(1,181) =$

Table 5.3. Mean Crossword Puzzle Skill Scores by Age Status and Teaching Type

	TEACHING TYPE	
AGE STATUS	TUTORING	SELF-TEACHING
Older	$-.04_a$	$.22_a$
Younger	$.11_a$	$-.36_b$

Note. Data are *Z*-scored. Means with different subscripts are significant at $p \leq .06$.

5.40, $p < .02$). In contrast, older self-teachers scored marginally better than younger self-teachers (F (1,151) = 3.78, $p < .06$). Among tutoring subjects, there was no age difference; among older subjects, there was no significant difference between those in the self-teaching and those in the tutoring condition.

None of the other multivariate main effects or interactions for crossword puzzle subjects produced significant *F*s, with one exception: High-ability subjects performed better than low-ability subjects (F (2,155) = 22.97, $p < .00001$). Subsequent univariate analyses indicated that this main effect was repeated for skill scores only (F (1,156) = 43.45, $p < .00001$). Although teaching type did not produce a significant multivariate main effect, it did yield a univariate main effect for skill of borderline significance (F (1,156) = 3.26, $p < .07$). As the means in Table 5.3 suggest, tutoring-condition subjects did better on crossword puzzles than self-teaching subjects.

The results for the paperfolding subjects were somewhat different. The interaction between age status and teaching type was not significant. However, there was a significant three-way interaction between age status, teaching type, and ability level (F (2,162) = 4.56, $p < .01$). Subsequent univariate analyses conducted to aid in interpreting this multivariate effect indicated that this three-way interaction was found to be significant for paperfolding skill (F (1,163) = 7.16, $p < .008$) but not for ability gain. The skill means associated with this interaction are presented in Table 5.4.

The group with the best skill score was the high-ability tutors. Note that high-ability tutors had much higher skill scores than low-ability tutors (F (1,156) = 14.05, $p < .001$). However, the comparison of the skill scores between high-ability tutors and high-ability self-teachers was only of borderline significance (F (1,42) = 3.32,

Table 5.4. Mean Paperfolding Skill by Age Status, Teaching Type, and Ability Level

AGE STATUS	ABILITY LEVEL	TEACHING TYPE: TUTORING	TEACHING TYPE: SELF-TEACHING
Older	High	$.52_a$	$-.09_a$
	Low	$-.47_b$	$-.00_a$
Younger	High	$.20_a$	$.19_a$
	Low	$.16_a$	$-.47_b$

Note. Data are Z-scored. Means with different subscripts are significantly different at $p \leq .03$.

$p < .08$). In addition, the contrast between high-ability tutors and tutees failed to yield a significant F. This suggests that even among high-ability subjects, tutoring was not associated with greater paper-folding skill than being tutored. In fact, low-ability tutors did less well than their tutee counterparts ($F(1,56) = 4.90, p < .03$). Furthermore, the contrast between high-ability tutors and low-ability tutees also was not significant.

An examination of the skill means for self-teaching subjects indicates that ability level appeared to have little effect among older subjects. Among younger subjects, high-ability self-teachers performed better than their low-ability counterparts ($F(1,56) = 4.95$, $p < .03$).

In addition to the significant three-way interaction, there was a significant multivariate main effect for ability level ($F(2,162) = 8.33$, $p < .004$). Subsequent univariate analyses indicated that this significant main effect was repeated for both ability gain ($F(1,163) = 7.81$, $p < .006$) and skill scores ($F(1,163) = 9.77$, $p < .002$). In both cases, individuals who started out with high spatial abilities had gained more at the end of the 10 sessions and performed paper-folding better.

Step 2. In order to determine whether the quality of tutoring affected the tutoring outcome for either tutors or tutees, the four tutoring behaviors were examined: instructing, directing, collaborating, and working alone. Since tutors were allowed to pursue their own teaching style, one might argue that the Step 1 analyses failed to test the essence of the sibling tutoring hypothesis, because some of the tutors did little teaching. Therefore, another series of analyses was conducted to test the sibling tutoring hypothesis. In these, an additional factor was included in the analyses to represent the extent to which the tutor had actively taught.

It was considered desirable to derive a single index of teaching behavior that would reflect, at one end, active teaching behavior, and at the other, passive teaching behavior. Initially, it seemed likely that the behavior categories of instructing, directing, and collaborating represented more active teaching styles than working alone. However, empirical support for this supposition was sought by factor analyzing the peers' ratings of these four behaviors. If these four behaviors demonstrated a pattern of relationships such that instructing, directing, and collaborating were positively and closely associated with each other whereas working alone was negatively and distantly associated with the other teaching behaviors, then there would be evidence that instructing, directing, and collaborating are teaching styles distinct from working alone.

The results of the principal components factor analysis with varimax rotation are presented in Table 5.5. Although the number of factors to be produced was allowed to vary, the factor analysis yielded a single factor with an eigenvalue of 1.28 accounting for 100% of the variance. The factor matrix presented in Table 5.5 supports the idea that instructing, directing, and collaborating are similar because they load together at one end of the matrix and distinct from working alone because working alone loads at the opposite end.

To further support this interpretation, each subject's factor scores on the teaching behavior factor was correlated with the subject's postsession ratings of how involved she had been in teaching and learning during the 10 sessions. This correlation was significant

Table 5.5. Factor Matrix of the Four Teaching Behaviors

TEACHING BEHAVIORS	FACTOR MATRIX
Instructing	.350
Directing	.599
Collaborating	.325
Working alone	−.834

Note. $n = 190$.

(r (189) = .23, $p < .001$), thereby indicating that subjects who reported being highly involved in teaching or learning used more collaborating, instructing, and directing.

Because of this support for instructing, directing, and collaborating as active teaching behaviors and working alone as a passive behavior, subjects in the tutoring condition were divided into two groups on the basis of their factor scores. Tutors who scored above the median were assigned to an active-tutor group, and those who scored below the median were assigned to a passive-tutor group.

This active/passive variable was entered into a multivariate analysis of variance which consisted only of subjects from the tutoring condition. The other two independent variables in this analysis were ability level and age status, which were defined in a fashion identical to that used in Step 1. Separate analyses were conducted for crossword puzzle and paperfolding subjects. The two dependent variables were ability gain and skill scores.

The results of these two multivariate analyses indicated that the addition of the teaching behavior variable had a greater impact on the crossword puzzle results than on the paperfolding results. For crossword puzzle subjects, teaching behavior interacted significantly with ability level (F (2,89) = 3.35, $p < .04$). Separate univariate analyses with skill and verbal ability gain found that this interaction was significant for skill scores (F (1,90) = 6.41, $p < .01$) but not ability gain. The crossword puzzle skill means are presented in Table 5.6.

High-ability subjects who were more active teachers had the highest skill scores. Planned comparisons between high- and low-ability active teachers were significant (F (1,48) = 28.52, $p < .001$). The difference between active and passive high-ability subjects was also significant (F (1,45) = 4.28, $p < .04$). Among low-ability subjects, there were no significant differences between active and passive teachers. For passive subjects, ability level did make a difference (F (1,48) = 10.93, $p < .002$), with high-ability subjects scoring higher than low-ability subjects.

In addition to this interaction, one other significant effect was produced by the multivariate analysis of the crossword puzzle data: Ability level produced a significant main effect (F (2,89) = 21.23, $p < .0001$). Subsequent univariate analyses indicated that this main effect occurred for skill scores (F (1,90) = 38.57, $p < .00001$), but not for verbal ability gain scores. Subjects who initially scored high on

Table 5.6. Mean Crossword Puzzle Score by Teaching Behavior and Ability Level

	TEACHING BEHAVIOR	
ABILITY LEVEL	ACTIVE	PASSIVE
High	$.91_a$	$.28_c$
Low	$-.47_b$	$-.38_b$

Note. Data are *Z*-scored. Means with different subscripts are significantly different at $p \leq .04$.

verbal abilities scored higher on crossword puzzle skill than those with low verbal abilities.

The multivariate analysis of paperfolding data produced only one significant main effect: Ability level produced a significant multivariate effect ($F\ (2{,}82) = 4.11$, $p < .02$). The two univariate analyses conducted on the spatial ability gain and paperfolding skill scores indicated that the main effect was found for the skill ($F\ (1{,}83) = 6.55$, $p < .01$), but not for ability gain. Like the crossword puzzle results, the paperfolding skill means indicated that individuals who initially scored high on spatial abilities scored higher on paperfolding skill than those with low spatial abilities.

Discussion

Study 2 produced stronger support for the sibling tutoring hypothesis than did Study 1. This support came from the analyses of the teaching behaviors used during tutoring, which indicated that among crossword puzzle subjects, those who took an active part in teaching and who had high abilities had higher skill scores than any other group. Comparable results were not found among paperfolding subjects, possibly because paperfolding represents fluid abilities, whereas crossword puzzles represents crystallized abilities for this sample. This interpretation is supported here by the finding that these subjects were more familiar with crossword puzzles than with paperfolding and that verbal skills are among those frequently categorized as crystallized, whereas spatial skills are more frequently categorized as fluid abilities.

This finding provides support for the sibling tutoring hypothesis because it indicates that at least for some subjects, taking an active teaching role is associated with significantly enhanced performance. The fact that this finding is true only for high-ability subjects is in conformation with the confluence model, which assumes that older children in a family have higher abilities than younger children. Therefore, the high-ability individual who actively teaches is analogous to the confluence model's conception of the older sibling in the sibling tutoring event.

Nonetheless, and despite the methodological refinements made in Study 2, these results failed to provide overwhelming support for the sibling tutoring factor. In general, older persons assigned to the role of tutor did not demonstrate either an ability gain or skill performance beyond that of their tutees or comparable individuals who were self-taught. This lack of association between tutoring someone younger and performance gains was found regardless of the type of ability examined. Further, the results indicate that skill was more readily influenced than either spatial or verbal abilities. Perhaps a significant gain in abilities is impossible to achieve with only 10 days of 30-minute-long training sessions.

Note that the overall results for the spatially trained subjects differed from the results for the verbally trained subjects. For spatially trained subjects, high-ability tutors were found to acquire relatively high skill scores. Unfortunately for the sibling tutoring hypothesis, their paperfolding scores were not significantly higher than the scores of either high- or low-ability tutees, nor did high-ability tutors score significantly higher than comparable self-teachers. Interestingly, high-ability tutors had higher paperfolding scores than low-ability tutors. This suggests that being cast as a tutor of spatial tasks has opposite effects for high- and low-ability individuals: High-ability tutors appear to benefit, whereas low-ability tutors appear to lose. Furthermore, the spatial training results indicate that low-ability subjects perform poorly when asked to teach themselves.

In contrast, the crossword puzzle subjects did demonstrate an interacting effect of differential age status and teaching type on puzzle skill. However, the means did not support the sibling tutoring hypothesis. On the contrary, the results gave support to the notion that self-teaching of crossword puzzles was less effective for younger than older subjects. This finding is probably best explained by considering the fact that the younger subjects were freshmen, whereas the older subjects were seniors. Perhaps freshmen have not yet acquired the self-teaching skills of seniors.

The results of Study 2 differed somewhat from those of Study 1. In Study 1, tutoring-condition subjects generally performed better than self-teaching subjects. Such was not the case in Study 2, in which no differences between tutoring-condition and self-teaching subjects were found. Perhaps these differences are attributable to the subjects' maturation level (i.e., Study 2's subjects were older than Study 1's) or to the greater selectivity of Study 2's subjects (i.e., college students presumably are more successful self-teachers than high school students). In addition, Study 1 found that the older subjects had stronger initial abilities than the younger subjects, a finding that strengthened the case for the analogy between the experimental dyads and sibling tutoring. However, older subjects in Study 2 scored better on initial verbal ability tests, but not on spatial ability tests, than younger subjects. This discrepancy may be attributable to the fact that the verbal abilities measured in Study 2 primarily represented crystallized abilities, which university education enhances, whereas the spatial abilities measured in Study 2 primarily represented fluid abilities, which university education rarely touches. Therefore, one would expect university seniors to have greater verbal abilities than freshmen, whereas one would expect little difference between seniors and freshmen on spatial abilities.

An important similarity between the results of Study 1 and Study 2 is that in both studies, low-spatial-ability subjects who self-taught performed poorly relative to low-ability subjects who were taught by others. In Study 1, low-ability self-teachers performed the worst of all subjects; in Study 2, they shared the worst-performance status with low-ability tutors. These results suggest that individuals who have low spatial abilities should not be expected to improve their performance on their own.

GENERAL DISCUSSION

The strongest support for the sibling tutoring hypothesis was provided by Study 2. Among subjects who actively taught verbal tasks, those with high abilities achieved higher skill scores than did either high-ability subjects who passively taught or low-ability subjects. Obviously, the generalizability of such a result is limited by the fact that a comparable finding was not repeated among subjects who taught spatial tasks. Furthermore, the results of both studies demonstrate that simply taking the tutor role does not lead to the acquisition of significantly better abilities than taking the tutee role or self-teaching the same task. These two studies demonstrate that ability level and the teaching style of the tutor are more important in determining an intellectual gain than age difference and taking a teaching role. Note also that the two studies consisted of subjects spanning an age range of 13 to 21 years. This age span represents the time at which Zajonc *et al.* (1979) have indicated that sibling tutoring begins to have its observable benefits on intellectual development.

In defense of the sibling tutoring effect, one must admit that the single-trial teaching session of the first study and the 10 trials of the second study are probably too brief to be analogous to the cumulative effect Zajonc and Markus envisioned. It is certainly possible that longer-lasting treatments could have brought about the effects expected for tutors. Nonetheless, 10 days of tutoring was long enough to bring about the tutor gains reported by Allen and Feldman (1973).

If these studies provide only qualified support for the sibling tutoring effect, it may be advisable to reconsider some of the alternative explanations suggested for the IQ discontinuities of only and last borns. For example, Zajonc and Markus speculated that only and last borns may be less wanted by their parents or may have more handicaps than other children. It is likely that a higher incidence of unwantedness and handicaps are present in only and last borns (Collins, 1982; Westoff & Ryder, 1977). Indeed, the major reason why only and last borns are the only or last child born in their families is that they were unwanted or handicapped.

In addition, two alternative explanations for the only–last-born handicap have been suggested. First, Blake (1981) proposed that the only–last-born handicap found in the original Dutch data used by Zajonc and Markus is attributable to the increased likelihood that these individuals were affected by the 1944–1945 Dutch famine. The men in the original sample were extremely young during this famine. Blake argues that the families that were hard hit by the famine stopped producing children. Therefore, within this cohort, the categories of only and last borns contain an overabundance of individuals nutritionally deprived during childhood.

Second, Falbo (1978) suggested that father absence contributed to the only-born handicap. Spouse absence is more common among women who have only one child than among women with more than one. According to the confluence model, the intelligence level of a family is determined by the combined intelligence levels of the members of the family, with adults generally having higher intelligence than children. Families with fewer adults and more children would produce children with lower intellectual abilities. Therefore, another reason why only borns may score lower than expected on intelligence tests is that only children as a group experience a higher incidence of father absence than others. As evidence for this alternative explanation, Claudy, Farrell, and Dayton (1979) found that when individuals from single-parent families were eliminated from their sample, the only-born discontinuity in intellectual abilities not only disappeared but also reversed itself. This explanation may also apply to last borns, although comparable information about the incidence of father absence among last borns is unavailable.

Overall, the current evidence suggests that although sibling tutoring may enhance children's intellectual development, other possible causes for the only–last-born handicap are as plausible and have as much or more empirical support. Although scientists are trained to find parsimonious explanations for observed differences, it may be that some differences between groups are attributable to multiple causes. In short, only and last borns may do worse than expected on intelligence tests for several reasons, including sibling tutoring, unwantedness, handicaps, and father absence.

REFERENCES

Allen, V. L., & Feldman, R. S. Learning through tutoring: Low-achieving children as tutors. *The Journal of Experimental Education*, 1973, *42*(1), 1–5.

Anastasi, A. *Psychological testing* (4th ed.). New York: Macmillan, 1976.

Belmont, L., & Marolla, F. A. Birth order, family size, and intelligence. *Science*, 1973, *182*, 1096–1101.

Berbaum, M. S., Markus, G. B., & Zajonc, R. B. A closer look at Galbraith's "Closer look." *Developmental Psychology*, 1982, *18*(2), 174–180.

Blake, J. Family size and the quality of children. *Demography*, 1981, *18*(4), 421–442.

Boyd, G. S. Reading achievement and personal adjustment: A study of the effects of participation as a tutor and as a pupil in an elementary school tutorial program (Doctoral dissertation, University of Alabama, 1969). *Dissertation Abstracts International*, 1970, *30*, 4764A–4765A. (University Microfilms No. 70-93, 29)

Brown, J. T. *Examiner's manual: The Nelson–Denny reading test.* Boston: Houghton-Mifflin, 1960.

Cattell, R. B. *Abilities: Their structure, growth, and action.* Boston: Houghton-Mifflin, 1971.

Claudy, J. G., Farrell, W. S., & Dayton, C. W. *The consequences of being an only child: An analysis of project TALENT data.* Final report to the National Institute of Child Health and Human Development, Contract No. NO1-HD-82854, 1979.

Cloward, R. D. Studies in tutoring. *Journal of Experimental Education*, 1967, *63*(1), 14–25.

Collins, M. S. *Parental reactions to a visually handicapped child: A mourning process.* Unpublished doctoral dissertation, The University of Texas at Austin, 1982.

Crenshaw Community Youth Study Association. *Summer Crash Tutorial Program.* Los Angeles: Crenshaw Community Youth Study Association, 1968. (ERIC Document Reproduction Service No. ED 029 766)

Devin-Sheehan, L., Feldman, R. S., & Allen, V. L. Research on children tutoring children: A critical review. *Review of Educational Research*, 1976, *46*(3), 355–385.

Duff, R. E. Effects of pupil-tutoring on self-perception and academic achievement of primary grade tutors and tutees (Doctoral dissertation, Southern Illinois University, 1973). *Dissertation Abstracts International*, 1974, *34*, 5473A–5474A. (University Microfilms No. 74-6262)

Ehly, S. W., & Larsen, S. C. *Peer tutoring for individualized instruction.* Boston: Allyn & Bacon, 1980.

Ellis, D. H. An analysis of achievement gains in mathematics classes which result from the use of student tutors (Doctoral dissertation, University of Utah, 1971). *Dissertation Abstracts International*, 1971, *32*, 1976A. (University Microfilms No. 71-24, 998)

Falbo, T. Sibling tutoring and other explanations for intelligence discontinuities of only and last borns. *Journal of Population*, 1978, *1*(4), 345–364.

French, J. W., Ekstrom, R. B., & Price, L. A. *Manual for kit of reference tests for cognitive factors.* Princeton: Educational Testing Service, 1963.

Galbraith, R. C. Sibling spacing and intellectual development: A closer look at the confluence models. *Developmental Psychology*, 1982, *18*(2), 151–173.

Morgan, R. F., & Toy, T. B. Learning by teaching: A student-to-student compensatory tutoring program in a rural school system and its relevance to the educational cooperative. *The Psychological Record*, 1970, *20*, 159–169.

Morita, H. The effects of cross-age tutoring on the reading achievement and behavior of selected elementary grade children (Doctoral dissertation, University of Southern California, 1972). *Dissertation Abstracts International*, 1972, *33*, 1374A. (University Microfilms No. 72-26, 041)

Pepler, D. J. *Naturalistic observations of teaching and modeling between siblings.* Paper presented at the meeting of the Society for Research in Child Development, Boston, April 1981.

Pepler, D. J., Abramovitch, R., & Corter, C. Sibling interaction in the home: A longitudinal study. *Child Development*, 1981, *51*, 1344–1350.

Peterson, P. L., & Janicki, T. C. Individual characteristics and children's learning in large-group and small-group approaches. *Journal of Educational Psychology*, 1979, *71*, 677–687.

Peterson, P. L., Janicki, T. C., & Swing, S. R. *Individual characteristics and children's learning in large-group and small-group approaches: Study II.* Technical Report No. 561, Wisconsin Research and Development Center for Individual Schooling, 1980.

Raven, J. C. *Guide to the standard progressive matrices.* Dumfries, Scotland: William Grieve & Sons, 1960.

Richer, H. M. Peer teaching as a facilitator of learning: Using conservation of substance as a measure (Doctoral dissertation, University of California, Los Angeles, 1973). *Dissertation Abstracts International*, 1973, *34*, 641A–642A. (University Microfilms No. 73-18646)

Rogers, M. S. A study of an experimental tutorial reading program in which sixth-grade underachievers tutored third-grade children who were experiencing difficulty in reading (Doctoral dissertation, University of Alabama, 1969). *Dissertation Abstracts International*, 1970, *30*, 4695A–4696A. (University Microfilms No. 70-9381)

Snapp, M., Oakland, T., & Williams, F. C. A study of individualizing instruction by using elementary school children as tutors. *Journal of School Psychology*, 1972, *10*(1), 1–8.

Webb, N. M. Group process and learning in an interacting group. *The Quarterly Newsletter of the Laboratory of Comparative Human Cognition*, 1980, *2*(1), 10–15.

Werth, T. G. An assessment of the reciprocal effect of high school senior low achievers tutoring freshman low achievers in English classes (Doctoral dissertation, Oregon State University, 1968). *Dissertation Abstracts International*, 1968, *29*, 1057A. (University Microfilms No. 68-14,882).

Westoff, C. F., & Ryder, N. B. *The contraceptive revolution.* Princeton: Princeton University Press, 1977.

Wu, P. P. C. The effects of a peer tutorial program on academic achievement and self-concept of low-achieving high school mathematics students (Doctoral dissertation, Florida State University, 1973). *Dissertation Abstracts International*, 1974, *34*, 5612A–5613A. (University Microfilms No. 74-6607).

Zajonc defuses IQ debate: Birth order work wins prize. *APA Monitor*, May 1976, p. 1.

Zajonc, R. B. Birth order and intelligence: Dumber by the dozen. *Psychology Today*, January 1975, pp. 37–43.

Zajonc, R. B., & Markus, G. B. Birth order and intellectual development. *Psychological Review*, 1975, *82*(1), 74–88.

Zajonc, R. B., Markus, H., & Markus, G. B. The birth order puzzle. *Journal of Personality and Social Psychology*, 1979, *37*(8), 1325–1341.

·6·

THE ONLY CHILD IN SINGLE-PARENT FAMILIES

DENISE POLIT

If one were to describe the typical American family of the 1950s or 1960s, the profile would most likely include a mother, a father and three or four children. In the 1970s the number of children would have dropped to two or three. However, describing a "typical" family of the 1980s is more difficult: A wider range of family structures and family sizes has come to form the fabric of American family life than was true in earlier decades. While many of us may continue to idealize the two-parent/two-child family, we can expect that a minority of children of this generation will turn 18 having been raised entirely in this familial context.

Of the many changes in family composition taking place in our society, two demographic trends are of particular relevance to this paper. First, substantially higher percentages of marriages are ending in separation or divorce than in the past. Between 1970 and 1980, the percent of children 18 or younger living with a single parent nearly doubled, from 11.9% to 19.7% (U.S. Bureau of the Census, 1980a). During this same period, family size (both expected and actual) was on the decline. In 1979, women aged 18 to 34 reported expecting an average of only 2.2 children. By comparison, in 1967 women of the same age expected an average of 3.1 children (U.S. Bureau of the Census, 1980b).

These trends in family size and divorce have converged to produce a dramatic increase in the number of single-mother/single-child families. In 1978, the average number of children living in families headed by a woman was 1.93, compared with 2.29 in 1970. Among divorced women under 30 in 1975, the largest group was

Denise Polit. American Institutes for Research, Washington, D.C. Current affiliation: Director, Humanalysis, Inc., Jefferson City, Missouri.

comprised of women with a single child (U.S. Bureau of the Census, 1979).

Although research on this family form is almost nonexistent, the popular sentiment appears to be that the absence of a husband and siblings in a family places the child at high risk of emotional disturbance[1] and the development of undesirable characteristics. This viewpoint is perhaps not surprising, given the generally negative stereotype of only children (see Chapter 1) and the common notion that divorce is traumatic to children. The "logical" conclusion is that a combination of these two undesirable states puts the child's mental health and social development in jeopardy.

Empirical support of this conclusion has not been published in the literature, although some clinical reports have alluded to the special risks of single-parent families with no males (e.g., female-headed families with only daughters) or with only one male (e.g., families with only sons). Only two studies have looked specifically at one-parent/one-child families and compared them with other kinds of families. In the study by Hawke and Knox (1977), 30 only children from one-parent families were compared with 138 onlies from two-parent families. The investigators reported that the one-parent families were very intense, that the single parents were troubled by their lack of a "second opinion," that the children complained about the household tasks they were expected to assume, and that the parents tended to view the only children as substitute mates.

Weiss (1979), on the other hand, drawing upon his extensive research with several hundred families of divorce, compared single-parent families with and without siblings. He concluded that the one-parent/one-child families are less hierarchial but have fewer opportunities for mutual support and closeness. The children in such families were reported to be more mature, to be the recipients of more parental protectiveness, and to lack the ally in going through the divorce process that their counterparts with siblings had. Weiss also observed that mother–son relations may be particularly strained

1. One indication that only children in divorced families are considered a high-risk group comes from a program announcement issued late in 1979 by the National Institute of Mental Health (NIMH). The announcement was for grants totaling approximately $1 million to study the impact of marital disruption on children. The NIMH program specifications indicated that research activities should focus on high-risk children, and only children were identified as one of eight categories in the high-risk population. No evidence was presented or referenced in support of this assertion.

in one-child families by pressures on the son to assume a spouselike role.

While both of these studies attribute certain negative outcomes to one-parent/one-child families, neither offers support to the view that the children's mental health is at substantially greater risk than that of other children. Furthermore, both of these studies used comparison groups that might have biased their conclusions. Hawke and Knox did not compare onlies and nononlies, and therefore they highlighted differences that might be attributable to the divorce; Weiss did not compare onlies from one- and two-parent families, and therefore he highlighted differences that might be attributable to family size. This bias might have been compounded by a tendency for the researchers to identify differential negative rather than positive outcomes.

The results reported in this chapter are based on a small, intensive study of one-parent/one-child families. These families were compared with both one-parent/multichild families and two-parent/one-child families drawn from a general population. Three broad areas are described here: (1) household structure and family functioning; (2) the children's characteristics and behaviors; and (3) family-size attitudes and satisfactions.

RESEARCH APPROACH

This research focused on families consisting of a divorced woman with an only child under the age of 19. For purposes of comparison, three other types of family units were included in the study: divorced mothers with two children, divorced mothers with three children, and two-parent families with an only child. These three comparison groups were included to permit an analysis of the effects of family size on the one hand, and household structure on the other, upon only children and their families.

A total of 110 families were included in the sample. The sampling design stratified the study group by the four family types and by the age of the child. In the case of two- and three-child families, a focal child was identified who met the age criterion for sample selection into one of three age groups (ages 0 to 6, 7 to 12, and 13 to 18). The sample consisted of 47 one-parent/one-child families,

22 one-parent/two-child families, 21 one-parent/three-child families, and 20 two-parent/one-child families.

Families were eligible to participate in the study if they belonged to one of the study groups defined by our sampling design and if they met the following sampling criteria: (1) *marital status*—for all family types, the adult member had to be either both legally *and* functionally divorced (i.e., not cohabiting) or married (i.e., not separated); (2) *length of divorce*—divorced women were eligible only if they obtained their divorce within three years of their interview; and (3) *custody*—in families involving a divorce, the custody of the child or children must have been awarded to the mother.

Respondents for the single-parent family groups were obtained by securing the names and addresses of women from divorce records in four counties in the Greater Boston area. This procedure was followed to ensure that families with different socioeconomic backgrounds and families living in communities with different population densities were represented in the sample.

Two-parent families with one child were identified through nominations by the single parents interviewed for this study. This procedure was used as a rough control for socioeconomic status, since referrals of this type are usually within the respondent's social network.

A summary of the major demographic characteristics of the sample, by family type, appears in Table 6.1. The groups differed in several background characteristics. The married women were, typically, well-educated, unemployed, financially secure, and non-Catholic. Single women with an only child most closely resembled the married women in education and financnes, but they were five times as likely as the married women to be working full time. Single women with two and three children were more likely to be living in lower-income communities and to be receiving public assistance than were members of the other two groups. Divorced women with one and two children were most likely to be currently enrolled in some educational program.

The data were collected by means of intensive, open-ended interviews with the 110 women and with 29 children in the 13-to-18 age range. All of the interviews were conducted in the respondents' homes, usually during the evening or on weekends. The interviews required an average of approximately 2 hours to conduct.

Table 6.1. Summary of Major Demographic Characteristics of Sample, by Family Type

CHARACTERISTIC	ONE PARENT/ ONE CHILD	ONE PARENT/ TWO CHILDREN	ONE PARENT/ THREE CHILDREN	TWO PARENTS/ ONE CHILD	TOTAL
Average age of mother	32.5	32.7	34.2	34.9	33.3
Average age of child	9.0	9.8	9.1	9.0	9.2
Average length of marriage prior to divorce	9.9	10.8	12.0	—	10.6
Percentage of mothers with no college education	38.3	36.4	57.1	25.0	39.1
Percentage of mothers currently in school	34.0	36.4	14.3	20.0	28.2
Percentage of Catholic mothers	44.4	40.9	42.9	25.0	39.8
Percentage of mothers with full-time jobs	79.5	36.8	50.0	15.8	52.7
Percentage of mothers living in rented quarters	59.6	50.0	57.1	15.0	49.1
Percentage of mothers for whom finances were rated a serious problem	17.0	36.4	33.3	10.5	22.9

In questioning the respondents, interviewers used a topic guide that identified the type of information to be solicited. Since the data obtained through the use of an interview guide (as opposed to a formal schedule) are not always comparable, a checklist was developed for use in the interviews with the mothers. The instruments used for the women (i.e., the checklist and interview guide) covered the following broad areas: marriage and the family; divorce-related issues; family-size issues; household structure and functioning; social network; dating and remarriage; family relationships; children's characteristics, feelings and activities; and background information.

The major mode of data analysis was qualitative. Transcribed interviews were reviewed, and commonalities across individuals (particularly within cells of the sampling design) were sought. The preliminary phase focused on the identification of themes and concerns shared by respondents and on issues of primary interest to this research. After this preliminary informal analysis, a categorical coding scheme with major content areas covered was developed so that a content analysis of the transcript could be performed.

Quantitative analyses were performed with the checklist data and with quantitative codes derived from the transcripts. The primary statistical tests were analysis of variance and χ^2 tests. The statistical procedures were used less as a test of statistically significant relationships than as a measurement of the extent to which the data conformed to the assertions developed in the content analyses.

Household Structure and Functioning

Research on the effects of divorce has tended to focus on effects to individual family members rather than to the entire family unit. This focus also characterizes research on the consequences of family size. Common sense suggests that decision making, division of labor, family finances, and family interactions are affected by the presence or absence of a father and by the number of children in a family. In this study, the effects of family form on various familial activities and experiences were examined. Three aspects of family life are highlighted here, because they represent aspects in which families with only children differed from those with siblings: division of labor, finances, and family reorganization after divorce.

Division of Labor

During the course of their interviews, the women were asked to describe how tasks were accomplished in their families. They were also asked for specific information about which family member or members were normally responsible for nine specific tasks: washing dishes, cooking meals, grocery shopping, making repairs, making beds, doing laundry, emptying trash, shoveling snow, and dusting/vacuuming. Both types of data provided strong support for the notion that family size is related to the division of labor in single-parent families.

As might be expected, only children in intact families were less likely to be involved in household chores than were children in other family forms. This absence of household responsibilities appeared to be related to the fact that many husbands participated in household work (thereby reducing the amount of work required of the women), but it also reflects the higher percentage of women in the two-parent families who did not work full-time and who therefore were free to devote time to housework. The women in the two-parent families typically indicated that their only children were assigned a very modest number of tasks—for example, picking up their own rooms, setting the table, and emptying the trash. However, most women in two-parent families complained that they had to nag their children to do their assigned chores. One married woman explained:

> There are certain responsibilities that I have to nag. He won't do them unless I nag . . . . I think the time that he does it [mow the lawn] after being told once is like once a year, perhaps at the very beginning of the year and thereafter he doesn't like doing it. We really have an awful go around about it. He does get paid for it and uh, I told him what I'm going to start doing is deducting money from his pay for every time I have to remind him or add to his pay if he does it with no hassle but that hasn't worked at all . . . . Vacations and summers he's supposed to make his bed and if I don't tell him to, it doesn't get done. He really doesn't do anything unless I tell him to. He'll say, "Stop nagging." And I'll say, "Well, you don't do it." It's a vicious circle.

Divorced women with an only child relied somewhat more than the married women on the assistance of their children and were less likely to meet with resistance. Still, in comparison with children with siblings, only children in single-parent households were assigned relatively few chores. Unlike the married women, the divorced women with one child (who were more likely to be working full-time) did not have a husband to pick up the slack. The end result was that women in one-parent/one-child families assumed responsibility for a larger share of the household labor than women in any other family type. Several of these women with only children admitted that they compensated for the heavy work load by not being overly fastidious about the cleaning:

> Well I feel tight for time *and* overloaded but I don't do everything—everything's just sort of . . . gets half done—you know, closing the closets when they're a mess . . . shoving things in, you know . . . I'll take one day and straighten it out, but things aren't very neat. It's neat enough, but nothing's immaculate.

Children in two- and, especially, three-child families participated in household chores to a much greater extent than only children. Several of the mothers with these two family types reported that the children did not gradually begin to assume more household responsibilities, but rather that they were assigned more tasks at the time of the separation to compensate for the missing family member. In such cases, the mother often explained to her children in rational terms what the family needs were and how they were expected to contribute. One woman with three children described how she handled it:

> You know, I'm trying to teach them that if the four of us work together, the work will be a lot easier for everybody. You know? So they're to pick up their own things. And I enforce that. If it means an argument with them, I do . . . 'cause we're a family unit and we've got to work as a family unit. And that means that, you know, not one person picks up or not two . . . but all of us work together. They all have chores. They all have allowances. But I stress the point to them that, "You know you're not getting allowance for doing the work because you should do the work." You know? "You're getting the allowance to save your money for whatever you feel that you should need. . . . You're not getting paid for doing work around the house because that's something you should do. And you shouldn't get paid for it. You should help."

As might be expected, household responsibilities increased with the age of the child in all family types. There was no tendency for girls to be assigned more chores than boys (or vice versa), but tasks did seem to be divided along traditional sex-role lines: Boys were more often expected to empty the trash, shovel snow, rake leaves, and so on, while girls were expected to help with cooking, vacuuming, grocery shopping, and washing dishes.

Table 6.2 summarizes the women's responses to questions about who performed nine specific household tasks. There were strong differences in household assignments among the four family types with respect to all chores except for doing the laundry. The majority of women did the laundry themselves, regardless of family form. The table also indicates that the husbands' contribution was greatest for chores that are generally considered "men's work"—shoveling snow and emptying trash. These activities tended to be shared in the single-parent families by the mother and her children, with somewhat less sharing in the one-parent/one-child families.

The responses to the nine specific questions have been summarized further by the creation of two composite indices of household responsibility. The first index is a total of the number of chores performed by the mother alone. The second index is a total of the number of chores the children either did on their own or did jointly with their mother. The analyses of these two measures of household labor are presented in Table 6.3. The analysis of the first index corroborates our earlier assertion that divorced women with an only child tend to do more of the household chores on their own. However, the second index highlights the fact that only children from two-parent families have the fewest responsibilities. The children in three-child families make the biggest contribution to the performance of household tasks.

Finances

The family's financial situation was a source of considerable stress in a sizeable number of single-parent families. Although some of the married women said that money was a problem, there was a very sharp difference in the financial status of women in one- and two-parent households.

The road to financial recovery was long and often painful for these divorced women. At the time of the divorce, many had felt helpless and hopeless about their ability to manage financially. The majority were not working at the time of the divorce, and only a few had skills that could be marketed at a wage sufficient to support a family. Many who had had prior work experience had lost confidence in their ability to secure a job. At the time of the interview, however, many of the women were beginning to get back on their feet financially. Still, money was the problem most frequently mentioned in the interviews.

Financial problems appeared to be considerably more severe in two- and three-child families than in families with an only child. Women with two or three children were often forced to collect welfare to support their families. One woman with three children, who was working as a secretary at the time of the interview but who had been on welfare when she was first separated, described her financial situation:

> I worry terribly about finances. I can't make ends meet from one week to the next. That's another stage I went through: You know I went through worrying about that and then I went through all that worrying about bills. They're not gonna get paid whether I worry or not, you know? When I pay them, I pay them. You know? And I always have. But now I just don't worry about it. So, you know, the goal for the family is just, I guess, having what everybody else has to make life pleasant enough: You know, to make sure there's food in the refrigerator. When my kids get to be college age, I want to see that they get into college. You know, that type of thing. My goals are to be able to make enough money to afford a family of four . . . comfortably . . . and still live together, you know, without working two or three jobs to do it.

At the time of the interview, this woman had not received child-support payments from her ex-husband for over three months, and she had been unable to pay rent during that three-month period.

Child-support problems were common in single-parent families, regardless of the number of children. In many such instances, the woman seemed resigned to the fact that she would have to make it on her own. Some husbands had been divorced because of alcoholism, and the women knew before the divorce that they could not expect court-ordered child support payments from their intermittently employed alcoholic ex-husbands.

Although child-support problems were evident in families of all sizes, the impact seemed to be greater in two- and three-child families than in families with one child. In part, this reflects the fact that more children bring more expenses and that the loss of child support is therefore more critical. But it also is related to the fact that women in

Table 6.2. Responsibility for Nine Household Tasks, by Family Type

		FAMILY TYPE			
TASK	RESPONSIBILITY*	ONE PARENT/ ONE CHILD ($n = 47$)	ONE PARENT/ TWO CHILDREN ($n = 22$)	ONE PARENT/ THREE CHILDREN ($n = 21$)	TWO PARENT/ ONE CHILD ($n = 20$)
Washing dishes§	Woman alone	60%	50%	30%	40%
	Woman and children	36	50	65	10
	Wife and husband	—	—	—	35
Cooking meals†	Woman alone	66	77	65	70
	Woman and children	32	18	35	0
	Wife and husband	—	—	—	25
Grocery shopping§	Woman alone	62	59	48	45
	Woman and children	34	41	52	10
	Wife and husband	—	—	—	45
Repairing things§	Woman alone	63	68	43	10
	Woman and children	19	18	33	5
	Husband alone	—	—	—	50
	Wife and husband	—	—	—	20
Making beds‡	Woman alone	48	18	19	55
	Woman and children	50	68	72	20
	Children alone	0	14	5	0

Doing laundry	Woman alone	77	77	75	75
	Woman and children	23	23	25	10
	Husband (or wife and husband)	—	—	—	15
Emptying trash§	Woman alone	45	27	19	25
	Woman and children	25	41	14	0
	Children alone	28	32	67	15
	Husband (or husband and wife)	—	—	—	55
Shoveling snow§	Woman alone	45	29	15	0
	Woman and children	26	57	45	10
	Children alone	12	10	35	0
	Husband (or husband and wife)	—	—	—	65
Dusting and vacuuming†	Woman alone	45	36	10	65
	Woman and children	51	55	86	5
	Husband (or husband and wife)	—	—	—	20

*Not all categories of responsibility are shown. When the percentage was uniformly small (e.g., for a "children and husband" or "outside help" response), the category was omitted. Therefore the percentages do not usually add up to 100%.

†Two-tailed χ^2 test is statistically significant at the .01 level.

‡Two-tailed χ^2 test is statistically significant at the .001 level.

§Two-tailed χ^2 test is statistically significant at the .0001 level.

Table 6.3. Analyses of Two Summary Indexes of Household Responsibility

	INDEX 1*		INDEX 2†	
FAMILY TYPE	*M*	*SD*	*M*	*SD*
One parent/one child ($n = 47$)	4.9	2.6	3.4	2.7
One parent/two children ($n = 22$)	4.4	1.8	4.3	2.1
One parent/three children ($n = 21$)	3.1	1.4	5.4	1.5
Two parents/one child ($n = 20$)	3.8	2.0	.9	1.1
	$F = 3.685, df = 3$ $p < .01$		$F = 16.67, df = 3$ $p < .0001$	

*Total number of chores performed by mother alone.
†Total number of chores performed with children's involvement.

two- and three-child families were more dependent on child support than women with an only child. Women with onlies were more likely to be working full time and were therefore more self-sufficient.

In conclusion, the single-parent families were generally beset with severe financial worries. The majority of these women experienced a major change in their standard of living after separating from their husbands. Many had been forced to find new lodgings. And even those who remained in their previous houses or apartments were generally struggling financially. Most of the divorced women were working, but only a handful earned over $10,000 per year. As a result, there was a strong dependency on child support and, in some cases, welfare payments or financial assistance from family members. Divorced women with two and three children had more financial problems than divorced women with one child.

Family Reorganization after Divorce

For the majority of divorced women, the departure of the husband from the household requires some major changes in the organization of family life. Burdens of household management and parenting previously shared by the husband and wife become the sole responsibility of the woman. Many of the activities cannot reasonably be handled by one person—for example, providing an income for the family and caring for young children.

At the time of our interviews, which typically took place 1 to 2 years after divorce and 3 or more years after separation, the families had for the most part attained an equilibrium. Decisions about whether or not to work, whether or not to pursue further education, what child-care arrangement to use, where to live, how to handle money, how to manage housework, and so on had been made before our contact with these women. But the transition to this status of equilibrium was slower, more painful, and less thorough in some families than in others.

Women who had been working before the separation had the fewest problems in reorganizing their families' lives. These women were not faced with having to start a new life for themselves, nor did they usually need to make decisions about child care. Some of the working women even commented that family organization was easier without a husband because there were fewer conflicts about household decisions and less housework to be done.

Although several themes relating to reorganization difficulties emerged in all three family-size groups, there appeared to be a relationship between successful reorganization and the number of children in the family.[2] On the whole, women with one child had had the easiest transition period, and the vast majority in this group indicated that their families were functioning smoothly and had arrived at a fairly stable condition. More of the single mothers with one child than those with two or three children had been working before the divorce; fewer had child-care problems; fewer had financial difficulties (in part because more had found full-time jobs); and fewer had had to find a new place to live after the divorce. Several of the women with an only child had made the transition easier for themselves by planning ahead and making provisions for the separation:

> I decided that I didn't think it was going to work out. I made it a point to start looking for a job. And it was only after I found it that we then physically separated. So Peter was in day care probably about six months before his father moved out of the house. I wanted to feel that I was financially self-sufficient before we separated. The transition to full-

2. The major themes relating to reorganization include maintaining an adequate standard of living; finding a job; finding someone to care for children; locating a suitable and affordable place to live; supervising and disciplining the children; managing the distribution of household tasks; making day-to-day decisions without backup, support, or advice.

> time work . . . it was the first full-time job I had ever had . . . so that was probably difficult in terms of just the demands on my energy, but other than that . . . it was fun.

The group that experienced the most severe problems in reorganizing their family life was the one-parent/three-child families. At the time of the interviews, many of these families had not yet attained a high degree of stability. For example, a sizeable number of these mothers were receiving welfare payments and were awaiting some event, such as the entry of all children into school or the completion of job training, before establishing themselves and providing an independent income for their families. For many of these women, the reorganization of their family life was complicated by the fact that they had a great number of personal problems to work through. For example, child abuse, alcoholism of the ex-husband, and wife battering were much more prevalent in these families than in the families with fewer children.

In summary, the transition from a two-parent household was difficult for the majority of the divorced women. However, single mothers with an only child appeared to be better equipped to handle this transition, in part because small families are more manageable and in part because the women were able to move into the labor force fairly quickly. A sizeable number of the three-child families had not yet attained the equilibrium and stability that characterized most families with fewer children. Dependence on outsiders and on welfare appeared to contribute to this condition, and problems of personal adjustment exacerbated it.

Consequences to the Children

The literature on divorce suggests that some children suffer serious problems as a result of their parents' marital breakup.[3] The literature on the effects of family size on a child's characteristics and behaviors has consistently documented differences among persons with different number of siblings. Given these two bodies of research, we might

3. However, studies of the consequences of divorce on children have often used clinical samples (i.e., children in therapy or counseling) or have failed to consider the effects of the marital discord that led to the divorce.

expect to find some marked differences among the four groups of children studied. Of particular interest for this research is the only child in a one-parent family. As noted in the introduction, clinicians and other researchers have hypothesized that only children with a single parent are particularly at risk of emotional difficulties, and for two reasons: (1) they have no siblings with whom issues surrounding the divorce can be jointly worked out, and (2) the emotional climate of households with only one adult and one child has been presumed to suffer from the absence of buffers. This section focuses on the children in the four groups and examines their adjustment to the divorce, social networks and peer relations, and personal characteristics and behaviors.

Adjustment to the Divorce

The mothers reported that their children had originally shown signs of distress when they first learned of the parents' intended separation. However, at the time of the interviews (typically 1 to 2 years after the divorce), the majority of children appeared to have adjusted to their new life circumstances successfully, which typically included having a working mother and a father who visited them once or twice a week.

Despite the generally high level of adjustment in this sample, a number of children were continuing to manifest distress or anger about the divorce. This was especially true of children in two-child families. While only 4% of the mothers of one child and 10% of the mothers of three said their children were still displaying distress about the divorce, 35% of the mothers of two admitted this. Here is how one mother of two described the anger and hostility of her older son:

> Craig went out one time and I heard glass breaking . . . and I looked out just to see who was doing it and it was Craig. He was throwing rocks at bottles to break them. And I called him in and, you know, I gave him a spanking. And I said, "You know you're not supposed to do that. Why did you do it?" And he said, "I was just thinking it was Dad's head every time I threw the rock."

Mothers in multichild families rarely indicated that their children had been helpful to each other in coping with the strains of the postdivorce period. In fact, differences in the way the children interacted with their absent father appeared to be a source of considerable friction. Furthermore, sibling rivalry and competition for the mother's attention after the divorce often undermined the potential for mutual support. In the two-child family, where sibling rivalry was particularly intense, siblings may have exacerbated feelings of insecurity stemming from the father's departure.

Social Networks and Peer Relations

The children's social networks included a range of adults (especially relatives) and peers. The children from the one-parent families tended to have a broader network of nonrelated adults in their lives than those from two-parent families. Regardless of family structure and the availability of adults, however, it was the children with no siblings who demonstrated the most comfort and adroitness in communicating with adults. The presence or absence of a father in the household did not appear to affect this tendency. Here are the observations of two mothers with one child:

> She can talk to adults as well as she can talk to children. And she does. She's not afraid to talk to adults. She never has been. She can carry on a conversation with an adult as easily as she can carry on a conversation with someone her age.

> She is quite comfortable with adults because she would be entertaining everyone, very full of fun, and she liked being with people, and she's just used to being with adults. And she wasn't used to the usual things we take for granted that youngsters would do.

Despite the stereotype of the lonely and unsociable only child, only children in this study did not, according to their mothers' reports, have any particular problems socially. On the contrary, it was the children from two-child families who were rated as significantly more likely than children in the other three groups to have trouble making or keeping friends, to be overly shy with children and adults, and to prefer being alone. Below, two mothers in two-child families describe their children's interpersonal problems:

> Cindy doesn't have too much self-confidence so she's kind of shy when it comes to kids her own age. It takes her a while to get in . . . you

know, mingle in. She's not outgoing. She made out a . . . I don't know what magazine or what. . . . There was a whole bunch of questions and she answered them. And she answered them really true to her own personality. It said, "Would you rather be always alone?" And then it said, "Always, never, most of the time . . ." like that . . . and "A good deal of the time." or something like that. She answered it [that] she would rather be alone more than she would rather be with other people. —*Girl, age 15, in a two-child family*

Derek has not had very many close friends at all. He had a close friend years ago who moved to Florida . . . and then no one really replaced him. He always just preferred to stay around home by himself and no matter how much I tried to get him to make friends, or to join a sports group or something, he wouldn't.—*Boy, age 15, in a two-child family*

In summary, children in one-parent/one-child families in this study did not appear to have any social handicaps. In fact, they fared better than the children with one sibling on several interpersonal ratings and were described as particularly comfortable with adult friends.

Behavioral and Emotional Patterns

Consistent with the pattern that emerged in the analysis of the children's adjustment to divorce and their interpersonal relations, the children in one-parent/two-child families were described by their mothers as having the greatest number of behavioral and emotional problems. For example, these children were significantly more likely to be characterized as closed and uncommunicative and as uncapable or unwilling to share their feelings than were children in the other three groups. Another problem area that was more commonly mentioned by the mothers of two children was the children's sensitivity and vulnerability to external criticism. The following excerpts illustrate this point:

If he wants something, he gets really hyper if he doesn't get it right then and there, if I don't get it. And he'll try to do it on his own. And he'll probably make a mess of it or drop it so he feels he's clumsy and he's wrong and now he gets depressed because he has done this wrong. He tries to do it right. He's so hyper. Because he tried to do it right. He gets really uptight about it. —*First-born son, age 6*

> He gets upset over any projects or anything he has to do in school that he thinks he can't do. He defeats himself and says he can't do it before he even tries it. He gets so keyed up over just any little thing that he has to do. He did have a period that he was going through that he didn't want to. . . . He wanted to kill himself. He wanted to get rid of himself. And he was threatening to jump out his bedroom window.
>
> —*First-born son, age 11*

Another problem that was more commonly cited in the two-child families was the mothers' concern about their children acting immature. The mothers often interpreted their children's "silly" or "clowning" behavior as an attention-seeking device:

> He sometimes acts very immature when he's with his friends. He's just very noisy and trying to show off . . . and stuff like that.
>
> —*First-born son, age 14*

> The only problem that she does have is . . . um . . . if she gets in front of a lot of people that she doesn't know . . . or . . . um . . . sometimes, depending on what kind of mood she is in during the month or two months . . . she goes into little regression patterns of acting like a baby . . . baby talking. And um she'll like, you know, she just talks like . . . babyish . . . and she'll make actions like . . . like you'd expect out of a two-year-old and be awkward . . . and make noises like . . . a two-year-old. —*First-born daughter, age 6*

The only children from single-parent families were not, as a group, rated differently than the children in the remaining two groups. In fact, except for the children with one sibling, the children in this sample were fairly similar and demonstrated low levels of behavioral or emotional problems, both at home and in school. None of the groups differed significantly from one another in terms of the following behaviors: sulks when unable to have his/her own way; cries with no apparent reason; has difficulty controlling temper; often daydreams; has trouble relaxing; is overly masculine or feminine; acts out at home; resists doing homework; or plays hooky.

Personal Characteristics

In general, the children in this sample were described as healthy, active, and fairly bright and independent. For the most part, the children from all four groups were similar in personal characteristics, with one or two notable exceptions.

Self-esteem was a characteristic that many of the mothers felt needed improvement in their children. However, the divorced mothers with two children were especially likely to rate their children's self-esteem as poor or fair. Here is how two mothers with two children described the situation:

> When she's with her friends . . . she'll see a group of her friends across the street. She won't walk over unless she's invited. Like she has no self-confidence . . . none at all. —*First-born daughter, age 15*

> He's having right now a lack of self-confidence problem in himself. We're getting feedback from Jason about, "I can't do A's and 90s; I can't skate as well as anyone else." —*First-born son, age 12*

Although a majority of the mothers were concerned about their children's self-esteem, most felt that their children were independent and capable of making decisions on their own. Only children, in particular, were rated as highly autonomous, regardless of whether one or two parents were present. One mother, describing her 5-year-old daughter, had this to say:

> Doreen is very definitely independent . . . and she definitely has a mind of her own . . . and she doesn't object to voicing it to anybody. She doesn't care. You ask her a question, and she'll answer it. It may not be the answer you're looking for but she's gonna hit you with it anyway. —*Only daughter, age 5, one-parent family*

Only children in one-parent families were also described as particularly mature and empathic for their age. Their mothers attributed this high level of maturity to the combined effects of the divorce and their opportunity as only children to spend a lot of time with adults:

> He's very mature. But he's always been mature . . . even when he was, you know, a little tike. Like some of the conversations that he will have with adults . . . I mean he's very aware of what's going on in the world . . . more so than I am. —*Only son, age 16*

> I think she's very mature. I mean . . . I can sit and talk to her like you and I are talking . . . whether I have a problem . . . at work . . . she'll listen to me. I also think because of the divorce, she's had to grow

> up a lot. Because I talked to her. This is the way it is . . . "I can't stand him; I hate him; But he's your father . . . he said he wasn't going to give us this . . . we did get the house and different things". . . . I just told her; I got tired of trying to keep things from her.
>
> —*Only daughter, age 8*

In summary, the children in this study were typically healthy, independent, and sociable, though many mothers felt their self-esteem was low. Mothers of two were especially likely to comment on their children's low self-esteem. Only children were described more frequently than other children as independent and, in the one-parent group in particular, highly mature for their age.

Family Size Issues

Like many other studies of family size, this study found that different family configurations affect both family life style and individual experiences and behaviors. We also examined family size issues directly by asking the mothers to discuss family size. Two aspects of family size are described below: children's satisfaction with their family size, and sibling relations.

Children's Satisfaction with Their Family Size

Children in all four groups frequently asked their mothers for a baby brother or sister, although these requests were least often made by those children who already had two siblings. Children with one sibling were about as likely as those with none to ask their mother to have another child. In two-child families, however, the children's requests for another sibling were seldom insistent and more often appeared to reflect a desire for a baby rather than a sibling *per se*:

> She's five and a half and . . . it's like . . . she goes . . . "I love babies. . . . Can't you have another baby and I'll help you take care of it?" You know. . . . And she does go around the neighborhood; whenever she sees one of the neighborhood babies, she's always kissing it and patting it.

In only-child families, requests for siblings ranged from casual to intense. Two women, when asked whether their only children asked about not having siblings, replied:

> No, um, I think she's probably made a comment or two but not a complaint. It was not a big deal and you know, what could I say, "I'm sorry, it just never happened."

> She used to ask every once in a while, when we were still married. But she doesn't anymore.

Casual discussions such as these appeared to be fairly common in one-child families. Some women, however, indicated that their only children had strong feelings about having no siblings:

> Well, she would really like a brother or sister very intensely. She's a very social child and would love to have people around. She'd love to be a part of a big, noisy Italian family with probably many generations and all sorts of things going on.

The intensity of an only child's request for siblings appeared to be strongly related to the mother's own desires for more children. For example, the mother of the girl who "used to ask" once in a while, quoted above, said, "I like having one child and I don't want another." Another divorced woman who was quite content with one child and who had no plans for other children described a conversation with her 6-year-old daughter:

> So now when she asks me [about having a baby], I'll say, "Well first of all, I'm not married, Katy. And second of all, when Mom does get married or if she does, I want to go to school. I want to finish my degree." You know? And she'll say, "Oh well . . . okay. Well then will you have one?" And I said, "Well, I don't know. We'll have to see, you know. [We'll have to] see how things go." But I said, "I'm getting older and, you know, you don't have babies after a certain age." And she said, "Oh . . . well okay."

On the other hand, a woman who herself seemed somewhat bitter about the fact that her husband's disability had prevented them from having more children said:

> I would like two or three. I think it's a shame because she [the daughter] seems to resent being an only child. She goes into other people's homes and she sees, you know, other activities. She feels it.

The apparent correlation between mothers' desires for additional children and their children's desire for siblings may reflect the mothers' projection of their own wishes on to their children. It could also reflect the children's identification with their mother and their shared values and feelings.

Children in three-child families rarely asked for more siblings. In several cases, the respondents felt that at least some of their children would have preferred not to have siblings:

> My older child still longs. . . . She was the first child and the first grandchild and she still longs to be the only one. She has a very difficult time sharing. And she often says, "I wish I were the only child." The other two don't say that, but at times I think they feel that too.

In these three-child families, the correlation described above was again evident, but in reverse: In those families in which the mother wished she had restricted her family size, the children more often expressed a desire (according to the woman) to be an only child.

Sibling Relations

With rare exceptions, the mothers of two or three children emphasized the negative aspects of their children's relations with each other. In virtually all multichild families the mothers complained of regular sibling squabbles. Here are two typical comments:

> Johnie and Adam fight continuously . . . 24 hours a day. They do not know how to play together at all . . . at all. —*Mother of three*

> The thing that irritates me a lot with my two is mine like to fight. They fight. And I can't stand it. I do not like the fight. I don't mind an occasional fight. You know, that seems, like, par for the course. But sometimes they're fighting from the time they're coming down the stairs in the morning 'til the time they're going back up the stairs to bed. —*Mother of two*

About one-third of the mothers of three asserted that sibling quarrels were a problem, while nearly two-thirds of the mothers of two indicated this to be the case. The mothers of two were more likely to report that their children's hostilities were not only quite lively but also sometimes violent. Physical aggression was noted by a substantial number of these women:

> The little one teases. You know, she's at the age where she teases. Of course she teases everybody. You know, but Catherine won't take it . . . so she'll just as soon hit her. And she's very strong . . . so she really hurts. In fact, one time she even hit her. She punched her in the head . . . and broke her own hand.

> They fight about where to sit when they're watching TV, or where they're gonna sit at the supper table, who's gonna take a bath first. . . . You know, things like that. And it usually turns into a fist fight or a brawl of some kind, you know. And they're at an age now where they pick at each other. You know, one will walk up like he's gonna punch the other one in the face, or maybe smack him or something.

> They do fight; and I don't mind fighting with words, but he would fight her physically. He would hit her and kick her and I became very, very concerned for her sake because he's extremely strong.

In these two-child families, the mothers acknowledged that the fighting usually resulted from competition for the mothers' attention. Sibling rivalry and arguments seemed particularly intense in those families in which one or both children apeared to be insecure about their mother's love. These women reported receiving frequent complaints about inconsistent discipline, unequal attention, and favoritism.

Although not all interactions among siblings were described negatively, descriptions of support and protection among siblings were infrequent. In only one instance did a woman describe her children as providing support for one another in a divorce-related experience. These reports on intense sibling rivalry are even more disturbing in light of some evidence (Kauffman, Hallahan, & Ball, 1975) that parents tend to underestimate sibling hostility.

In summary, sibling quarreling and competition were problems in the great majority of two- and three-child homes. Few of the women attributed this problem to the divorce. In most cases, the basis for the rivalry appeared to have been established long before the fathers' departure. However, several women noted that the problem was worsening, although whether the problem was aggravated by the divorce or by the children's growing older is difficult to assess in the absence of a comparison group of intact multichild families.

DISCUSSION

The results of this study failed to support the hypothesis that only children are more at risk of emotional disturbances after a divorce than children with siblings. Of the three groups of one-parent families studied, the group with single children appeared to have the smoothest household functioning and the most favorable psychosocial outcomes among family members. Only children in both the married and divorced groups manifested personal traits that have been observed in a growing number of studies: They were bright, mature, independent, and comfortable in adult company. Behavioral or emotional problems were relatively rare.

These findings are at odds with both clinical observations and with the results reported earlier by Weiss (1979), which have indicated poorer outcomes for children without siblings in the post-divorce period. Several possible explanations of the clinical judgments should be considered: First, clinical personnel may be biased by the negative stereotypes attached to both only children (Almodovar, 1973; Griffith, 1973; Thompson, 1974) and their parents (Polit, 1978). Another possibility is that clinicians attribute a high degree of disturbance to onlies because only children represent a disproportionate percentage of their case loads. However, only children are overrepresented in families of divorce, so one would expect that a high percentage of children receiving therapy or counseling following a divorce would be onlies. A third explanation is that parents of only children have more resources than those with more than one child for seeking professional help for divorce-related distress. Our data on the financial situation of divorced families are consistent with this interpretation. Additionally, there is some evidence to support the view that parents of onlies are more inclined than parents with more than one child to pursue follow-up mental-health services for their children (Howe & Madgett, 1975). These various explanations are not mutually exclusive, and it seems plausible that they might, in combination, account for clinicians' perceptions that onlies are more vulnerable to postdivorce distress than nononlies.

The failure of this study to confirm Weiss's observations could be attributed to several factors. First, bias could be present in the analyses of the qualitative materials, either by Weiss or by the present author. Weiss's conclusions may be colored by only-child stereotypes; the present author has, on the other hand, been engaged in research that dispels the only-child myth and might, therefore, have biases in the opposite direction. However, the quantitative analyses of the mothers' ratings in the present study were entirely consistent with the qualitative analyses: In both, the two-child families were found to have the most negative outcomes, while the one-child families, on the whole, did rather well. Weiss's interpretations are not substantiated by any quantitative or objective evidence.

A second explanation for the differences between the two studies is that both used relatively small and select samples of one-parent families. It is possible that well-adjusted one-parent/one-child families and poorly adjusted one-parent/two-child families were overrepresented in the present sample. Refusal rates were highest in the one-parent/one-child category. If one assumes that the primary underlying cause of refusal to participate in a study of this type is maladjustment or distress that the woman prefers not to expose, then the higher refusal rate among women in one-parent/one-child families would require a reconsideration of the finding that members of this group of families have adjusted relatively well to the divorce. However, the data from this study do not support this interpretation. Undoubtedly, several of those who refused were disinclined to be interviewed because of ongoing emotional difficulties or problems in family reorganization. Yet emotional distress was clearly not absent among those who were willing to participate in the study. The divorce-related issues and problems raised by these single mothers are comparable to those cited by divorced women in other studies. In other words, we were by no means interviewing only successful adapters. The most common reasons cited for refusing to be interviewed were lack of time and lack of interest. Women in one-parent/one-child families disproportionately cited these reasons as the cause of their nonparticipation. In our sample, we found that women in this group were more likely than other women to be working full time, to be dating one man seriously, and to be actively pursuing a busy schedule of leisure and educational activities. It seems reasonable, then, that these women were more apt to refuse an interview because they were busy and doubted the personal value of spending two or three hours with a stranger.[4] If this interpretation is correct (and there is at least partial support for it in the data), then the group differences in personal functioning and family equilibrium revealed in this study may, if anything, be understated.

A third possibility for the discrepancies between the present findings and those of Weiss concerns the nature of the samples. Weiss's research did not focus on family size issues but rather examined broad issues relating to divorce and single parenthood among a sample chosen primarily by means of marital and parenting status. The present study, by contrast, was designed to investigate the consequences of family size within the context of single-parent families. To the extent possible, birth order was consciously controlled: The focal child for whom the mothers' ratings were obtained was the first born. We specifically sought to avoid comparing onlies with later-born children. This control certainly appears defensible. There is, for example, considerable evidence documenting differences in parental interactions with first borns and later borns (e.g., Jacobs & Moss, 1976; Lewis & Kreitzberg, 1979; Thoman, Turner, Leiderman, & Barnett, 1970). There is also a possibility of physiological differences (Maccoby, Doering, Jacklin, & Kraemer, 1979). Thus, first borns from multichild families would appear to be the logical comparisons for onlies, who are also first borns. On the other hand, a number of studies have found differences in personality and behavior between onlies and first borns (e.g., Eisenman & Taylor, 1979; Feldman, 1978). These differences might reflect the effect of siblings, the effect of differential parental treatment upon the arrival of a second child, and so on. In any event, it is possible that the exclusion of later-born children from this study and their inclusion in Weiss's research contributed to the discrepancies in the findings reported. Some aspects of this interpretation will be discussed at greater length below.

If one assumes that the findings reported here do not reflect major biases in either the analysis or the sample selection, then one must next consider why the onlies in the one-parent families fared so

4. In fact, a higher rate of refusal for this group than for other groups might indicate a lower degree of emotional distress, since many women found the interview session therapeutic.

well, particularly in comparison to the children from two-child families. The reasons are undoubtedly complex, but we review below two theoretical positions that might account for the observed family size differences.

Social Learning Theory Explanation

Social learning theory asserts that socialization is effected, to a large extent, by a modeling process. That is, behaviors are learned by means of observation of and identification with other people. Parents, especially mothers, are primary role models for the developing child (Bandura & Walters, 1963).

In the present study, the relative success of only children in adapting to the separation and divorce of their parents may reflect behaviors learned from their mothers' response to the situation. The interviews with the mothers of only children were permeated with a sense of their strength, self-confidence, and optimism. These women typically had lives that they enjoyed and careers or career plans to which they were dedicated. They were more likely than women with more than one child to have ended the marriage themselves after deciding that the relationship had failed. In this respect, and in others that emerged in the interviews, these mothers appeared to be the most introspective, most planful, and most in touch with their needs of any of the women interviewed. Consistent with other research (e.g., Falbo, 1978), these women were highly autonomous, which could explain the high degree of independence of their children. The women were also most likely to be working full time, the least likely to be having financial difficulties, and the most likely to be dating another man seriously. In short, these women had adjusted well to their new roles as single mothers, and therefore they provided their children with an effective model for coping with the loss of an important family member.

The mothers with two children, by contrast, were most likely to continue to grieve the loss of their ex-husbands and, perhaps equally important, the loss of a life style. That life style, which these women had typically accepted prior to the divorce with few reservations, included the traditional role of housewife living in a suburban neighborhood with a husband and their children. They had had, prior to their divorce, the kind of family that our cultural stereotype of families portrays as "normal." When the marriages of the women with two children ended—most typically when their husbands left them—they appeared to have fewer defenses than the other divorced women for coping with the situation. Many of these women seemed bitter about having been betrayed and were cautious about considering remarriage. From a social learning point of view, this maternal model of postdivorce adjustment could account for their children's prolonged bereavement and troubled interpersonal relations (e.g., these children were more closed and noncommunicative than others).

Social learning theory might also be useful in explaining the children's articulated preferences about additional siblings. Those only children who were least insistent about wanting a sibling were children whose mothers themselves preferred having no more children. Those onlies who were reported to be most critical of their only-child status had mothers who were disappointed with not having had more children. For the most part, this latter group consisted of the married women, many of whom had experienced health or infertility problems.

In summary, social learning theory would predict that parents who exhibit ongoing grief and depression after a marital dissolution will have chlidren who also have problems coping with the divorce. That prediction was supported in the present study. Our data suggest that women with an only child may be more in control than other women of the divorce itself, the decision to restrict their families to one child, and their life styles after the divorce.

Adlerian Explanation

Despite the controversy surrounding the empirical research that has been conducted relating to birth order (see, for example, Kammeyer, 1967; Manaster, 1977; Schooler, 1972), there is some intuitive appeal to the Adlerian view that situational determinants within the family constellation—notably the position that a child occupies—are important in the development of a child's character (Ansbacher & Ansbacher, 1956). Adler places particular emphasis on the power struggles that develop among siblings. With reference to first borns, Adler posits that dethronement on the arrival of a sibling is an especially important event in the child's development. For first borns who are not dethroned (i.e., who are only children) there is no competition for parental affection and support. Thus, some of the differences found in the present research might reflect differences between first-born onlies and first borns with siblings.

Much of the birth-order research has grouped onlies and first borns together, but a number of studies that have analyzed the characteristics of these groups separately have found them to be different. Furthermore, research that has focused on actual family interactions, especially mother–child interactions, has supported Adler's basic premise that a dethronement occurs upon the arrival of a second child. Dunn and Kendrick (1980), for example, conducted an intensive observational study of 41 mothers and their first-born children before and after the birth of a second child and found that there were decreases in maternal attention and play, increases in confrontation, and changes in the locus of initiating interaction after the second child was born. The work of Kidwell (1978) suggests that such changes in parental treatment have an impact on the children's perceptions regarding parental affection and respect. In her study, 1,255 first borns and 381 onlies in junior and senior high school were compared in terms of perceived parental affect. The onlies of both sexes rated parents of both sexes significantly higher on parental enjoyment of them and parental warmth than did their peers with siblings, even when social class, respondents' age, and intactness of the family were controlled.

The data collected in the present study about the children's behavioral and emotional problems and their personal characteristics may be interpreted as evidence that dethronement has some negative effects on development. However, negative consequences were observed primarily in the two-child, not in the three-child, families. Two possible explanations for this discrepancy can be considered: First, while the focal child in the two-child family was almost always the older sibling, the sampling design forced us to use children other than first borns in some of the three-child families. That is, the quota sampling procedure that ensured an adequate representation of children from the 0-to-6, 7-to-12, and 13-to-18 age groups made it virtually impossible to find a sufficient number of divorced women with all three children under age 7. Thus, most of the focal children in the 0-to-6 age group from three-child families were not the first borns in their families.

A second explanation for the behavior and personality differences between the children from the two- and three-child families concerns struggles among the siblings for power, parental attention, and affection. Sibling rivalry and hostilities were particularly intense in the two-child families. Whether this pattern also characterizes siblings in two-child and three-child intact families cannot be determined from our data. But the interviews suggest that the divorce situation may interact with family size in its effect on sibling relations. The mothers were judged, on the basis of their interviews, to favor one child over the other in three out of four two-child homes.[5] Typically, the preferred child was the older. In the three-child families there were fewer instances of clear-cut favoritism and a less pronounced preference for the eldest.

At first glance, this information might appear to be inconsistent with the finding that the first born in the two-child families (who was generally the mother's "favorite") had more difficulties than the children in three-child families—and, according to their mothers, than their younger siblings. But a closer inspection of the interview transcripts revealed that a not infrequently mentioned comment of the mothers of two was that the younger child had been the father's favorite: Each parent had paired off with a particular child. One might have predicted that the departure of the father would have had a more dramatic impact on his favorite than on the mother's favorite. However, as was observed in our study and in other studies of divorce, divorce does not necessarily decrease substantially the amount of time fathers spend with their children and often increases the quality of that time. By contrast, divorce often means less interaction between a mother and her children: Employment and dating, for example, are two activities that may be related to a marital disruption and that take the mother out of the home. Additionally, divorced women may feel a greater obligation to be more democratic in the affection and discipline they mete out once the younger children lose their champions. Thus the older child, who may have been accustomed to the ongoing presence and special treatment of the mother, may suffer more deprivation of parental attention than the younger sibling after a divorce.

Thus the data from our study provide some evidence in support of both Adlerian and social learning theory. Both of these frame-

5. Based on independent ratings by two raters, with over 90% interrater agreement.

works concern intrafamilial dynamics that, in any event, appear to be more critical to the outcomes of a divorce than family size *per se*.

This study, although based on a small number of families, yielded some patterns that were both internally consistent and consistent with other research, notably work on only children. Although the findings are tentative and the interpretations offered are speculative and clearly in need of verification, the burden of proof regarding the extreme "vulnerability" of only children in single-parent families lies with those who have made the claim.

REFERENCES

Almodovar, J. P. Existe-t-il un "syndrome de l'enfant unique"? *Enfance*, 1973, *3–4*, 233–249.

Ansbacher, H. L., & Ansbacher, R. R. (Eds.). *The individual psychology of Alfred Adler*. New York: Basic Books, 1956.

Bandura, A., & Walters, R. H. *Social learning and personality development*. New York: Holt, Rinehart & Winston, 1963.

Dunn, J., & Kendrick, C. The arrival of a sibling: Changes in patterns of interaction between mother and first-born child. *Journal of Child Psychology and Psychiatry and Allied Disciplines*, 1980, *21*(2), 119–132.

Eisenman, R., & Taylor, R. E. Birth order and MMPI patterns. *Journal of Individual Psychology*, 1979, *35*(2), 208–211.

Falbo, T. Reasons for having an only child. *Journal of Population*, 1978, *1*(2), 181–184.

Feldman, G. The only child as a separate entity: Differences between only females and other first-born females. *Psychological Reports*, 1978, *42*(1), 107–110.

Griffith, J. Social pressure on family size intentions. *Family Planning Perspectives*, 1973, *5*, 237–242.

Hawke, S., & Knox, D. *One child by choice*. Englewood Cliffs, N.J.: Prentice-Hall, 1977.

Howe, M. G., & Madgett, M. E. Mental health problems associated with the only child. *Canadian Psychiatric Association Journal*, 1975, *20*(3), 189–194.

Jacobs, B. S., & Moss, H. A. Birth order and sex of siblings as determinants of mother–infant interaction. *Child Development*, 1976, *47*, 315–322.

Kammeyer, K. Birth order as a research variable. *Social Forces*, 1967, *46*, 71–80.

Kauffman, J. M., Hallahan, D. P., & Ball, D. W. Parents' predictions of their children's perceptions of family relations. *Journal of Personality Assessment*, 1975, *39*(3), 228–235.

Kidwell, J. S. Adolescents' perceptions of parental affect: An investigation of only children vs. first borns and the effect of spacing. *Journal of Population*, 1978, *1*(2), 148–166.

Lewis, M., & Kreitzberg, V. S. Effects of birth order and spacing on mother–infant interactions. *Developmental Psychology*, 1979, *15*(6), 617–625.

Maccoby, E. E., Doering, C. H., Jacklin, C. N., & Kraemer, H. Concentrations of sex hormones in umbilical-cord blood: Their relation to sex and birth order of infants. *Child Development*, 1979, *50*(3), 632–642.

Manaster, C. J. Birth order: An overview. *Journal of Individual Psychology*, 1977, *33*(1), 3–8.

Polit, D. Stereotypes relating to family size status. *Journal of Marriage and the Family*, 1978, *40*, 105–114.

Schooler, C. Birth order effects: Not here, not now! *Psychological Bulletin*, 1972, *78*(3), 161–175.

Thoman, E. B., Turner, A. M., Leiderman, P. H., & Barnett, C. R. Neonate–mother interaction: Effects of parity on feeding behavior. *Child Development*, 1970, *41*, 1103–1111.

Thompson, V. D. Family size: Implicit policies and assumed psychological outcomes. *Journal of Social Issues*, 1974, *30*, 93–124.

U.S. Bureau of the Census. Divorce, child custody and child support. *Current Population Reports*, Series P-23, No. 84, 1979.

U.S. Bureau of the Census. Marital status and living arrangements: March, 1980. *Current Population Reports*, Series P-20, No. 365, 1980. (a)

U.S. Bureau of the Census. Population profile of the U.S., 1980. *Current Population Reports*, Series P-20, No. 363, 1980. (b)

Weiss, R. S. *Going it alone*. New York: Basic Books, 1979.

·7·

THE ONLY CHILD AS A YOUNG ADULT: RESULTS FROM PROJECT TALENT

JOHN G. CLAUDY

INTRODUCTION

One of the most widely held beliefs in Western society is that the only child is somehow "disadvantaged" relative to children with siblings. The origin of this belief is obscure, but allegedly authoritative pronouncements on the subject can be traced back to at least 1907, when the eminent American psychologist, G. Stanley Hall, stated, "Being an only child is a disease in itself" (Hall, 1907). Such opinions have greatly influenced the thinking and even the actions of large numbers of persons. Indeed, Solomon, Clare, and Westoff (1956) reported that one of the most frequently cited reasons for having a second child was to prevent the first child from being an only child.

During both the recent and more distant past, a large number of reports and articles relating family size and/or birth order to characteristics of individuals, both children and adults, have been published. However, because of a number of problems either with their design or execution, these studies have failed to provide an unequivocal answer to the question of how the only child is different, if indeed this is the case.

Thus the basic purpose of the study described here was to seek reliable information on the consequences of being an only child. That is, we sought to explore whether and in what ways only children differ from children with siblings. To accomplish this, data collected as a part of Project TALENT were used. Project TALENT is a large-scale, long-term research project intended to aid in understanding the

John G. Claudy. American Institutes for Research, Palo Alto, California.

nature and development of the talents of America's young men and women. Project TALENT was initiated in 1960, when the students attending a representative 4.5% sample of U.S. high schools were administered a battery of tests and questionnaires over a 2-day period. Some 400,000 students in grades 9 through 12 attending the 1,225 selected schools comprised the sample. The 1960 battery tested students' aptitudes, achievements, interests, and activities. In addition, some 395 questions were asked about the students' backgrounds, educational and occupational expectations, attitudes, social life, work habits, and so forth. Follow-up surveys, conducted 1, 5, and 11 years after the expected year of high school graduation, have inquired about such things as age at marriage, marital status, number of children, post-high-school education, occupation, and other activities. Among the questions asked in 1960 were several related to birth order and family size. The results to be presented here are based on subsamples of the ninth- and twelfth-grade Project TALENT participants, most of whom were 15 or 18 years of age at the time they took the test battery in 1960.

It appears justified to assert that no other data base exists that can match TALENT's simultaneous satisfaction of the following criteria: a large, heterogeneous, nationally representative sample tested with a wide variety of cognitive, psychological, educational, occupational, and demographic indexes measured longitudinally over a multiyear span.

Thus the major utility of the TALENT data base for studying the consequences of being an only child lies in the availability in the data base of large, comparable samples of only children and their peers from multichild families. The number of only and nononly children is large enough so that differential consequences for the two groups can be reliably studied. Moreover, data from the only children and the comparison group are available for several points in the groups' adolescent and young adult lives, so that long-term consequences of being an only child can be investigated. These data are comprehensive enough to include a wide and rich variety of cognitive, sociopsychological, achievement, and demographic consequences of being an only child for the individuals involved.

This is not to say that findings from the study contain the complete picture with respect to such consequences. Project TALENT's data base was not specifically designed for the study of the consequences of being an only child; therefore it lacks information on a number of variables that would have been included in an ideal study. However, the very real advantages realized in the use of extant data compensate for this lack. Another limitation of the study lies in the fact that the TALENT population consists of individuals who were in grades 9 through 12 in 1960; thus most of the findings from the study are only generalizable to the population of individuals reaching grade 9. However, because schooling in this country is generally mandatory through age 16, the TALENT population remains close to being nationally representative, especially for the 1960 ninth graders, and thus this limitation is not a major one. Perhaps more serious is the fact that findings from the study apply only to persons born in the early 1940s. Of course, to study the long-term consequences of being an only child, one must of necessity wait 15 to 30 years. In this sense the study's findings are as current as is theoretically possible.

DESCRIPTION OF THE SAMPLE

The individuals constituting the sample used in this study are a subsample of Project TALENT participants who were in either the ninth or twelfth grade in 1960 and who responded to the follow-up survey conducted 11 years after their expected date of high school graduation. A total of 48,987 individuals met these two criteria. From this large sample of cases, a stratified random subsample of 3,221 cases was selected so as to simultaneously match, as closely as possible, the parameters in the middle column of Table 7.1.

Based on the four stratification variables listed in Table 7.1, a total of 36 sampling cells were defined. For each of these sampling cells, a target number of cases based on the desired target marginal parameters was calculated. These target numbers served to guide the selection of cases. This approach ensures that, for example, approximately 50% of the cases were ninth graders; that approximately 50% of the ninth graders were females; that approximately 50% of the ninth-grade females were only children, and so forth.

The right-hand column in Table 7.1 presents the actual marginal parameters obtained when the sample was selected. The 3,221 individuals in the final sample divided as shown in Table 7.2.

Our decision to limit the analyses to Project TALENT participants who were only children or children from two-child families who were living with both parents in 1960 was based on several

Table 7.1. Parameters of Stratification Variables Used in Sample Selection

STRATIFICATION VARIABLES	TARGET MARGINAL PARAMETER (%)	OBTAINED MARGINAL PARAMETER (%)
Ninth graders in 1960	50	49.0
Twelfth graders in 1960	50	51.0
Females	50	49.6
Males	50	50.4
Only children	50	46.2
First borns of two	25	27.4
Second borns of two	25	26.4
Parental family in upper quarter on SES	33.3	31.7
Parental family in middle half on SES	33.3	36.6
Parental family in lower quarter on SES	33.3	31.7
Living with both parents in 1960	100	100

considerations. Primary among these was the fact that this was a study of the consequences of being an only child and not of family size *per se*. Accordingly, although some sort of comparison group was required, it was felt that inclusion of multiple alternatives to the single-child family might tend to obscure the meaning of the results or focus attention on family size rather than only-child effects.

For a couple, the two most viable alternatives to having an only child are having no children or having two children. Since the Project TALENT sample contains no individuals from families without children, the two-child family was selected as the comparison group. Because of the sampling procedure employed, the children from two-child families were divided approximately equally between first borns and second borns. This led to the question of whether the only children should be compared with first borns of two, second borns of two, or both. Our decision was to combine all children from two-child families into a single comparison group. This decision was based on the obvious but nonetheless important fact that all two-child families, except those of twins, are composed of a first-born and a second-born child. Thus, even though first borns of two may differ from second borns of two, and they may thus differ differentially from only children, a couple with two children cannot choose to have two first borns or two second borns. They must have one of each.

A third decision was that within the comparison group of children from two-child families, no attempt would be made to take the sex of the sibling into account. Thus, for example, within the group of ninth-grade males from two-child families, the siblings could be younger or older, male or female. This decision was made because, given the current state of medical science, parents have no control over the sex of their offspring.

A factor that might have been controlled but was not because the necessary information is lacking in the Project TALENT data, was age spacing between siblings. Accordingly, the spacing between the comparison group members and their siblings can be as little as 9 months to as much as 20 years or more. To the extent that a large proportion of the comparison group members are greatly different in age from their sibling, they are more likely to be similar to only children, thus masking differences between the two groups.

A final decision reflecting on the design of the study was to limit the sample to individuals living with both of their parents in 1960. This step was taken in an attempt to eliminate one of the potential confounding factors in only-child research: that a higher proportion of only children than of children with siblings come from one-parent families. The strength of this confounding is illustrated in the data presented in Table 7.3, based on a random sample of 1,000 Project TALENT ninth graders. Falbo (1978) in particular has postulated that this higher prevalence of one-parent families, particularly with female heads of household, may account for at least some of the only-child decrement in performance found by Zajonc (Zajonc & Markus, 1975).

The study sample thus consisted of two groups of Project TALENT participants who responded to the 11-year follow-up

Table 7.2. Sample Composition by Subgroup

	n
Ninth-grade female only children	342
Ninth-grade females from two-child families	441
Ninth-grade male only children	366
Ninth-grade males from two-child families	428
Twelfth-grade female only children	382
Twelfth-grade females from two-child families	433
Twelfth-grade male only children	399
Twelfth-grade males from two-child families	430

Table 7.3. Relationship between Family Size and Living in a Two-Parent Family

NUMBER OF CHILDREN IN FAMILY	PERCENTAGE LIVING WITH BOTH PARENTS
1	71
2	85
3	83
4 or more	77

survey: (1) only children who were living with both parents in 1960; and (2) children from two-child families, regardless of the sex and their age relationship with their sibling, who were living with both parents in 1960. Both of these groups were further divided into four subgroups: ninth-grade females; ninth-grade males; twelfth-grade females; and twelfth-grade males. All analyses were carried out within these grade/sex subgroups.

The classification of the study cases into the various cells of the sampling design was based on the Student Information Blank (SIB) questions asked of Project TALENT participants in 1960 (see Figure 7.1). Examination of questions 221, 222, and 223 reveals that the number of children in the family is based not necessarily on the number of children born to the parents but rather on the number of children in the household. In most cases all the children in the household are the natural children of the parents, but this potentially broader definition makes Project TALENT data inappropriate for testing hypotheses about differential intrauterine or physiological effects.

As might be expected, some people did not respond consistently to questions 221, 222, and 223. For example, a respondent might have indicated that there were two living children in his or her family on question 221, and then have indicated on questions 222 and 223 that he or she had two older sisters and one older brother. Such persons could not be properly categorized and were eliminated from the study.

A critical question regarding the use of longitudinal data such as those provided by Project TALENT is whether differential attrition or nonresponse rates reduce or destroy the comparability of the

Figure 7.1. Student Information Blank questions.

220. With whom are you now living: that is, who are the heads of the house?
  a. Mother and father
  b. Mother only
  c. Father only
  d. Sometimes with my mother, sometimes with my father
  e. Mother and stepfather
  f. Father and stepmother
  g. Grandparents, aunt, uncle, or cousins
  h. Brother or sister
  i. Foster parents (not relatives)
  j. Someone not listed above
221. What is the total number of living children in your family? Include yourself, together with all full brothers and sisters, half-brothers and sisters, stepbrothers and sisters, and foster brothers and sisters. Include those not now living in your home.
  a. 1
  b. 2
  c. 3
  d. 4
  e. 5
  f. 6
  g. 7
  h. 8
  i. 9
  j. 10
  k. 11
  l. 12 or more
222. How many of your brothers, half-brothers, foster brothers, or stepbrothers are older than you? Do not count your own twin brother.
  a. None
  b. 1
  c. 2
  d. 3
  e. 4
  f. 5
  g. 6
  h. 7
  i. 8
  j. 9
  k. 10
  l. 11 or more
223. How many of your sisters, half-sisters, foster sisters, or stepsisters are older than you? Do not count your own twin sister.
  a. None
  b. 1
  c. 2
  d. 3
  e. 4

(continued)

Figure 7.1. (*Continued*)

f. 5
g. 6
h. 7
i. 8
j. 9
k. 10
l. 11 or more

various subgroups. Accordingly, this issue was examined before the analyses were conducted. On the basis of this examination it can be stated that although there has been selective attrition in the TALENT sample, there does not appear to have been *differential* selective attrition within the two groups studied. That is, while the typical 11-year follow-up respondent was somewhat higher than the typical 1960 TALENT participant in academic aptitude and socioeconomic status, only children and children of two-child families do not appear to have been affected differently relative to their 1960 groups. Thus we feel confident in the use of Project TALENT data.

DEPENDENT VARIABLES

A total of 131 dependent variables covering a wide range of possible consequences were examined in this study. The majority of these data were collected during the initial data collection in 1960, when the Project TALENT participants were in high school. The remaining data were collected by mailed questionnaires in either 1971 or 1974, when the respondents were about 29 years old. Data on a larger number of variables are available from 1960, because the initial 1960 survey required 2 days of the participants' time, whereas the 11-year follow-up survey required an hour or less of the participants' time. The dependent variables selected for inclusion in the study are not an exhaustive set of the possible variables. However, they do represent those variables available in Project TALENT which, in the opinion of the project staff and based on a review of the related literature, presented the greatest probability of showing significant differences, if such differences exist.

ANALYSIS PROCEDURES

The primary statistical analysis procedure employed was analysis of covariance with the effects of socioeconomic status being covaried out. For those dependent variables that were measured on nominal or ordinal scales, χ^2 analyses were performed. Our initial plan was to control socioeconomic status (SES) effects experimentally by means of sample selection. However, a preliminary comparison of only children with children from two-child families revealed that these two groups significantly differed in SES in two of the four grade/sex combinations—ninth-grade females and ninth-grade males. Accordingly, to ensure that SES effects had been removed, further analyses were run with SES covaried out.

All analyses were carried out using the Statistical Package for the Social Sciences (SPSS) computer program library, as implemented at the Stanford University Center for Information Processing.

RESULTS

For convenience and clarity of presentation the variables have been organized into 10 categories:

1. Cognitive abilities
2. Personality characteristics
3. Occupational interests
4. Social life
5. Health-related concerns
6. Activities
7. Education and academic achievement
8. Marriage and childbearing
9. Work-related concerns
10. Mobility

Within each of the categories, except the first four, for which there are no follow-up variables, and the last category, for which there are no 1960 variables, variables collected in 1960 are presented first, followed by variables collected during the follow up. Because the Project TALENT variables are not widely available and thus their statistical properties are not generally known, the actual means obtained by only children and individuals from two-child families are not presented. Instead, for each of the four grade/sex groups we indicate whether onlies are higher than, lower than, or equal to individuals from two-child families ($1 > 2$, $2 > 1$, $=$). Because the majority of the comparisons between only children and individuals from two-child families are nonsignificant, this mode of presentation seems to facilitate identification and examination of trends. A second column for each grade/sex comparison indicates the level of statistical significance achieved.

Cognitive Abilities

Perhaps the most surprising set of findings in the study arose in the area of cognitive abilities. It has been found repeatedly that the intellectual functioning of onlies is below expectation (Belmont & Marolla, 1973; Claudy, 1976; Zajonc & Markus, 1975).

Contrary to most of the previous findings, only children in the present study performed *better* than the average of children from two-child families on a variety of cognitive tasks. The variables in the cognitive cluster included creativity, abstract reasoning, mechanical reasoning, mathematics, English, reading comprehension, general/specific information, and a composite measure of IQ, all measured in 1960. Of the 32 possible comparisons between onlies and nononlies (eight measures times four groups), onlies scored higher on 25 comparisons, were equal on 4 comparisons, and scored lower in only 3 comparisons, as shown in Table 7.4. A sign test applied to these directionality differences shows that onlies were significantly higher in cognitive abilities overall ($p < .001$). In addition, four of the individual differences were significant—these were IQ, mathematics, reading comprehension, and general/specific information. All significant differences involved ninth-grade females, and onlies scored higher than nononlies in each instance.

Why was this pattern of results obtained? A likely explanation can be found in the fact that only children in the present study (as well as nononlies) were chosen from families in which both parents were present. A recent study by Falbo (1978) suggests that a considerable portion of the intellectual deficit found for only children results from their being overrepresented in single-parent families. (Note the supporting data from Project TALENT in the section on

Table 7.4. Cognitive Abilities

VARIABLE	DIRECTION AND SIGNIFICANCE OF DIFFERENCE			
	NINTH-GRADE FEMALES	TWELFTH-GRADE FEMALES	NINTH-GRADE MALES	TWELFTH-GRADE MALES
Total, 395-item general/ specific information test	1 > 2 †	1 > 2	1 > 2	1 > 2
Reading comprehension	1 > 2 †	1 > 2	1 > 2	1 > 2
Total, 5-part English test	1 > 2	1 > 2	2 > 1	1 > 2
Total, 3-part math test	1 > 2 *	1 > 2	1 > 2	1 > 2
Mechanical reasoning	1 > 2	2 > 1	=	1 > 2
Abstract reasoning	1 > 2	=	=	1 > 2
Creativity	1 > 2	=	2 > 1	1 > 2
Composite IQ score	1 > 2 *	1 > 2	1 > 2	1 > 2

*Significant at .05 level.
†Significant at .01 level.

sample selection.) Falbo presented her argument to counter the notion that onlies suffer because they lack the opportunity to tutor younger siblings (Zajonc, 1976). It should be noted, however, that the original confluence model (Zajonc & Markus, 1975) (as opposed to the expanded "tutoring" version) can handle the single-parent findings quite well: The intellectual environment of a family declines markedly when one parent leaves. Moreover, the tutoring explanation accounts for last-child as well as only-child deficits.

In any event, the study described here seems to have been the first large-scale study to look specifically at only children from two-parent homes. Far from being disadvantaged, the onlies in this sample appear to be at least equal and probably superior to those from two-child families in terms of cognitive and intellectual functioning. At the least, this finding casts some doubt on tutoring explanations of intellectual development; at the most, it suggests that only children from normal family situations are as intellectually advantaged as the original confluence theory would predict.

Personality Characteristics

An important part of the 1960 TALENT battery of tests and measures was the Student Activities Inventory. This inventory consisted of 150 self-descriptive items dealing with aspects of a student's personality. Students were asked to rate how well each item described them, using a 5-point scale that ranged from "extremely well" to "not very well."

The items have been grouped into 10 scales, each consisting of from 5 to 24 items. The scales are calmness, culture, impulsiveness, leadership, maturity, self-confidence, sociability, social sensitivity, tidiness, and vigor. Examples of items from the calmness scale are "I am calm," "People consider me level-headed," and "I often lose my temper" (scored negatively). Scale scores were derived by summing individual item scores within a scale.

Although the Student Activities Inventory is not strictly a personality measure, it resembles one very closely and will be treated as such in the present discussion. Table 7.5 shows the differences between only and nononly children on each of the inventory's 10 scales. Directionality in the table refers to a greater amount of the trait in question, that is, more calmness, more sociability, and so on.

Table 7.5. Personality Characteristics

VARIABLE	DIRECTION AND SIGNIFICANCE OF DIFFERENCE			
	NINTH-GRADE FEMALES	TWELFTH-GRADE FEMALES	NINTH-GRADE MALES	TWELFTH-GRADE MALES
Calmness	=	1 > 2	=	=
Culture	1 > 2	1 > 2	=	1 > 2
Impulsiveness	1 > 2	=	2 > 1	=
Leadership	=	2 > 1	=	1 > 2
Maturity	1 > 2 *	1 > 2 *	1 > 2	1 > 2
Self-confidence	=	1 > 2	2 > 1	=
Sociability	2 > 1 *	2 > 1 *	2 > 1	2 > 1
Social sensitivity	1 > 2	1 > 2	=	1 > 2
Tidiness	1 > 2	1 > 2	1 > 2	1 > 2
Vigor	=	1 > 2	2 > 1	=

*Significant at .05 level.

No significant differences (or nonsignficant trends) were found between onlies and the average of two-child families in calmness, impulsiveness, leadership, self-confidence, or vigor. The differences that did reach significance, or for which a trend was apparent, form a remarkably coherent picture. Onlies were found to be more cultured, mature, socially sensitive, and tidy than nononlies, whereas nononlies were found to be more sociable. In brief, only children behave more like adults than do nononly children. This finding is not unexpected. Many investigators have theorized that onlies, growing up without siblings, tend to model adult behavior more than that of other children; adults are the only other people in a single-child home.

Those few studies (including the present one) that have found that only children are intellectually superior to nononly children have speculated that this might be attributable to a linguistic modeling effect: Only children imitate their parents' (not their siblings') language behaviors and thus become verbally adept at an early age (Cropley & Ahlers, 1975). This in turn aids their performance in school and on language-based intelligence tests. The present findings suggest that only children may tend to imitate other aspects of their parents' behavior, thus evidencing greater maturity, culture, tidiness, and social sensitivity than their high school peers. The observation that onlies are less sociable than nononlies might be a practice effect—only children lack siblings to interact with while growing up. This is a tenuous argument, however, since the very lack of siblings is thought to increase affiliative tendencies among only children. It is hard to imagine that affiliative tendencies are completely independent of sociability, but it is possible: Onlies may tend to affiliate under stress but may remain less sociable under normal circumstances.

In summary, only children did appear to possess more adult characteristics than the nononly comparison group. The evidence concerning one other factor associated with only children, independence, was mixed: Only children did not differ from nononly children in leadership ability or self-confidence, but they were less sociable.

Occupational Interests

As a part of the original TALENT data collection, an inventory was developed to survey the occupational interests of high school youth.

The Interest Inventory consists of 205 items dealing with 122 occupations and 83 activities. Students were asked to respond to each item, disregarding its educational requirements, salary, and social standing; responses were based on a 5-point scale ranging from "I would like this very much" to "I would dislike this very much."

The 205 items were divided (*a priori*) into 17 composite scales, each designed to measure interest in a broad occupational area. The scales are physical science, biological science, public service, literary, social service, artistic, musical, sports, hunting/fishing, business management, sales, computation, office work, mechanical/technical, skilled trades, farming, and labor.

Table 7.6 shows the relative interest expressed in each of these areas by only children and those from two-child families. Though few of the differences reached significance, some interesting trends appear in the data. There are six areas for which no trends are evident: public service, social service, artistic, business management, sales, and farming. However, if we consider those areas in which at least three of the four groups showed the same directionality for onlies and nononlies, the following pattern emerges: Only children have greater interest in physical science, biological science, music, computation, and literary areas, while nononly children have greater interest in sports, hunting/fishing, office work, mechanical/technical, skilled trades, and labor. This is a remarkably consistent set of findings and may represent the first time that onlies have been so neatly differentiated from nononlies in terms of interests. It should be noted as well that this finding is not confounded with socioeconomic status: SES has been partialled out in all analyses.

Why should only children score higher on white-collar, scientific, cerebral occupations while nononly children score higher on blue-collar, manual, outdoors activities? Two answers can be suggested. First, only children (at least in the present sample) performed at a higher intellectual level than nononly children. It could be expected, then, that they would tend to choose occupations calling for thought as opposed to manual labor. Second, it has long been postulated that only children receive an exaggerated amount of parental attention and encouragement to achieve. Although this parental drive may have negative effects, it may also instill in only children a desire to obtain the maximum possible education and a tendency to gravitate toward the more socially prestigious occupations.

Table 7.6. Occupational Interests

VARIABLE	DIRECTION AND SIGNIFICANCE OF DIFFERENCE			
	NINTH-GRADE FEMALES	TWELFTH-GRADE FEMALES	NINTH-GRADE MALES	TWELFTH-GRADE MALES
Physical science, engineering, math	1 > 2	1 > 2	1 > 2	2 > 1
Biological science and medicine	1 > 2	1 > 2 *	2 > 1	1 > 2
Public service	2 > 1	=	1 > 2	2 > 1
Literary, linguistic	1 > 2	1 > 2	1 > 2	1 > 2
Social service	2 > 1	1 > 2	=	2 > 1
Artistic	1 > 2	=	1 > 2	2 > 1
Musical	2 > 1	1 > 2 *	1 > 2	1 > 2
Sports	2 > 1	2 > 1	2 > 1	2 > 1
Hunting/fishing	2 > 1	2 > 1	2 > 1	2 > 1
Business management	2 > 1	1 > 2	=	1 > 2
Sales	1 > 2	2 > 1	2 > 1	1 > 2
Computation	2 > 1	1 > 2	1 > 2	1 > 2
Office work	2 > 1	2 > 1	1 > 2	2 > 1
Mechanical/technical	2 > 1	2 > 1	1 > 2	2 > 1 *
Skilled trades	2 > 1	2 > 1	2 > 1	2 > 1 *
Farming	1 > 2	=	2 > 1	2 > 1
Labor	2 > 1	1 > 2	2 > 1	2 > 1

*Significant at .05 level.

Social Life

Four items of information collected in 1960 provide information on the social life of Project TALENT participants. These variables, which are presented in Table 7.7, were: percent of participants who were dating, age when they went on their first date, average number of dates per week, and a composite measure of the intensity of the participants' overall social life. While only one of the individual comparisons is statistically significant, a highly consistent pattern of trends is evident. In all 11 cases where differences occurred, the differences favored nononly children. This is significant by means of the sign test, $p < .001$.

Among those individuals who were dating, there were no differences between only children and children of two-child families in the age at which they started dating. However, a greater proportion of individuals from two-child families were dating, and, on the average, they were dating more frequently and had a more active social life. This trend, while at variance with Bonney's (1949) finding that only children may be more socially outgoing, is consistent with our finding that individuals from two-child families receive higher average scores on the TALENT sociability scale. Thus, it appears justified to state that onlies are a little less social than nononlies, at least in terms of interactions with their peers in high school.

Health-Related Concerns

Somewhat paradoxical predictions can be made regarding the relative health of only and nononly children. On the one hand, only children do not have to compete with siblings for (perhaps scarce) family resources. Thus they are most likely to receive the benefits of optimal nutrition and medical care. On the other hand, there is evidence that births subsequent to the first are easier on the mother and that parents sometimes cease having children if the first one is physically or mentally handicapped. Other factors may be operative as well: A large number of pregnancies may lead to uterine fatigue in a woman; communicable diseases tend to linger in larger families as they get passed from one member to another. On balance, large families are probably somewhat disadvantaged with respect to smaller families in

Table 7.7. Social Life

VARIABLE	DIRECTION AND SIGNIFICANCE OF DIFFERENCE			
	NINTH-GRADE FEMALES	TWELFTH-GRADE FEMALES	NINTH-GRADE MALES	TWELFTH-GRADE MALES
Percentage who were dating	2 > 1	2 > 1	2 > 1	2 > 1
Age when went on first date (among those who were dating)	=	=	=	=
Average number of dates per week	2 > 1	2 > 1	=	2 > 1
Intensity of social life	2 > 1 *	2 > 1	2 > 1	2 > 1

*Significant at .05 level.

terms of health; within small families, however, the costs and benefits of being an only child may be roughly equivalent.

The findings from the present study are at least consistent with this latter null hypothesis: Only children did not differ consistently from the average of two-child families in reported health. Ninth and twelfth graders were asked in 1960 to rate their health (1) up to age 10 and (2) during the 3 years preceding the TALENT survey. They were also asked a series of specific health-related questions (concerning, for example, their vision, hearing, illness history, etc.); the answers to these were combined for the present analysis into a single composite health-status measure. Finally, ninth graders were asked in the 11-year follow-up whether they were suffering from any activity-limiting health problem.

Table 7.8 shows the results when onlies were compared to nononlies on these four variables. Of 14 possible differences, nononlies reported better health in 6 cases (two were significant); onlies reported better health in 6 cases (two were significant); and the two groups were equivalent in 4 cases. It is clear from this pattern that neither group is particularly advantaged with respect to health. The only subpattern discernible in Table 7.8 is a tendency for nononly males to have reported better health in 1960. If this trend is real, however, it seems to have disappeared by the time of the follow-up survey.

The lack of health differences between only children and those from two-child families is not really surprising. As noted above, effects of family size and birth order on health may be visible only in larger families, in which ease of birth, uterine fatigue, and competition for resources can become critical factors. The one hypothesis that might best distinguish onlies from children with siblings—the notion that parents would stop at one child if that child were physically disadvantaged—was not corroborated in the present study.

Activities

Data were collected in 1960 on the extent to which students engaged in any of 29 different activities; follow-up data were gathered when the respondents were about age 29 concerning 2 additional activities as well. Examples of high school activities include sports, hobbies,

Table 7.8. Health-Related Concerns

	DIRECTION AND SIGNIFICANCE OF DIFFERENCE			
VARIABLE	NINTH-GRADE FEMALES	TWELFTH-GRADE FEMALES	NINTH-GRADE MALES	TWELFTH-GRADE MALES
Health up to age 10	2 > 1	=	2 > 1 *	2 > 1 †
Usual health during past 3 years	1 > 2	=	2 > 1	2 > 1
Composite health status	=	1 > 2	1 > 2	2 > 1
Chronic health problems‡	1 > 2 *	§	=	§

*Significant at .05 level.
†Significant at .01 level.
‡11-year follow-up question.
§Not applicable. Was not asked of this grade/sex group.

reading, and crafts; follow-up respondents were queried on their newspaper- and magazine-reading habits.

The full list of activities is shown in Table 7.9, along with the differences between only and nononly children on each activity. For this set of results, directionality will be ascribed if any of the following criteria is met:

1. At least three of the four groups show the same directionality.
2. Two groups show the same directionality, and neither of the other two groups shows opposite directionality.
3. One group shows significant directionality, and none of the other groups shows opposite directionality.

These standards appear to be fair for two reasons. First, the patterns that emerge when the data are viewed in this way are very coherent. Second, because of the number of cases for which only/nononly equivalency is *expected* (e.g., girls in athletics; boys in cooking), it would be overly strict to demand, for example, three same-direction groups before ascribing directionality.

Using these criteria, Table 7.9 can be summarized as follows:

1. Only children participated to a greater extent than nononly children in:
    a. extracurricular activities
    b. extracurricular reading
    c. collecting (stamps, coins, etc.)
    d. clubs
    e. hobbies
    f. raising animals, having pets
    g. acting, singing, dancing
    h. music
    i. photography
2. Nononly children participated more than only children in:
    a. sports
    b. high school leadership roles
    c. team activities (baseball, basketball, etc.)
    d. hunting and fishing
    e. woodworking
    f. cooking

Table 7.9. Activities

VARIABLE	DIRECTION AND SIGNIFICANCE OF DIFFERENCE			
	NINTH-GRADE FEMALES	TWELFTH-GRADE FEMALES	NINTH-GRADE MALES	TWELFTH-GRADE MALES
High school leadership roles	2 > 1	2 > 1	2 > 1	1 > 2
Number of clubs belonged to in past 3 years	1 > 2	1 > 2	=	1 > 2
Variety of extracurricular activities	1 > 2	1 > 2	1 > 2	1 > 2
Degree of participation in extracurricular activities	1 > 2	1 > 2	1 > 2	1 > 2
Athletic team memberships in past 3 years	=	=	2 > 1	1 > 2
Frequency of playing baseball, football, basketball in past 3 years	2 > 1 ‡	=	2 > 1 *	=
Level of participation in sports	2 > 1	2 > 1	2 > 1	2 > 1
Athletic awards since ninth grade	=	=	2 > 1	2 > 1
Amount of extracurricular reading	1 > 2 *	1 > 2 †	1 > 2	1 > 2
Variety of hobbies	2 > 1	1 > 2	1 > 2	2 > 1

Degree of participation in hobbies	1 > 2	1 > 2 *	1 > 2	2 > 1
Frequency of raising/caring for animals or pets in past 3 years	1 > 2	1 > 2	=	=
Frequency of drawing, painting, decorating, or sculpting in past 3 years	=	=	=	=
Art awards received since ninth grade	=	=	1 > 2	=
Frequency of auto or mechanical repairs in past 3 years	=	=	=	2 > 1
Frequency of collecting rocks, coins, stamps, etc., in past 3 years	1 > 2	1 > 2	1 > 2	1 > 2
Frequency of cooking in past 3 years	2 > 1 *	=	=	=
Frequency of making jewelry, pottery, or leatherwork in past 3 years	=	=	=	2 > 1 *
Frequency of making/repairing electrical equipment in past 3 years	2 > 1 *	=	=	=
Frequency of gardening/raising flowers or vegetables in past 3 years	2 > 1	1 > 2	1 > 2	2 > 1

(*continued*)

Table 7.9. (*Continued*)

VARIABLE	DIRECTION AND SIGNIFICANCE OF DIFFERENCE			
	NINTH-GRADE FEMALES	TWELFTH-GRADE FEMALES	NINTH-GRADE MALES	TWELFTH-GRADE MALES
Frequency of hunting/ fishing in past 3 years	2 > 1	=	2 > 1	=
Frequency of doing metal work in past 3 years	=	=	=	2 > 1
Frequency of building model ships, planes, cars, etc., in past 3 years	2 > 1	=	1 > 2	1 > 2
Frequency of public acting, singing, or dancing in past 3 years	=	1 > 2	1 > 2	=
Number of music awards received since ninth grade	=	1 > 2 *	=	1 > 2
Frequency of working with photo equipment in past 3 years	=	=	=	1 > 2 *
Frequency of sewing, knitting, crocheting, or embroidering in past 3 years	=	=	=	=

Frequency of woodworking or cabinetmaking in past 3 years	=	=	2 > 1	2 > 1
Number of awards received since ninth grade in student govt., Boy Scouts, Girl Scouts, YMCA, YWCA, etc.	2 > 1	1 > 2	=	1 > 2
How often read newspaper§	‖	=	‖	1 > 2
Amount of time spent reading newspapers or newsmagazines§	1 > 2	‖	1 > 2	‖

*Significant at .05 level.

†Significant at .01 level.

‡Significant at .001 level.

§11 year follow-up question.

‖Not applicable. Was not asked of this grade/sex group.

g. jewelry making, pottery making, etc.
h. electrical/electronic crafts

3. At age 29, onlies spent more time than nononlies reading newspapers and news magazines.

This pattern suggests some consistent and coherent differences between only and nononly children. Only children tended to engage in activities that are solitary (collecting), intellectual (reading), and artistic (music, drama, photography). Nononly children tended to engage in activities that are group oriented (team sports) and practical (woodworking, cooking). These are some exceptions to this pattern, but overall the findings are remarkably uniform.

These results are reminiscent of the findings with respect to the sample's occupational interests. Only children received higher scores on the scientific, artistic, and intellectual scales, whereas nononly children tended to receive higher scores on the scales related to the manual trades. These career-related interests appear to be nicely matched with the students' high school activities. Although popular stereotypes of the only child have been avoided, the data on activities tend to reinforce one such stereotype: that of the only child as more of a loner or social isolate. Other findings in this study suggest that onlies are in fact somewhat less sociable than nononlies. The extent to which only children perceive this and are troubled by it remains to be seen, however.

Educational and Academic Achievement

The bulk of the evidence from past studies with respect to education and academic achievement has been that children from small families exceed those from large families in these areas. This may in part reflect the higher intelligence of the former, although one study (Chopra, 1966) found the relationship to hold even when intelligence was partialed out. Achievement needs in general have also been found to be greater among those from small families. This may account for part of the educational-achievement differences.

While this study revealed few individually significant differences between onlies and those from two-child families on academic and educational achievement, the pattern of differences (onlies higher in 48 out of 56 comparisons) was again significant by the sign test, $p < .001$. In addition, all of the individually significant differences favored onlies. The variables examined under this topic included 16 from the High School Information Blank and 5 from the 11-year follow-up, as shown in Table 7.10.

On four variables, significant differences appeared across two groups, a generally rare occurrence in this study. The four variables are:

1. Proportion of participants in an academic high school curriculum
2. Self-perception of reading skills
3. Self-perception of writing skills
4. Study habits and attitudes

If there is a pattern here, it seems to involve a combination of higher academic skills, particularly verbal skills, and a greater need to achieve academically. High school grades were significantly higher for onlies in one group (ninth-grade females) as well, reinforcing this pattern. The only significant difference beyond high school relates to the greater amount of education expected among twelfth-grade female onlies. The follow-up data collection showed this group to have received significantly more education than twelfth-grade female nononlies at age 29, suggesting that the high school expectations had been fulfilled.

Thus, in general the findings support those of earlier studies in that they show that children of smaller families attain higher educational and academic outcomes than those of larger families. What has been added is evidence that this pattern extends even to one-child families. The reasons onlies outscore nononlies seem to derive from their greater cognitive abilities (a finding of this study that runs counter to most past findings) and onlies' greater achievement orientation. It should be remembered, however, that only a few significant differences were found among the many variables and groups examined, and that while the general pattern of differences shows onlies outscoring nononlies, most differences are slight.

Marriage and Childbearing

As a part of both the 1960 and the 11-year follow-up surveys, data were collected about the Project TALENT participants' expectations and outcomes relative to marriage and childbearing. Table 7.11

Table 7.10. Educational and Academic Achievement

VARIABLE	DIRECTION AND SIGNIFICANCE OF DIFFERENCE			
	NINTH-GRADE FEMALES	TWELFTH-GRADE FEMALES	NINTH-GRADE MALES	TWELFTH-GRADE MALES
Proportion of participants in an academic high school curriculum	1 > 2	1 > 2	1 > 2 *	1 > 2 *
High school grades	1 > 2 *	1 > 2	1 > 2	1 > 2
Self-perception of reading skills	1 > 2	1 > 2 *	1 > 2	1 > 2 †
Self-perception of writing skills	1 > 2 *	1 > 2	1 > 2	1 > 2 *
Study habits and attitudes	1 > 2 †	1 > 2 †	1 > 2	1 > 2
Number of hours of study per week	1 > 2	1 > 2	1 > 2	1 > 2
Number of science awards received since ninth grade	=	=	=	=
Number of math awards received since ninth grade	=	=	=	=

Number of foreign language awards received since ninth grade	=	=	=	=
Number of awards for writing, debate, or oratory received since ninth grade	=	=	=	=
Degree of agreement that "success in life depends upon ability and effort, not how much education one has"	2 > 1	2 > 1	=	2 > 1
Degree of agreement that "girls should go to college only if they plan to use their education on a job"	=	=	=	1 > 2
Degree of agreement that "more girls should go to college because the country is going to need more trained women to fill important jobs"	1 > 2	1 > 2 *	=	=
Degree of agreement that "it is not necessary to have a college education in order to earn a good salary or be a leader in the community"	2 > 1	1 > 2	=	2 > 1
Amount of education expected	1 > 2	1 > 2 †	1 > 2	1 > 2

(*continued*)

Table 7.10. (*Continued*)

VARIABLE	DIRECTION AND SIGNIFICANCE OF DIFFERENCE			
	NINTH-GRADE FEMALES	TWELFTH-GRADE FEMALES	NINTH-GRADE MALES	TWELFTH-GRADE MALES
Amount of education parents want participant to have	1 > 2	1 > 2	1 > 2	=
Amount of education completed‡	1 > 2	1 > 2 †	1 > 2	1 > 2
Attended noncollege post-secondary school‡	1 > 2	§	2 > 1	§
College program was to prepare participant for a specific occupation‡	2 > 1	1 > 2	1 > 2	2 > 1
Participant attended college‡	1 > 2	1 > 2	1 > 2	1 > 2
High school considered of value "all things considered"‡	§	1 > 2	§	=

*Significant at .05 level.
†Significant at .01 level.
‡11-year follow-up question.
§Not applicable. Was not asked of this grade/sex group.

presents the results obtained when only children and individuals from two-child families were compared on the 12 variables in this category. Of the 12 variables, all but 2 were collected during the 11-year follow-up survey.

With the exception of one variable, number of children, the results for this category of variables is much like that for most of the other categories. That is, although few differences are statistically significant, a number of consistent trends occur. When they were in high school, individuals from two-child families expected to marry younger and to have more children than onlies. The accuracy of these expectations is reflected in two questions asked during the 11-year follow-up survey. With regard to the number of children the TALENT participants had parented, one of the most strongly supported findings of this entire study is that individuals from two-child families had more children than did only children. This finding was statistically significant for three of the four groups. There is no consistent trend across the four groups with regard to the age at first (or only) marriage among those ever married. Table 7.11 shows that the two ninth-grade groups were consistent with each other and differed from the two twelfth-grade groups. However, since it is difficult to attribute real cohort differences to groups born just 3 years apart, it seems reasonable to state that age at marriage was not different for the individuals included in this study. In agreement with this finding is the fact that there were no trends in the age of the spouse at the time of the participants' first marriage. However, for the ninth graders of the original survey, the only group of whom the question was asked, the spouses of only children tended to have more education than did the spouses of persons from two-child families. This finding is consistent with the finding that only children had completed more education than had individuals from two-child families.

The probability of a person marrying by about age 29, or of marrying more than once by that age, was not related to whether he or she was an only child or from a two-child family. But it appears that individuals from two-child families were more likely to be divorced by age 29. Finally, there were three follow-up questions, asked only of former ninth graders, related to their expected and ideal family sizes at about age 29. Both males and females from two-child families expected to have more children of their own than did only children. This is of course in agreement with the finding that by about age 29, individuals from two-child families did in fact have

Table 7.11. Marriage and Childbearing

VARIABLE	DIRECTION AND SIGNIFICANCE OF DIFFERENCE			
	NINTH-GRADE FEMALES	TWELFTH-GRADE FEMALES	NINTH-GRADE MALES	TWELFTH-GRADE MALES
Age when participant expects to marry (asked when in high school)	1 > 2 *	1 > 2	1 > 2	1 > 2
Number of children expected (asked when in high school)	1 > 2	2 > 1	2 > 1	2 > 1
Proportion of participants ever married‡	2 > 1	1 > 2 *	2 > 1	=
Proportion of those ever married who were divorced‡	2 > 1	2 > 1	=	2 > 1
Number of times married‡	=	=	=	=
Age when first married among those ever married‡	2 > 1	1 > 2	2 > 1	1 > 2

Age of spouse when married among those ever married‡	2 > 1 *	=	1 > 2	=
Spouse's amount of education among those ever married‡	1 > 2	§	1 > 2	§
Number of children‡	2 > 1 *	2 > 1 *	2 > 1	2 > 1 †
Number of children expected (asked on follow-up)‡	2 > 1	§	2 > 1	§
Participant's best possible family size‡	1 > 2 *	§	2 > 1	§
Ideal family size for typical couple‡	1 > 2	§	2 > 1	§

*Significant at .05 level.
†Significant at .01 level.
‡11-year follow-up question.
§Not applicable. Was not asked of this grade/sex group.

more children. However, when these same former ninth graders were asked to specify their own best possible family size and the ideal family size for a typical couple, different results were obtained. In these two situations female onlies gave larger numbers than did females from two-child families. The results were reversed for males, with individuals from two-child families obtaining larger averages. Since these questions were asked only of former ninth graders, it is not clear if these results represent real sex differences.

To summarize:

1. Only children expect to, but do not in fact, marry at an older age.
2. Only children expect to and do in fact have smaller numbers of children, and they further expect their ultimate family sizes to be smaller.
3. The spouses of only children have greater amounts of education but do not differ in average age from the spouses of nononlies.
4. Only children are less likely to be divorced by age 29.

Work-Related Concerns

This section addresses the question: What are the effects of being an only child on work-related activities? Data are available on 13 variables related to this question for all four groups in the sample and on an additional 9 variables for the twelfth-grade groups. Results of the comparisons are presented in Table 7.12. The first 8 variables come from the Student Information Blank administered while the participants were in either the ninth or twelfth grade. The last 14 variables are from the follow-up data collection done when participants were approximately age 29.

Of the 68 cells in which differences might appear in Table 7.12, onlies exceeded nononlies in 22 cases, were equal in 28 cases, and were exceeded by nononlies in 18 cases. This is a numerically balanced picture. However, the pattern varies between the first four variables, which reflect work activities in high school (where nononlies exceeded onlies), and the other variables, which reflect career plans and achievement (where onlies exceeded nononlies).

One explanation for the higher scores of nononlies on high school work activities might be that those from two-child families had a greater economic need to earn money while in high school. Another might be that those from two-child families had more contacts, through their sibling and their sibling's friends, that allowed them to obtain jobs. Three of the individual items (numbers 2 through 4) that contributed to the work-activities composite are also presented to show the source of some of the differences found in the composite.

Two other items revealed significant differences between participants from one-child families and those from two-child families. The first pertains to ninth-grade females. These young women, if from one-child families, had more definite occupational plans. This may suggest greater career ambition, or perhaps a higher awareness of the need to work. Perhaps these young women conform to the Bossard and Boll (1956) perceptions that single-child families stress ambition, achievement, competition, and planning, whereas larger families stress cooperation, conformity, and consensus (although two-child families are hardly "large"). Any such conclusion should be tempered by the many variables that failed to reveal this difference, however, and by the failure of the differences to appear among participants from the twelfth-grade female group or either of the male groups.

Finally, twelfth-grade males from one-child families were more likely to have moonlighted, that is, to have "held one or more *extra* jobs in addition to [their] regular job." This finding appears to fit in with no particular pattern or hypothesis.

To summarize, the chief finding concerning work-related activities is that only and nononly children are remarkably similar. Those from two-child families are somewhat more likely to work and earn money in high school; female only children have more definite career plans. But the number of significant differences is small in light of the many variables examined, and on balance, little evidence was found suggesting that only children differ from their two-child family counterparts on work-related activities.

Mobility

Twelfth graders were asked two questions in the follow-up survey concerning their mobility since high school. The first question asked how many times they had moved since high school, and the second question asked how far they had moved since high school.

Table 7.12. Work-Related Concerns

VARIABLE	DIRECTION AND SIGNIFICANCE OF DIFFERENCE			
	NINTH-GRADE FEMALES	TWELFTH-GRADE FEMALES	NINTH-GRADE MALES	TWELFTH-GRADE MALES
Work activities composite§	2 > 1 ‡	2 > 1	2 > 1	2 > 1 ‡
Number of hours per week participant spent doing chores around the house	2 > 1	2 > 1	2 > 1	2 > 1
Age when participant began earning money	2 > 1	2 > 1	2 > 1	2 > 1
Number of hours per week participant worked for pay during the school year	2 > 1	2 > 1	=	2 > 1
Desire to make a career in the military service	=	1 > 2	1 > 2	2 > 1
Definiteness of occupational plans	1 > 2 †	1 > 2	=	=
Expected earnings 20 years after high school	1 > 2	1 > 2	2 > 1	=
Expected financial well-being in lifetime	1 > 2	=	1 > 2	1 > 2
Participant is employed‖	1 > 2	1 > 2	=	1 > 2
Participant is a housewife‖	=	1 > 2	#	#
Composite measure of job satisfaction‖	1 > 2	=	1 > 2	=
Fit between job and long-range plans‖	=	=	=	=

Earnings (adjusted to hourly rate)‖	2 > 1	1 > 2	1 > 2	=	
Participant has "moon-lighted"§‖	#	1 > 2	#	1 > 2	*
Participant has changed careers‖	#	=	#	=	
Participant has been retrained‖	#	1 > 2	#	1 > 2	
Participant has been in the Peace Corps‖	#	=	#	=	
Participant has been in Vista‖	#	=	#	=	
Participant has lived over-seas‖	#	1 > 2	#	=	
Participant has lived in a commune‖	#	=	#	=	
Participant has been a "dropout from society"‖	#	=	#	=	
Participant has been on welfare‖	#	=	#	=	

*Significant at .05 level.
†Significant at .01 level.
‡Significant at .001 level.
§See text for explanation.
‖11-year follow-up question.
#Not applicable. Was not asked of this grade/sex group.

Table 7.13 presents the findings based on these questions. It can be seen that there were no significant differences between only children and the average of two-child families in terms of mobility. Further, there are no apparent trends or patterns in the data: The mobility of onlies was greater in one instance, less in two instances, and equivalent in one instance to that of nononlies.

There is little prior work with which the present finding can be directly compared. Claudy, Gross, and Strause (1974) note that children from large families tend to be less mobile than those from small families; that trend was not evident in the present data. Although one might argue that two-child families are not large, a better way of conceptualizing the issue might be to ask how large a family must be before differences appear between only and nononly children. The present study was limited to two-child families as a comparison group, but it is clear that such families are "large" enough to lead to some differences between onlies and nononlies, such as those in cognitive abilities.

CONCLUSIONS AND IMPLICATIONS

From a statistical point of view the results of this study can be summarized by stating that there were few individually significant differences between outcomes for only children and children of two-child families. While such a statement is technically accurate, it does not do justice to a number of important trends exhibited by the results, several of which were significant in the aggregate. Viewing the results as a whole, it appears that the only child is not disadvantaged relative to individuals from two-child families and may, in fact, be in a slightly advantageous position. The reasons for this conclusion can perhaps be best explained by the following summary of results. Relative to individuals from two-child families, only children:

1. Received higher scores on cognitive tests
2. Appeared to be more cultured, mature, socially sensitive, and tidy, but less sociable
3. Were more interested in white-collar, scientific, cerebral occupations and activities and less interested in blue-collar, manual, or outdoor occupations and activities
4. Had a less intense social life
5. Did not differ in terms of health

Table 7.13. Mobility

VARIABLE	DIRECTION AND SIGNIFICANCE OF DIFFERENCE			
	NINTH-GRADE FEMALES	TWELFTH-GRADE FEMALES	NINTH-GRADE MALES	TWELFTH-GRADE MALES
Number of times moved since high school*	†	2 > 1	†	=
Distance moved since high school*	†	1 > 2	†	2 > 1

*11-year follow-up question.

†Not applicable. Was not asked of this grade/sex group.

6. Spent more time in solitary, intellectual, and artistic activities and less time in group-oriented and practical activities
7. Were more academically oriented in high school and showed greater academic achievement by age 29
8. Married better-educated spouses and had fewer children
9. Worked less during high school but had higher long-term occupational and financial expectations
10. Were more often employed at the time of the follow up, but received approximately equal pay
11. Did not differ in terms of mobility

While none of the differences was large in absolute terms, the total picture that emerges is one in which the only child appears to be more academically oriented and "adult-like," though less social and more of a loner. It is difficult to conceive of such a person as disadvantaged. However, this picture is consistent with some of the popular stereotypes of the only child, though there is no evidence regarding the most common only-child stereotype, that of the only child as a spoiled child.

This study differed from most previous investigations of only children in finding that only children are intellectually and academically advantaged with respect to their nononly peers. This finding is even more remarkable in light of the fact that the *least sensitive* set of comparisons possible was carried out, in that only children were contrasted with those from two-child families. Two-child families cannot, by any standard, be considered large. The onlies in the current study might have appeared even more advantaged if they had been compared to children of six-child families, for example.

The likely explanation for the results obtained in this study has already been alluded to—both samples came exclusively from families in which both parents were present. Although it is known that a disproportionate number of onlies come from single-parent families, and although at least one investigator has argued that this accounts for previously found deficits among onlies (Falbo, 1979), ours appears to be the first large-scale study to control for this factor. The results are enlightening. Onlies who have grown up in two-parent homes simply do not show the intellectual deficits that have traditionally been ascribed to only children.

These presumed deficits led Zajonc (1976) and Zajonc and Markus (1975) to expand the confluence model of family size and birth-order effects. They postulated that only and last-born children, having no siblings to tutor, would suffer intellectually relative to what the original confluence model would predict. The present findings suggest that this tutoring explanation may be unnecessary, at least for onlies. It is still possible, of course, that lack of tutoring opportunities may help explain last-child deficits and that even two-parent only children perform slightly below the original confluence prediction; the present study could not examine these questions.

Within the context of the long history of research on the only child (and in addition to the substantive findings), this study seems to be of particular importance because of several methodological strengths related to the specification and selection of the sample:

1. The sample is large and representative.
2. Both sexes are included.
3. Two grade cohorts are included.
4. Data were collected during young adulthood.
5. The variables cover a wide range of areas.
6. Parental SES is carefully controlled for.
7. Only children and first borns are not grouped together.
8. A potential problem, the overrepresentation of onlies among one-parent families, is eliminated.

For all of these reasons, this study appears to provide more reliable results than the vast majority of studies of the only child.

The most important implications of this study relate to the advice and counsel that might be given to potential parents. Based on the results of this study, we can see no good reason for not having an only child. A childless couple who are considering having children should have no concern about having an only child. Likewise, a couple with a single child who are considering having a second child should base their decision on factors other than a desire to avoid raising an only child. We found no evidence of major negative consequences of being an only child.

ACKNOWLEDGMENTS

The author expresses his appreciation to William S. Farrell, Jr., and Charles W. Dayton, who assisted in the conduct of the study upon which this chapter is based.

The study described here was performed pursuant to Contract No. NO1-HD-82854 from the National Institute of Child Health and Human Development

(NICHD). The opinions expressed here are solely those of the author and do not necessarily reflect the policies or opinions of NICHD or its staff.

REFERENCES

Belmont, L., & Marolla, F. A. Birth order, family size, and intelligence. *Science*, 1973, *182*, 1096–1101.

Bonney, M. E. A study of friendship choices in college in relation to church affiliation, in-church preferences, and length of enrollment in college. *Journal of Social Psychology*, 1949, *29*, 153–166.

Bossard, J. H. S., & Boll, E. S. *The large family system: An original study in the sociology of family behavior.* Philadelphia: University of Pennsylvania Press, 1956.

Chopra, S. L. Family size and sibling position as related to measured intelligence and academic achievement. *Journal of Social Psychology*, 1966, *70*, 133–137.

Claudy, J. G. *Cognitive characteristics of the only-child.* Paper presented at the meeting of the American Psychological Association, Washington, D.C., September 1976.

Claudy, J. G., Gross, D. E., & Strause, R. D. *Two population studies* (Technical report). Palo Alto, Calif.: American Institutes for Research, October 1974.

Cropley, A. J., & Ahlers, K. H. Development of verbal skills in first-born and only boys. *Journal of Biosocial Science*, 1975, *7*, 297–306.

Falbo, T. Sibling tutoring and other explanations for intelligence discontinuities of only and last borns. *Journal of Population*, 1978, *1*, 349–363.

Falbo, T. *Folklore and the only child: A reassessment.* Unpublished manuscript, The University of Texas at Austin, 1979.

Hall, G. S. In Smith, T. L. (Ed.). *Aspects of childhood life and education.* Boston: Ginn, 1907.

Solomon, E. S., Clare, J. E., & Westoff, C. F. Fear of childlessness, desire to avoid an only child, and children's desires for siblings. *Milbank Memorial Fund Quarterly*, 1956, *34*, 160–177.

Zajonc, R. B. Family configuration and intelligence. *Science*, 1976, *192*, 227–236.

Zajonc, R. B., & Markus, G. B. Birth order and intellectual development. *Psychological Review*, 1975, *82*, 74–88.

·8·

WITHOUT SIBLINGS: THE CONSEQUENCES IN ADULT LIFE OF HAVING BEEN AN ONLY CHILD

H. THEODORE GROAT
JERRY W. WICKS
ARTHUR G. NEAL

THE SOCIAL AND DEMOGRAPHIC CONTEXT

The United States, along with the vast majority of other industrialized nations, is experiencing a period of extremely low fertility. Projections of these trends indicate that by about the year 2020, deaths should outnumber births. Should this occur, it would imply a total lifetime fertility rate of only 1.5 births per woman. To place this in historical perspective, such a low level of fertility has never been found for an actual cohort of women (Westoff, 1978).

Partly in response to these trends, there has been considerable speculation on the future of marriage and the family. Some scholars, for example, are forecasting a return to patterns of earlier marriage and larger families (Easterlin, 1978; Lee, 1976). This cyclical perspective draws upon the observed relationships between previous increases in births over a period of years and declining cohort fertility. The high fertility in the 1950s was produced by the small cohorts of the 1930s; children born in the 1950s in turn contributed the very low fertility of the 1970s. Thus, should the cycle be repeated, the small 1970s cohorts would generate yet another swing toward higher fertility a decade or two from now.

H. Theodore Groat, Jerry W. Wicks, and Arthur G. Neal. Department of Sociology, Bowling Green State University, Bowling Green, Ohio.

Many demographers and sociologists, however, relate very low current fertility to what they perceive to be fundamental and far-reaching changes in the social and normative structures of the larger American society (e.g., Bumpass, 1973; Ryder, 1979; Westoff, Thus radical improvements in contraceptive technology, along with the wide diffusion of sterilization and abortion, have helped create conditions both reflective of and conducive to changing institutional arrangements with respect to marriage and the family. Virtually all married Americans now use contraception to avoid or delay pregnancy. And while such a high degree of fertility control portends a so-called perfect contraceptive society, it also suggests that annual fluctuations in fertility rates may be somewhat more volatile than in the past—more responsive to changing short-term economic conditions. But what of the long run?

Normatively, in the United States people traditionally have been pressed into a preference for marriage and parenthood, and for at least two children rather than for an only child. Recently, however, striking changes in marriage patterns have been widely observed: increases in rates of divorce and separation, in the incidence of cohabitation, in the proportion of the population not married, and in the proportion of births occurring out of wedlock. In combination with an unprecedented contraceptive efficacy, sterilization, and the availability of abortion, these trends constitute an overall depressant on fertility, a separation of sex from reproduction, a separation of reproduction from marriage, and a weakening of marriage as a "permanent" arrangement between the sexes. As Westoff (1978) has observed, each of these phenomena is related to the changing status of women—especially to their increasing economic independence. Given the magnitude of economic inequality between the sexes that still exists, Westoff asks us to "imagine the consequences for marriage and fertility of a society in which men and women are economically equal and independent!" (Westoff, 1978, p. 81).

Along similar lines, Ryder has emphasized changes in the family institution as the key to our dwindling fertility. Tracing the family from its premodern forms as a basic economic unit, he concluded that in its contemporary and highly specialized form "the child has come to mean rather little to the parent today, and the parent rather little to the child" (Ryder, 1979, p. 365). In other words, structural change in the family institution has generated a different set of valuations of children. From this perspective, parenthood is viewed by prospective parents today more as a highly conscious cost accounting (costs vs. benefits) than it was, perhaps, during any other period of history. Generational bonds, once conjoined by functional concerns of parent for child and child for parent, have given way to a bond based largely (and more tenuously) on the affective notion of love (Hoffman, Thornton, & Manis, 1978).

If we predict a further decrease in sexual inequality and sexual interdependency in the near future, present low levels of fertility seem destined to persist or even to reach yet lower levels. As more and more young women opt to combine employment and parenthood or to avoid parenthood altogether, the proportions of women ending up with fewer than two children seem likely to increase. Indeed, this is precisely what is happening now. Over the past 15 years the proportion of women completing their childbearing with fewer than two births has gone from 18% to 36%, accounting for approximately one-third of the decline in cohort fertility (Ryder, 1979).

There is thus every reason to believe that the last frontier of modern fertility decline will involve a greater normative acceptance of voluntary childlessness and the one-child family. Recent data on birth expectations among 18-to-24-year-old women indicate that, among white women, nearly 12% report "none" and about 10% "one" child as their expected lifetime fertility (U.S. Bureau of the Census, 1977). Thus among this age and race category, childlessness is given a somewhat greater preference than having an only child. Two-child (51%) and three-child (18%) families remain the overwhelming choices. Nonetheless, should a modification occur in the popular folklore surrounding the only child, which seems likely, normative proscriptions against the one-child option should gradually erode.

FOLKLORE AND THEORY

Perhaps, as stated by the authors of a recent book on the only child, "the time for the one-child family has come" (Hawke & Knox, 1977, p. xi). Certainly parents and prospective parents have long been under the influence of a popular folklore that holds that "being an only child is a disease in itself," as the eminent psychologist G. Stanley Hall has been quoted as saying (Fenton, 1928, p. 547). Increasing concerns about the quality of social and economic life, however, in combination with changing family life styles, do seem to call for a new look at what has been described as the "only-child syndrome" (Messer, 1968).

In the abstract, and assuming a rational decision-making process, we might expect all couples who are contemplating parenthood to consider objectively the advantages and disadvantages, the relative costs and benefits, of having a single child. But this in turn would require the availability of a catalog of scientifically generated and unequivocal research findings on the only child. No such catalog currently exists, although recent research seems likely to contribute to a relatively firm empirical foundation (see, for example, Blake, 1981; Claudy, Farrell, & Dayton, 1979; Hawke & Knox, 1978; Moore, 1981; Pines, 1981; Polit, Nuttall, & Nuttall, 1980). The research record has never convincingly demonstrated the existence of stereotypical traits associated with only-child status. The popular notions of onlies as somehow handicapped, emotionally or psychologically, simply are not supported by the scientific literature (Falbo, 1977; Hawke & Knox, 1977; Terhune, 1975). Much of the research on onlies, moreover, has been confounded by various methodological shortcomings and confusing if not contradictory findings. Thus enough ambiguity exists that perhaps we should not be surprised by the strong aversion among Americans generally to the prospects of having only one child. Beyond this, however, we believe there are several reasons why only children have become so enmeshed in a folklore, largely negative in its overtones, in the minds of so many people.

First, pronatalism has long been characteristic of American culture (Blake, 1972; Peck & Senderowitz, 1974). Childbearing takes place in a sociocultural environment that influences people to behave in certain ways and not to behave in other ways. In virtually all societies, human beings have been organized into family structures whose functions are involved with the social control of reproductive behavior. Mechanisms of socialization and sex-role differentiation, for example, lead to expectations among offspring that they will in turn someday marry and have children of their own. Much of adult social life, in fact, is organized around the activities of married couples and their children. Freedom of choice, therefore, is always exercised only within a normative and organizational context. The net result, for generations of Americans, is that marriage and parenthood have seemed to comprise features of the "natural" human condition. Individuals have made their reproductive decisions within this institutional context.

As Blake (1972) has suggested, because marriage and parenthood have been almost ascribed statuses, people have generally made their reproductive choices within a sociocultural milieu that constrains them to marry rather than not marry, to have children rather than remain childless, and to have at least two children instead of only one. And to this day the modal or "ideal" family size for most Americans is two or three children. This "small" family size is perceived to be affordable, to provide for sibling interaction, and to allow for a child of each sex. Such a stereotypical family type has of course been imprinted on the public consciousness by a varied and ubiquitous popular culture. The mass media, for instance, have used the family image of mother and father with two or three children to advertise everything from detergents to station wagons.

Under the circumstances, it does not seem surprising that one-child families have traditionally been viewed as incomplete or hardly real families at all. But as we have seen, the institutional mechanisms of the family have been changing, and over the next decade or so the normative structure may permit greater freedom of choice with respect to family size. On the face of it, single-child families would seem to have some distinct advantages (Hawke & Knox, 1977). Having an only child, for instance, allows for the experience and rewards of parenthood without a sense of overwhelming parental responsibilities. Compared with two or more children, expenses are less, restrictions on the parents are fewer, and the burdens of child care are of shorter duration. Why, then, don't more couples choose the one-child family? The answer, we suspect, in addition to remaining pronatalist sentiment, is that the mass media continue to report an "expert opinion" on the only child that is mostly negative in its implications.

Two recent examples from widely read syndicated columnists should illustrate our point. George Crane (1979), author of the "Worry Clinic," recently advised his readers not to marry someone who had been an only child. Only children, as compared to sibling children, according to Crane, tend to be more rigid in their religious and political views, crave attention, are more irritable, strive to exert greater dominance in their marital relationships, and as a result are more likely to get a divorce. Prospective parents are therefore urged to have at least three children!

Niki Scott (1979), author of a syndicated column, "Working Woman," recently wrote on the special problems entailed in having only one child. Only children are not *necessarily* deprived, she points out, but they do have "a special need for outside activities" to keep them from being overly lonely or turning into "miniature adults."

Writing in *The New York Times Magazine*, Alfred Messer, a psychiatrist, summed up many popular ideas that, collectively, comprise a kind of "only-child syndrome." Only children, according to Messer (1968), are more serious, with heightened senses of responsibility. They also tend to be involved as "peacemakers" in parental conflicts and to be less secure (feeling that they can't "measure up" to their parents' expectations). Further, only children are likely to have special problems when they become parents themselves, caused largely by the potential rivalry between parent and child. Thus, because there are "special hazards" with the one-child family, Messer concluded by recommending that parents of only children consider adopting a second child "in order to give their family more emotional balance" (p. 91).

In focusing on the psychological characteristics of only children and in making reference to "clinical" studies and subjects in "therapy," articles such as Messer's in many ways typify a vast popular conception of only children as selfish, lonely, maladjusted, and in other respects "high risk" (Thompson, 1974). As Falbo (1977) points out, relatively little popular or scientific attention has been given to the more positive attributes of having or being an only child. As we have seen, the combination of pronatalist sentiment (Blake, 1972; Peck & Senderowitz, 1974; Russo, 1976) and selective "scentific" reports has provided a foundation for thinking about only children in largely negative terms.

Beyond all this, however, there are indeed several theoretical reasons for *expecting* only children to differ from their counterparts with siblings. These theoretical rationales can be reduced to a relatively small number of explanatory mechanisms (Terhune, 1974), each of which common sense tells us should make a difference between onlies and siblings.

First, each family cares for its children with some finite amount of resources that must be distributed among members of the family. Incomes are limited, of course, as is the time parents have to spend with other members of the family. All else being equal, then, small family size should be converted into advantages of numerous kinds: nutrition and health, educational attainment, and perhaps such personality characteristics as independence and self-esteem. On the other hand, the same logic might be used to argue that onlies are more likely than siblings to be overindulged or spoiled.

Another principle of family size differences involves the pattern of social interactions: As family size decreases there is likely to be a concomitant concentration of interaction between family members. Children in small families seem likely to receive more care and attention; they are also likely to have greater expectations placed on them by their parents. This is where a kind of popular psychology of the only child enters the picture. To the extent that parents expect the achievements of their offspring to provide them with satisfaction, their children will be expected to achieve. In the case of the single child, of course, one child is all the parents have to provide this satisfaction for them. And so it is with other forms of social exchange between parents and child—the only child must provide for a portion of exchange value that would likely be shared if siblings were present in the family. Again, then, although concentrated parental attention may be an advantage to children in small families generally, it makes at least "common" sense to expect only children to be more susceptible to certain kinds of stressful conditions. In the eyes of many people, therefore, the end result is likely to be an "insecure" only child.

It also seems that children in small families would be more likely to go outside the home for companionship and stimulation. To the extent that this actually occurs, the child would of course be exposed to a greater variety of stimuli in the larger social world. In the case of only children, for whom affiliative needs presumably would most likely be realized through extrafamilial activities, a sense of self-reliance and independence might very well be the end result. It could also be argued, however, that these same conditions are likely to produce insecure and anxious children.

Another theoretical reason for expecting differences between onlies and children with siblings is that only children are also first-born children. Thus birth order, as distinct from number of siblings, is associated in both the scientific literature and in popular lore with implications for patterns of personality development and achievement. For example, a vocabulary of popular psychology is frequently drawn upon to explain differences between the oldest child, the middle child, and the baby in the family. Because birth-order differences presumably imply different patterns of teaching and learning within family structures, we might expect differences between first borns and later borns to show up in such areas as intellectual and academic achievement. But this line of reasoning assigns special advantages to the first borns with one or two siblings, while underlining the fact that only children lack the opportunity to tutor younger siblings (Zajonc, 1976).

Finally, children in large families may be exposed to greater authoritarianism than children in small families (Terhune, 1974). Thus the only child might be brought into family decision making at an earlier age, and under more equalitarian conditions, than children with siblings. But does this mean that an only child is likely to be socialized in the direction of more democratic principles or to become more demanding and inflexible than others?

The point of this discussion is that both social psychological theory and common sense tell us that only children should be different in certain respects. From this position, however, there is no clear path for concluding what such differences are likely to be, how important they are, or under what conditions they are likely to be found. And even if we knew precisely what differences were likely to distinguish onlies from children with siblings, not everyone would evaluate the differences the same way: A child who seems spoiled and aggressive to one person may appear self-reliant and independent to another. The popular labeling of personality characteristics traverses a series of fine lines between the bad and the good in us all (Gergen, 1973).

THE STUDY

Much research on only children, as well as birth order, has been based at least implicitly on the assumption that the differential family constellations in which a child is socialized are reflected in later adult behavior. Only children, or nononly children in particular birth-order positions, are believed or theorized to experience childhood conditions that develop relatively enduring personality characteristics. The further assumption is that these personality characteristics are important enough to affect major life events (Falbo, 1977). A considerable portion of the research on only children, however, has been based on samples of children or adolescents and has concentrated on personality as opposed to behavioral consequences. Hence very little is actually known about the behavioral consequences, in key areas of adult life, of having been an only versus a sibling child. Thus, it behooves the research community to test under rigorous conditions the extent to which only children are indeed disadvantaged (or advantaged) vis-à-vis other children who grow up within a social context of sibling relationships. The indicants of advantages and disadvantages should also be operationalized around dimensions of social life that are generally agreed to be consequential.

The research reported here is an attempt to add to the literature on only children through a concentrated examination of possible differences between onlies and nononlies within a broad range of adult behaviors. In our judgment, the more important consequences of being an only child are likely to be expressed during the years of entry into adult status, marriage, parenthood, and employment; involvement in various lines of activity, especially during the early fecund years, seem to us most likely to have enduring consequences.

Drawing upon a developmental framework for the analysis of data, we have concentrated on a search for significant behavioral differences between men and women who were onlies vis-à-vis those who were not. The adults in our sample were traced through their educational achievements, patterns of family formation, and occupational and economic attainment. Throughout, the strictest controls permitted by the data were utilized to test for significant differences that might have been attributable to only- versus nononly-child status. Our working hypothesis was straightforward and parsimonious: Men and women who grew up as only children would not differ significantly from men and women who grew up with one or more siblings.

If the reasons for expecting only children to differ from sibling children are indeed valid, and if enduring and important personality characteristics distinguish the adult behavior of onlies from nononlies, then we would expect to reject our null hypothesis at several points in the analysis. Our reasoning was that any underlying personality differences, to the extent that they are truly consequential, should be reflected in behavioral outcomes in later adult life.

Data

The data for this study were obtained from Cycle I of the National Survey of Family Growth (NSFG). This survey, conducted in 1973 by the National Center for Health Statistics, provided detailed information on family formation, fertility expectations, contraceptive behavior, educational and employment histories, aspects of child and maternal health care, and many social and economic characteristics of both husbands and wives. The data base thus supplied us with measures of the fundamental events of adult life that to a large extent had remained untested in the context of differential sibling status.

The final sample drawn for the NSFG, after preparatory fieldwork, was derived from a five-stage probability design (a detailed description of the sample design is included in French, 1978). Based on initial interviews, 10,879 women were selected for the final sample. Personal interviews, averaging 70 minutes in length, were conducted with these women. A total of 9,797 women completed the interviews, for a completion rate of 90.2%. From the somewhat larger target population of currently or ever-married women between the ages of 15 and 44, inclusive, living in the United States, we restricted our analytic sample to 7,512 currently married couples, of which 5.8% of the wives and 6.1% of the husbands had grown up as only children.

Finally, the NSFG data were weighted by the National Center for Health Statistics to the statistical requirements of a broad series of demographic, ethnic, and religious categories. Thus the data permitted direct generalization to the more than 26 million currently married couples in which the wife is between 15 and 44 years of age.

Our independent variable was sibling status. This variable was measured by response to a question asking how many babies had been borne by the respondent's mother, as well as by the respondent's answer to the same question about her husband's mother. Because the sample was comprised of adults, only-child status was unlikely to have been contaminated by additional, subsequent fertility in the parental generation. In other words, given the nature of the sample, we can be quite confident that "only" status is what is implied by the category label.

Our dependent, or outcome variables, were clustered into three major categories: educational attainment, family formation, and socioeconomic achievement. Education was measured by the highest number of years of schooling completed. Both family formation and socioeconomic achievement, however, were measured by reference to more than a dozen specific variables. Age at marriage, age at parenthood, number of children, and desired family size, for example, were among the numerous measures of family formation. The socioeconomic indicants included various measures of employment status relative to marriage and fertility, occupational prestige, and several personal and family-income variables. Whenever it was appropriate and an adequate measure existed, identical analyses were carried out for both husbands and wives in each of these clusters. For the sake of parsimony, only a representative sampling of the much greater list of variables in the original study is included in the tables in this chapter.

Finally, the NSFG data were supplemented by published data from the 1970 U.S. census. Recalculations of these data permitted us to determine the national distributions of only children by such socioeconomic background variables as mother's education, father's occupation, and family income.

Findings

The Distribution of Onlies

As a starting point, and to profile the general incidence of only-child status and its distribution within a series of demographic and sociocultural categories, an overview of the data is shown in Table 8.1. These data are limited to a national probability sample of currently married women still in their childbearing years, and to their husbands, regardless of age.

Table 8.1 shows that 5.8% of the wives and 6.1% of the husbands were only children. This slight sex differential probably reflects both the sex ratio at birth and the preference for male offspring (Coombs, 1977; Markle, 1974; Williamson, 1978). That is, not only is the first-born child somewhat more likely to be male than female, but parents may also be somewhat more likely to terminate their fertility if their first born is a son rather than a daughter. In addition, the husbands in our sample were somewhat older than the wives; thus they more frequently fell into the birth cohorts from which larger proportions of only children originated.

Historically, the pattern of one-child families, as one would expect, has inversely paralleled the increase in American fertility since the 1930s. Children born in the decade of the Depression, for example, were more than twice as likely to grow up without siblings as were children born during the baby boom of the 1950s. To illustrate, 7.7% of the 1929–1934 birth cohort of wives were onlies, in contrast to merely 3.0% of the 1955–1959 cohort. Clearly, having only one child has not been a popular choice for the overwhelming majority of parents of the past few decades. More recently, however,

Table 8.1. Percentages of Wives and Husbands Who Were Only Children, by Selected Demographic and Social Categories

	WIVES		HUSBANDS	
	NUMBER (1,000's)	PERCENT	NUMBER (1,000's)	PERCENT
Total	26,422	5.8	26,422	6.1
Birth cohort				
1955–1959	402	3.0	62	6.9
1950–1954	3,964	3.3	2,305	3.2
1945–1949	6,105	4.8	5,391	5.0
1940–1944	5,330	5.7	5,084	6.3
1935–1939	4,707	7.2	4,697	7.6
1929–1934	5,915	7.7	8,883*	6.5
Race†				
Whites	24,028	5.9	23,680	6.1
Blacks	2,078	4.7	2,024	6.7
Others	317	3.0	718	3.2
Religion				
Protestant	17,134	5.9	16,527	6.2
Catholic	7,623	5.1	7,664	5.3
Jew	440	15.4	464	8.2
Other	1,226	5.2	1,768	7.6
Ethnic origin				
European	18,601	6.2	17,122	6.6
Hispanic	1,666	3.8	1,588	3.5
African	1,951	5.0	2,024	6.7
Other‡	4,204	5.2	5,689	5.0
Place of residence				
Metropolitan	18,462	6.5	18,462	6.6
Nonmetropolitan	7,961	4.2	7,961	4.8
Region of residence				
Northeast	5,357	7.4	5,357	6.7
North central	6,942	5.0	6,942	5.3
South	8,828	6.0	8,828	6.0
West	5,295	5.0	5,295	6.6

Note. This table excludes a small number of wives and husbands who were adopted and for whom data on sibling status were not reported.

*This number includes husbands born before 1929 and therefore older than 44.

†Racial classification for wives was determined by interviewer observation; for husbands, race was classified from data reported by the wives on the ethnic origins of their husbands.

‡The "Other" category includes wives who reported themselves or their husbands as Asian, American Indian, "American," or "Other," specified as other than American.

concomitant with the general fertility decline of the 1960s and 1970s, increasingly larger percentages of young wives have reported an expected lifetime family size of only one child (U.S. Bureau of the Census, 1978). Between 1960 and 1976, for example, the percentage of wives 18 to 39 years old who reported expecting only one child increased from 7.0% to 10.8%. Hence an increase in the proportion of families completing their childbearing in the 1980s and 1990s with only one child seems likely .

The prevalence of onlies also varies somewhat by race, religion, ethnicity, and residence. For instance, slightly larger percentages of white than black wives, of black than white husbands, and of Protestants than Catholics, had grown up as only children. Only-child status was more prevalent among the Jewish segment of the married population than among any of the other classifications shown in Table 8.1. To illustrate, 15.4% of Jewish wives and 8.2% of Jewish husbands were raised as only children. These data are of course consistent with the generally lower fertility of American Jews compared with Catholics and most Protestants, which has been routinely documented in the demographic literature (e.g., Ryder & Westoff, 1971).

Beyond the religious differentials, only children were somewhat more likely than sibling children to be of European ancestry and to be living in metropolitan areas in the northeastern region of the country. Thus, these patterns of only-child status follow closely the more general patterns of fertility differentials within American society.

In an additional series of analyses, we cross-classified the data by various combinations of the variables shown in Table 8.1. The results of these more detailed analyses accentuated the major conclusion derived from the data in Table 8.1, that by far the most significant differentials in sibling status are those obtained by birth cohort. Regardless of race, religion, residence, or region, the data showed a consistent pattern of decline between the older birth cohorts and the younger birth cohorts in the percentages of wives and husbands who were only children. Among the numerous cross-classifications, the highest percentage of wives (8.9%) and husbands (7.8%) who were only children were those born before 1940 and residing in metropolitan communities. In contrast, only 1.5% of wives and 1.7% of husbands born since 1950 and living in nonmetropolitan communities were only children.

Collectively, these analyses provided us with an overview of the distribution of adult onlies by combinations of demographic and sociocultural characteristics. These data did not tell us, however, how these adult onlies were distributed by the socioeconomic characteristics of their families of origin. Because family of origin has such obvious and significant implications for later life achievements, it is important to determine insofar as possible the socioeconomic characteristics of the families that have generated only children. If, for example, certain socioeconomic categories of the adult population contribute significantly more than others to the pool of only children, then only children in the aggregate would be the recipients of whatever advantages or disadvantages might accrue to people who grow up within the context of particular socioeconomic characteristics.

Unfortunately, the 1973 National Survey of Family Growth did not include questions on the family background characteristics of the adult respondents. This was a potentially serious limitation, which we dealt with in two ways. First, U.S. census materials were analyzed to determine the extent to which the distributions of only children and one-child families were skewed along each of several socioeconomic dimensions. Second, once the patterns of educational attainment by sibling status were determined, educational attainment was then controlled in the subsequent analyses of family formation and socioeconomic achievement. Our reasoning was that one of the most, if not *the* most, important advantages or disadvantages likely to accrue to children who grow up in different socioeconomic strata is that of years of schooling completed. Hence by comparing the patterns of family formation and economic achievement between adult onlies and siblings, net of educational attainment, we were able to test our null hypothesis while largely neutralizing the differential effects of socioeconomic origin. Although this procedure was inferior to having complete information on the relevant variables, the seriousness of the data limitations may be partially evaluated on the basis of what the census data reveal with respect to the distributions of only children and one-child families.

Socioeconomic Characteristics of Families of Origin

There are several ways of looking at the phenomena of onliness, or the one-child family, as they are distributed according to the social and economic characteristics of the parent generation. First, for example, we may compare the percentages of only children born to women within selected socioeconomic categories. This would give us the percentage of only children born to women with certain characteristics. Second, we may compare the percentages of all married women, again by socioeconomic categories, who have given birth to only one child. This distribution would provide us with an overview of the incidence of one-child families. Finally, we may compare the percentage distributions of all women within socioeconomic categories with the percentage distributions of all only children born to women in those same categories. If the aggregate distribution of only children is significantly skewed in the direction of some socioeconomic characteristics of family of origin, such as education or income, this latter set of comparisons would clearly demonstrate it.

In the larger study from which our data are drawn, we addressed each of the above comparisons with a series of analyses, based on data from the 1970 U.S. census, of the social and economic characteristics of the parent generations of only children. The analytic distinctions between the three comparisons were apparent in the results. For instance, among ever-married white women 40 years of age and over, those with less than a high school education had a somewhat lower proportion of only children than those in higher educational categories. There were virtually no differences, however, between high school graduates and those who attended college. Overall, 6.2% of children born to white women and 5.4% of children born to black women were only children.

Although the percentage of children who were onlies was quite small, we found that having an only child, by comparison, has not been such an uncommon occurrence among American families. That is, in computing the proportions of ever-married women who had given birth to a single child, we found that 16.5% of white women and 17.3% of black women were parents of an only child. Among ever-married white women, there was very little variation in the percentage distributions by educational attainment. In contrast, the percentages of black women with only children increased from 17% among those with less than a high school education to 21.5% among those with four or more years of college.

For purposes of exploring the significance of socioeconomic background variables with respect to the NSFG sample, the most relevant question is whether women with selected socioeconomic characteristics contribute disproportionately to the total pool of only children. Table 8.2 shows the distributions of all women ever married,

Table 8.2. Percentage Distribution of Ever-Married Women and Ever-Married Women with Only Children, by Education

	WHITE WOMEN		BLACK WOMEN	
YEARS OF SCHOOL COMPLETED	ALL WOMEN EVER MARRIED (%)	ALL ONLY CHILDREN (%)	ALL WOMEN EVER MARRIED (%)	ALL ONLY CHILDREN (%)
Less than 4 years of high school	53.4	51.2	77.9	76.3
4 years of high school	30.8	32.4	14.3	14.7
1–3 years of college	9.6	10.1	4.1	4.3
4 or more years of college	6.2	6.3	3.7	4.6

Note. Limited to women 40 years of age and over. Calculated from U.S. Bureau of the Census. *Census of Population: 1970.* Subject reports, Final Report PC(2)-3A, Women by Number of Children Ever Born, Tables 36–37. (Rounded percents do not always add up to 100.)

and of all their only children, as percentages of the totals within educational groupings. For example, women with four or more years of college comprised 6.2% of all ever-married women over 40 in 1970; in turn, 6.3% of all only children were borne by women in this educational category. In other words, although slightly larger percentages of college-educated than non-college-educated women bore an only child, their contribution to the total number of only children was very close to their proportionate contribution to the total number of women under consideration. Within each educational category, in fact, we found a very close correspondence between the distributions of ever-married women, both white and black, and their only children. Thus in the aggregate, on a national basis, women with varying amounts of education have not contributed disproportionately to the total number of only children.

We replicated this analysis by the additional socioeconomic variables of husbands' incomes and occupations, with the same results. That is, women contributed to the pool of only children in very close approximation to their distributions within each of the income and occupation categories. These findings suggest that the following analyses, based as they are on national probability data, are unlikely to reflect differences in the socioeconomic status of families of origin.

Educational Attainment and Family Formation

Educational attainment and age at first marriage are highly correlated behaviors, largely because continuing one's education is typically associated with a postponement of marriage. Both of these behaviors also represent pivotal decisions within a relatively short time span for most young adults. More important, the highly correlated decisions of when to terminate one's education and when to marry are replete with implications for a variety of later life achievements. For instance, occupational achievement is clearly related to years of education (Kamens, 1977; Sewell, Haller, & Ohlendorf, 1970), and patterns of family formation, such as the number and spacing of children, have of course been associated with age at marriage (Bumpass & Westoff, 1970). For these reasons, then, we began our analysis of the outcome variables with a series of tests for differences between onlies and nononlies with respect to both educational attainment and age at marriage.

Table 8.3 lists adjusted means and proportions for educational attainment, age at marriage, and several additional family-formation variables. This and Table 8.4 summarize the key findings with respect to several representative variables. In the original study, numerous other related variables were analyzed in a similar way and subjected to additional controls through various data-partitioning procedures. We will make reference to these other variables and analytic procedures in discussing the results shown in Tables 8.3 and 8.4.

Multiple classification analysis (MCA) was the multivariate statistical technique (Andrews, Morgan, Sonquist, & Klem, 1975) utilized throughout this phase of the study. One of the advantages of this technique is its ability to examine relationships among a large number of predictor variables with levels of measurement at the nominal or ordinal level, and of a dichotomous nominal or interval level dependent variable within the context of an additive model. We have limited the obtained results in Tables 8.3 and 8.4 to the means or proportions, the β values, and the F-ratio tests for significance. The β value measures the relationship between the independent and dependent variables after adjusting for all other independent variables, whereas the F-ratio tests approximately whether or not a predictor, after controlling for all other predictors, explains a significant portion of the variance in the dependent variable. For each variable, separate analyses were performed for whites and nonwhites and, where the data permitted, for both husbands and wives.

Numerous studies have documented higher levels of educational attainment for only children as compared to children from larger families. Among the strongest evidence yet of differentials in educational attainment between onlies and nononlies was that reported by Bayer (1966) on the basis of a large-scale longitudinal survey of thousands of high school seniors in the early 1960s. His data, which utilized several important controls for socioeconomic status, led to the conclusion that only children were more likely than first-, intermediate-, or last-born children to continue their education beyond the high school level. This finding held within each of the socioeconomic levels examined.

Table 8.3 shows significant differences in mean years of education between onlies and nononlies among white wives and husbands. Only-child wives completed an average of 13.13 years of education, whereas their counterparts with siblings completed 12.26 years. Similarly, husbands who were onlies had more years of education (13.76) than those who were not (12.66). These differences in adjusted means among wives and husbands reached statistical significance at the .001 level. Beyond the results shown in Table 8.3, we also partitioned the data for white wives and husbands by separate age categories, with comparable results. That is, for both sexes within both partitioned age cohorts (younger vs. older), onlies were found to have a statistically significant educational advantage over siblings.

We also examined educational differences among white wives and husbands by whether or not both parents were present in the home when the children were 14 years of age. Our reason for this additional control is that only children are more likely to be products of single-parent homes than nononly children (Falbo, 1978). In other words, one reason why parents may have only one child is that one of the parents is absent. Because children from homes broken by the absence of one parent are presumably subjected to different environmental circumstances than others, it is important to test for only versus nononly differences within intact as well as broken family arrangements. Our results from this additional analysis showed clearly that onlies, in comparison with nononlies, completed more years of schooling regardless of parental composition at age 14. Educational advantages accruing to onlies were evident among those who grew up in intact as well as broken homes.

The results shown in Table 8.3 thus corroborate previous research, which has indicated an advantage to onlies over siblings in educational achievement. These findings, however, should be approached with some caution. For one thing, they are limited to whites; none of the differences in education among nonwhites reached statistical significance. Moreover, despite the statistical significance of the educational differences among whites, sibling status actually explained very little variance in number of years of schooling completed. For instance, having been an only versus a nononly child typically accounted for no more than 1 or 2% of the variance in education across our separate comparisons by sex, age, race, and the parental composition of families of origin.

Many of the negative stereotypical notions about only children focus on presumed psychological characteristics such as egotism, selfishness, and inability to get along well with others. To the extent that these profiles are accurate and significant, we might expect onlies to exhibit personality attributes that would be converted into differential patterns of behavior in later life. Presumably onlies, if

Table 8.3. Adjusted Means and Proportions for Educational Attainment and Representative Family Formation Varibles among Wives and Husbands, by Sibling Status

	WHITES				NONWHITES			
	WIVES		HUSBANDS		WIVES		HUSBANDS	
WEIGHTED NUMBERS (1,000's)	ONLIES ($n = 1427$)	NONONLIES ($n = 22{,}590$)	ONLIES ($n = 1448$)	NONONLIES ($n = 22{,}222$)	ONLIES ($n = 108$)	NONONLIES ($n = 2287$)	ONLIES ($n = 158$)	NONONLIES ($n = 2585$)
Years of education*	13.13	12.26	13.76	12.66	11.02	11.57	11.14	11.16
β	.11		.10		.05		.01	
Significance of F	.001		.001		—		—	
Age of marriage†	19.72	19.79	25.74	24.40	18.93	20.19	24.50	25.23
β	.02		.06		.07		.03	
Significance of F	—		—		—		—	
Proportion previously married‡	.13	.13	.19	.14	.26	.15	.30	.21
β	.01		.04		.07		.05	
Significance of F	—		—		—		—	
Proportion premaritally pregnant§	.16	.17	.14	.17	.28	.36	.46	.30
β	.01		.02		.04		.08	
Significance of F	—		—		—		—	

Number of pregnancies‖	2.41		2.56	2.43		2.56	2.83		2.96	2.80		2.90
β		.02			.01			.01			.01	
Significance of F		—			—			—			—	
Number of children‖	1.99		2.16	2.09		2.62	2.06		2.16	2.51		2.50
β		.02			.05			.01			.00	
Significance of F		—			—			—			—	
Desired family size‖	2.60		2.78		#		2.15		2.80		#	
β		.03						.09				
Significance of F		—						—				

*Means adjusted for birth cohort and religion.

†Means adjusted for birth cohort, education, and religion. Data for wives are for first marriage; data for husbands are for current marriage.

‡Means adjusted for birth cohort, education, age at marriage, and religion.

§Means adjusted for birth cohort, education, and religion.

‖Means adjusted for birth cohort, education, age at marriage, family income, and religion.

#Not available.

Table 8.4. **Adjusted Means and Proportions for Representative Socioeconomic Achievement Variables among Wives and Husbands, by Sibling Status**

	WHITES				NONWHITES			
	WIVES		HUSBANDS		WIVES		HUSBANDS	
WEIGHTED NUMBERS (1,000's)	ONLIES ($n = 1427$)	NONONLIES ($n = 22{,}590$)	ONLIES ($n = 1448$)	NONONLIES ($n = 22{,}222$)	ONLIES ($n = 108$)	NONONLIES ($n = 2287$)	ONLIES ($n = 158$)	NONONLIES ($n = 2585$)
Years employed prior to marriage*	1.20	1.17	†		1.25	1.28	†	
β	.02				.01			
Significance of F	—				—			
Years employed since first marriage‡	4.02	3.59	†		3.28	4.75	†	
β	.02				.05			
Significance of F	—				—			
Weeks employed prior to interview§	20.47	20.20	†		18.17	25.32	†	
β	.00				.07			
Significance of F	—				—			

Proportion employed as professionals or managers§	.18		.18	.38		.34	.10		.13	.15		.16
β		.00			.02			.02			.00	
Significance of F		—			—			—			—	
Occupational prestige*		†		43.46		42.17		†		35.31		34.98
β					.02						.01	
Significance of F					—						—	
Family Income*	15,082		14,434	15,351		14,452	11,302		12,103	12,104		11,663
β		.02			.03			.02			.01	
Significance of F		—			—			—			—	

*Means adjusted for birth cohort, edcuation, age at marriage, and religion.
†Not available.
‡Means adjusted for birth cohort, education, number of children, years since first marriage, and religion.
§Means adjusted for birth cohort, education, number of children, and religion.

they are in the aggregate that much different from siblings, would not follow normative patterns of family formation, such as those related to age at marriage, frequency of divorce, and the spacing and number of children. The remaining data shown in Table 8.3, therefore, are directed toward tests of these hypotheses concerning patterns of family formation.

The first family-formation variable shown in Table 8.3 is age at marriage. For many reasons, age at marriage has important consequences for later life achievements. Patterns of childbearing, for instance, in terms of both numbers and spacing, are related to differential age at marriage. Other things being equal, early marriage is associated with premarital pregnancy, lower educational attainment, a faster tempo of childbearing, and higher rates of divorce. These family formation sequelae, in turn, are thought to be predictive of lower rates of female labor-force participation, as well as lower occupational achievement and lower earnings. In short, men and women who postpone their marriage to ages beyond the average for their peers are believed to benefit in the long run through greater probability of success in various life endeavors, including marriage itself.

Do only children marry at significantly older or younger ages than children with siblings? The data shown here for white and nonwhite wives and husbands indicate a qualified negative answer to this question. Although there are some apparent differences in the raw data on mean age at marriage across the paired comparisons by sex and race, in no instance do these differences reach statistically significant levels. Thus with controls for age, education, and religion, no discernible pattern of differences in age at marriage was revealed. We also partitioned these data by educational level (high school or less vs. college) and age (younger vs. older cohorts), testing for differences within each of these categories, with similar results. No significant differences in age at marriage were found by sibling status.

Only children, compared to siblings, are often considered to be more likely to be rigid, to crave attention, to be irritable, and to strive for dominance in their marital relationships. Presumably, they are also more likely to be divorced. Within the limits of our data, we have also tested this hypothesis. The data for white wives and husbands do not provide support for the divorce hypothesis. Indeed, there are no differences whatever by sibling status between the proportions of white wives who had been previously married. Among the husbands, those who were only children do indeed include higher proportions of the previously married than their counterparts with siblings. These differences in the raw data, however, do not reach statistically significant levels. Among the nonwhite comparisons, the differences between proportions by sibling status appear impressive. Again, though, the raw data are misleading. The original, unweighted sample of nonwhite wives (from which data for both wives and husbands were collected) was quite small. Thus the distributions of variables within the subsamples shown for nonwhites reflect potential distortions based on a very small unweighted number of wives and husbands in the only-child category. In a statistical sense we cannot be confident that the differences shown in the proportions of previously married husbands and wives accurately reflect the distributions we would find in the larger population of currently married women and men.

While we feel confident that the burden of proof is on those who believe that onlies are significantly more likely than siblings to divorce, we are also cognizant that we have not measured the incidence of divorce *per se*. Rather, we have measured the presence or absence of at least one previous marriage in a sample of currently married men and women. To the extent that divorced onlies differ from divorced nononlies in the propensity for remarriage, therefore, our findings may differ somewhat from those obtained from another kind of sample. For these reasons, then, we believe that this topic may deserve further investigation with different samples and more complete data on marital histories.

Much has been written about the implications not only of age at marriage but also of the timing of the first birth, especially for women, for the later achievement of life rewards (Davis, 1972; Furstenberg, 1976; Pohlman, 1969; Presser, 1971, 1973, 1974, 1975). A basic premise of this literature is that early marriage and early childbearing are associated with larger completed family size (Bumpass & Mburugu, 1977; Trussell, 1978). In part this is because of the strong association between early marriage and premarital pregnancy (Baldwin, 1976) as well as the longer duration of exposure to the risk of pregnancy; also included, however, is the notion of a constraining influence of the parenthood role on the probabilities that other, alternative roles, especially for the mother, will have time to develop (Presser, 1971, 1973, 1974).

Early childbearing, including premaritally conceived but legitimate births, has also been associated with other facets of life achievement. Educators and parents alike, for instance, have long been concerned over the disruptive influence of early parenthood on the educational, occupational, and social interests of adolescents and young adults. Bacon (1974, p. 333), for example, has emphasized the "stress-engendering acceleration of role transitions" that may lead to various "social pathologies." Because early childbearers tend to complete less schooling than others (Furstenberg, 1976; Mott & Shaw, 1978), they also tend to be relatively disadvantaged in the job market, not to mention the lost opportunities for personal and intellectual growth. Husbands and fathers, of course, are also likely to be young and relatively less educated, resulting in a lower family income (Coombs, Freedman, & Pratt, 1970). Therefore, there is convincing evidence that not only the young parents but also their children are vulnerable to adverse and long-lasting social and economic consequences (Baldwin & Cain, 1980; Hofferth & Moore, 1979).

With the above issues in mind, the question here is whether or not there are substantial and significant differences in the patterns of pregnancy and childbearing between onlies and nononlies. In the NSFG data, approximately 17% of the white wives and 35% of the black wives who had at least one child were premaritally pregnant. A birth occurring within 7 months after marriage was operationally defined as the result of a premarital pregnancy.

Are wives and husbands who were only children significantly more or less likely to have experienced a premarital pregnancy than those who were not only children? The data shown in Table 8.3 provide an overwhelmingly negative answer. Among white wives and husbands, the adjusted proportions show only insignificant differences in premarital pregnancy rates by sibling status. Among nonwhites, the pattern is not so clear. Female onlies were less likely than female nononlies to have been premaritally pregnant; but the opposite trend is revealed for the nonwhite men. In the latter instance the data approach but do not reach a level of statistical significance.

More important, although we have not included additional statistical information in this summary table, the squared partial correlations between sibling status and premarital pregnancy rates for whites and nonwhites alike ranged from only .001 to .008. In other words, sibling status, net of the control variables, did not explain even a moderate amount of variance in premarital pregnancy. Having been an only child versus a sibling child, in this instance, did not matter.

Another perspective on the entry into parenthood may be gained by limiting the analysis to women with at least one live birth and testing for differences by sibling status in the timing of the first birth relative to timing of the first marriage and the age of the mother. These separate analyses showed that among both wives and husbands there was a trend toward onlies delaying their first births somewhat longer than nononlies. The most striking difference in this regard was found among nonwhite wives, among whom the first-birth interval for onlies was 26 months in contrast to only 16 months for nononlies. This was one of a very few statistically significant differences (.05 level) obtained by sibling status from among dozens of comparisons in the original study. No significant differences by sibling status were found, however, in our series of tests for differences in the mean ages of mothers at the birth of the first child.

In simplistic terms, different people have different numbers of children for two basic reasons: (1) they want or desire a specific number of children, and (2) they have different capacities (biological, economic, social, psychological, informational, etc.) for having the number of children that they want. Theoretically, there are reasons with respect to each of these factors why we might expect differences between onlies and siblings. Since children are socialized in large part within a family context, it would be surprising if the number of siblings one had did not enter into the development of motivations for differing numbers of children of one's own. In addition to this, and to the extent that the efficacy of fertility control may be taken as an indication of general mastery and planning, onlies may also differ from nononlies in their overall fertility behavior for the same reasons that have been discussed in the research literature for expecting differences in educational and occupational achievement. Both of these avenues to differential fertility behavior are addressed with reference to the final variables listed in Table 8.3.

We have approached this topic with reference to several studies that have demonstrated, using fairly large samples, a weak association between size of family of origin and the child's own eventual family size (Berent, 1953; Bumpass & Westoff, 1970; Burks, 1941; Duncan, Freedman, Coble, & Slesinger, 1965; Huestis & Maxwell, 1932). Of the studies that have separated onlies from first borns, the results confirm that onlies both desire and have fewer children. Westoff and his colleagues (Westoff, Potter, Sagi, & Mishler, 1961), for example, found that the lowest mean number of children was among wives with no siblings. In a later study (Westoff, Potter, & Sagi, 1963), the smallest number of children desired by the wife after the birth of the second child, and the lowest average number of pregnancies following the second live birth, occurred among Protestant women with no siblings. These patterns were not replicated, however, among Catholics or Jews. Westoff and Potvin (1967), on the other hand, found in their study of college women and fertility values that the number of children desired was smallest for women with no siblings, regardless of religious affiliation.

Table 8.3 lists data on the number of pregnancies and number of children ever born by the sibling status of both wives and husbands. Data on desired family size among wives (corresponding data for husbands were not available) are also shown. No statistically significant relationships are revealed for any of these three outcome variables, although there is a generally consistent trend in the data toward lower fertility for onlies as compared to nononlies. For example, the lowest adjusted mean numbers of both pregnancies and children are found among white wives and husbands without any siblings. With one exception, a similar pattern is shown for the nonwhite sample. The results for desired family size among wives are similar: Onlies desire somewhat fewer children than siblings; among nonwhite wives the difference in desired family size by sibling status (2.15 versus 2.80) approaches statistical significance.

We also explored the issue of fertility control by addressing the incidence of unwanted pregnancy (data not shown in the tables). The unwantedness of a pregnancy was determined in the NSFG data by the wives' responses to a series of questions about the circumstances of each pregnancy. Virtually no differences were found in the mean number of unwanted pregnancies by our major analytic variables; nor did the data reveal a discernible pattern or trend. Thus, insofar as fertility control is an indicant of mastery and control over important life events, onlies and siblings appear to be remarkably similar in this respect.

In conclusion, sibling status is not an important predictor of subsequent fertility outcomes. Compared to the relative importance of several control variables included in our regression equations (education, age at marriage, income, and even religion), having been an only versus a nononly child is virtually meaningless.

Occupational and Economic Achievement

In a highly competitive society with relatively high rates of social mobility such as the United States, status and prestige are characteristically assigned on the basis of individual achievement in education, occupation, and income (Blau & Duncan, 1967; Coleman & Rainwater, 1978). Much of the research in this area begins with the assumption that "a fundamental trend toward expanding universalism characterizes industrial society" (Blau & Duncan, 1967, pp. 429–30), implying the presence of a socioeconomic continuum on which virtually all individuals and families can be ranked on the basis of occupation, income, education, and skills (Becker, 1965; Mincer, 1974). Although this research tradition has not gone unchallenged, considerable evidence has accrued that suggests the presence of a popular version of socioeconomic achievement in these terms (Coleman & Rainwater, 1978). Thus the concerns and aspirations of parents for their children are routinely framed within this kind of achievement-oriented context. For our purposes, then, the question is quite straightforward: Are there differences between only and sibling children that in later adult life are likely to be converted into significant advantages or disadvantages, net of or in combination with other factors, with respect to socioeconomic status?

There are indeed reasons, drawn both from the empirical and theoretical literature, for expecting some differences in the socioeconomic achievements of onlies and nononlies. Overall, for example, numerous studies have suggested that children from smaller families are advantaged relative to those from larger families. In terms of intelligence (Belmont & Marolla, 1973; Eysenck & Cookson, 1970) academic achievement (Eysenck & Cookson, 1970; Schachter, 1963), educational and material aspirations (Turner, 1962), need for achievement (Rosen, 1961) and related variables, children from smaller families generally have been found to be somewhat higher achievers, more ambitious, and more independent than children from larger families.

Similar results may be found in the birth-order literature, which of course is closely related to the research on family size. Thus firstborn and early-born children, as well as children from smaller families generally, are described in the literature as more intelligent (Belmont & Marolla, 1973) and better academic achievers (Schachter, 1963; Altus, 1965) than later-born children and children from larger families.

The theoretical explanations offered for these obtained differences in children by family size and birth order were examined earlier. Suffice it to state here that differences in family resources (income, time, energy, etc.) and family configurations (interactions, sibling interaction patterns, etc.) carry the weight of most theoretical rationales.

On the face of it, these findings and theories suggest that only children should be advantaged in several respects. After all, onlies are necessarily first borns and members of the smallest families. Yet they are also last borns, and this may be a major reason why the extant research sometimes shows them as intermediate between first-born and later-born children in several characteristics. For example, with respect to intelligence onlies are sometimes reported as superior (Cropley & Ahlers, 1975) but more often as occupying an intermediate position in comparison with first and later borns (Belmont & Marolla, 1973). Comparisons of onlies with nononlies on academic achievement generally report an advantage for onlies (Poole, 1974; Schachter, 1963). Summarizing these and other findings of a more subjective nature, Terhune (1974) concludes that onlies may be characterized by such traits as ambition and drive.

Table 8.4 lists summary data for three sets of achievement-related variables: the employment experiences of married women, the nature of employment among wives and husbands, and level of family income. Each of these variables is representative of a much larger number of similar variables that were also analyzed in the original study.

The great increase in female labor-force participation over the past few decades has of course been widely noted. Not as generally recognized, perhaps, is the change in the characteristics of women comprising this segment of the labor force. For example, since 1940 middle-class women, especially, have been increasingly combining household and employment responsibilities. Moreover, it is clear that children are no longer the same deterrent they were in the past to the employment aspirations of married women (Oppenheimer, 1969). One of the most dramatic trends of recent years, in fact, has been the sharp increase in labor-force participation among mothers with preschool children (Waite, 1981).

Collectively, these trends involve a change in the traditional patterns of women's marital employment. There is an increasing tendency for women to work outside the home at any stage, or all stages, of the family-forming process. For purposes of the present research, these trends are important because they relate to differential avenues for the attainment of socially valued goals, economic as well as noneconomic in nature. Other things being equal, for instance, the employment of both husbands and wives obviously contributes to the financial well-being of families. Beyond this, however, the timing and pattern of women's employment are implicated in a host of differentials related to family formation, including age at marriage and the number and spacing of children (Groat, Workman, & Neal, 1976; Groat, Wicks, Neal, & Hendershot, 1982). Childbearing, therefore, may be viewed in part as the result of interactions between costs, barriers, and facilitators that motivate women to seek some combination of both familial and nonfamilial gratification.

The preference for employment outside the home has also been related to sex-role orientation (Scanzoni, 1975). Thus such experiences as college education and premarital employment may be viewed as achievements associated with a greater emphasis on so-called modern, as opposed to traditional, sex-role orientations. To the extent that women work before marriage, after marriage but before the birth of the first child, or at other stages in the family-formation process, for example, we may view these extrafamilial activities as general indicants of socioeconomic achievement. With this in mind, our first concern here is with the question: What is the influence of sibling status on the employment activities of women during their early adult years?

The first three outcome variables shown in Table 8.4 address this question. On the average, with adjustments made for several control variables, both wives who had siblings and those who did not worked just over 1 year before their first marriages. The data show a weak trend among white wives toward onlies having longer durations of employment than siblings. Among the nonwhite wives, however, where the number of onlies is quite small, the data show a reverse trend by sibling status. Neither of these inconsistent patterns reaches a statistically significant level. Similarly, during the 12-month period before the NSFG interviews, there were virtually no differences in duration of employment among white wives. For nonwhites, on the other hand, nononlies tended to have longer durations of employment than onlies, though these differences also were insignificant in any statistical sense.

In a separate analysis, we tested for differences between the proportions of only and nononly wives not currently employed who expected to look for or return to work sometime in the future. No trends or significant differences were found. Finally, limiting our analytic sample to wives who had given birth to one or more children, we tested for differences by sibling status in the durations of employment in both the first and second birth intervals as well as since the birth of the last child. None of these analyses resulted in a significant difference between only and nononly wives.

Table 8.4 includes two variables related to the kind or nature of the employment of wives and husbands. Husbands' occupations were coded in the NSFG data on the basis of the Hodge–Siegel Prestige Score originally designed for use with the 1960 U.S. census (U.S. Department of Commerce, 1978), and the occupations of both wives and husbands were coded by the much broader 1970 census occupational classification. The combined Professional (including technical and kindred) and Managerial (including administrators, except farm) category we are using in Table 8.4 includes a wide diversity of white-collar occupations characteristically associated with high levels of income and educational attainment.

Our first question, then, is whether onlies, compared to nononlies, are disproportionately represented in the professional and managerial occupations. Under controlled conditions, the answer is "no" among both wives and husbands, whites and nonwhites alike. Similarly, the occupational prestige scores for the husbands failed to reveal differences by sibling status. We also analyzed the occupational prestige scores of the husbands by the sibling status of the wives, and found that wives who were only children were not significantly more or less likely than their counterparts with siblings to be married to men with high levels of occupational prestige.

The final variable shown in Table 8.4 is family income. Because income can be converted into so many other symbols of achievement and is so directly related to differential life changes, it is not surprising that Americans typically consider income as a preeminent criterion for status evaluation (Coleman & Rainwater, 1978). Our concern here is limited to the extent to which having been an only versus a nononly child is related to income. The differences in family income by sibling status, for both sexes, are minimal.

We also tested for personal (in contrast to family) income differences and for income for wives by current as well as most recent employment. Additionally, we examined the economic achievements of wives in terms of their relative contributions to the total incomes of their families. Again, no significant results were obtained.

In brief, on the basis of a wide range of achievement variables, we conclude that having been an only rather than a nononly child, net of such other factors as education, age, and age at marriage, simply does not make much difference.

SUMMARY AND CONCLUSIONS

Present demographic trends in the United States portend an increasing interest among couples in both voluntary childlessness and one-child families. Viewed in the historical context of the trend toward more efficacious means of fertility control, the present low level of fertility suggests that the last frontier of modern fertility decline may encompass a greater normative acceptance of these smallest family-size options. While it seems obvious that no society is likely to tolerate, indefinitely, the extremely low fertility implied by these fertility choices, it also seems clear that the range of normatively acceptable family sizes may come to include these lower limits. Whether or not this happens will no doubt depend in large part on the general public perception of the consequences for a couple of having no children, and of the consequences for a child as well as the parents of having only one child. Thus the issue of whether having been an only versus a sibling child has major consequences in later adult life is important, since the weighing of perceived costs and benefits of family-size options among couples in a "contracepting" society is presumably based increasingly on the process of rational decision making.

Most of the previous research on only children has been limited to samples of school-age children, adolescents, and college students. Relatively little empirical work has focused on what happens to onlies versus nononlies in later adult life. If personality differences between onlies and siblings do exist, for example, the most relevant question for prospective parents might well be whether or not these differences really matter in later adult life; that is, are there truly consequential behavioral outcomes that are more likely to characterize onlies than siblings? The present report, therefore, has traced a cross-sectional sample of adult men and women through their educational achievements, patterns of family formation, and such extrafamilial participations as occupational and economic attainment.

What implications can we draw from this study? We have documented the fact that among a national probability sample of currently married men and women there are very few significant differences in a series of behavioral outcomes by whether or not the adults grew up as only rather than nononly children. Moreover, the one clear significant difference that did emerge, educational attainment, showed only children at somewhat of an advantage over their sibling counterparts. The decision to have more than one child, then, in order to avoid having an only child, would seem to be misplaced. No evidence was found of any negative consequences for onlies, compared to nononlies, in patterns of behavior in adult life.

ACKNOWLEDGMENT

This chapter is drawn from a much larger study completed for the Center for Population Research, NICHD (Contract NIH-NO1-HD-92806). See Groat, Wicks, and Neal (1980).

REFERENCES

Altus, W. D. Birth order and academic primogeniture. *Journal of Personality and Social Psychology*, 1965, *2*, 872–876.

Andrews, F. M., Morgan, J. N., Sonquist, J. A., & Klem, L. *Multiple classification analysis*. Ann Arbor, Mich.: Institute for Social Research, 1975.

Bacon, L. Early motherhood, accelerated role transition, and social pathologies. *Social Forces*, 1974, *52*, 333–341.

Baldwin, W. H. *Adolescent pregnancy and childbearing: Growing concerns for Americans*. Washington, D.C.: Population Reference Bureau, 1976.

Baldwin, W. H., & Cain, V. S. The children of teenage parents. *Family Planning Perspectives*, 1980, *12*, 34–43.

Bayer, A. E. Birth order and college attendance. *Journal of Marriage and the Family*, 1966, *28*, 480–484.

Becker, G. S. *Human capital: A theoretical and empirical analysis, with special reference to education*. New York: National Bureau of Economic Research, 1965.

Belmont, L., & Marolla, F. A. Birth order, family size, and intelligence. *Science*, 1973, *182*, 1096–1101.

Berent, J. Relationship between family sizes of two successive generations. *Milbank Memorial Fund Quarterly*, 1953, *31*, 39–50.

Blake, J. Coercive pronatalism and American population policy. In R. Parke, Jr., & C. F. Westoff (Eds.), *U.S. Commission on Population Growth and the American Future* (Vol. VI). Washington, D.C.: U.S. Government Printing Office, 1972.

Blake, J. The only child in America: Prejudice versus performance. *Population and Development Review*, 1981, 7, 43–54.

Blau, P. M., & Duncan, O. D. *The American occupational structure*. New York: Wiley, 1967.

Bumpass, L. L. Is low fertility here to stay? *Family Planning Perspectives*, 1973, *5*, 67–69.

Bumpass, L. L., & Mburugu, E. K. Age at marriage and completed family size. *Social Biology*, 1977, *24*, 31–37.

Bumpass, L. L., & Westoff, C. F. *The later years of childbearing.* Princeton: Princeton University Press, 1970.

Burks, B. Social promotion in relation to differential fecundity. *Human Biology,* 1941, *13,* 103–113.

Claudy, J. G., Farrell, W. S., & Dayton, C. W. *The consequences of being an only child: An analysis of Project TALENT data.* Palo Alto, Calif.: American Institutes for Research, 1979.

Coleman, R. P., & Rainwater, L. *Social standing in America.* New York: Basic Books, 1978.

Coombs, L. C. Preferences for sex of children among U. S. couples. *Family Planning Perspectives,* 1977, *9,* 259–265.

Coombs, L. C., Freedman, R., & Pratt, W. H. Premarital pregnancy and status before and after marriage. *American Journal of Sociology,* 1970, *75,* 800–825.

Crane, G. Worry clinic. *Daily Sentinel Tribune,* Bowling Green, Ohio, April 16, 1979, p. 24.

Cropley, A. J., & Ahlers, K. H. Development of verbal skills in first-born and only boys. *Journal of Biosocial Science,* 1975, *7,* 297–306.

Davis, K. The American family in relation to demographic change. In R. Parke, Jr., & C. F. Westoff (Eds.), *U.S. Commission on Population Growth and the American Future* (Vol. 1). Washington, D.C.: U.S. Government Printing Office, 1972.

Duncan, O. D., Freeman, R., Coble, J. M., & Slesinger, D. P. Marital fertility and the size of family of orientation. *Demography,* 1965, *2,* 508–515.

Easterlin, R. A. What will 1984 be like? Socioeconomic implications of recent twists in the age structure. *Demography,* 1978, *15,* 397–432.

Eysenck, H. J., & Cookson, D. Personality in primary school children: Family background. *British Journal of Educational Psychology,* 1970, *40,* 117–131.

Falbo, T. The only child: A review. *Journal of Individual Psychology,* 1977, *33,* 47–61.

Falbo, T. Sibling tutoring and other explanations for intelligence discontinuities of only and last borns. *Journal of Population,* 1978, *1,* 349–363.

Fenton, N. The only child. *Journal of Genetic Psychology,* 1928, *35,* 546–556.

French, D. K. *National survey of family growth, cycle I: Sample design, estimation procedures, and variance estimation.* Department of Health, Education, and Welfare, National Center for Health Statistics, Series 2. Washington, D.C.: U.S. Government Printing Office, 1978.

Furstenberg, F. F., Jr. The social consequences of teenage parenthood. *Family Planning Perspectives,* 1976, *8,* 148–164.

Gergen, K. J. Social psychology as history. *Journal of Personality and Social Psychology,* 1973, *26,* 309–320.

Groat, H. T., Wicks, J. W., & Neal, A. G. *Differential consequences of having been an only versus a sibling child.* Final report to the Center for Population Research, NICHD, 1980.

Groat, H. T., Wicks, J. W., Neal, A. G., & Hendershot, G. E. *Working women and childbearing: United States.* Department of Health and Human Services, National Center for Health Statistics, Series 23, No. 9. Washington, D.C.: U.S. Government Printing Office, 1982.

Groat, H. T., Workman, R. L., & Neal, A. G. Labor force participation and family formation: A study of working mothers. *Demography,* 1976, *13,* 115–125.

Hawke, S., & Knox, D. *One child by choice*. Englewood Cliffs, N.J.: Prentice-Hall, 1977.

Hawke, S., & Knox, D. The one-child family: A new life style. *The Family Coordinator*, 1978, *3*, 215–219.

Hofferth, S. L., & Moore, K. A. Early childbearing and later economic well-being. *American Sociological Review*, 1979, *44*, 784–815.

Hoffman, L. W., Thornton, A., & Manis, J. D. The value of children to parents in the United States. *Journal of Population*, 1978, *1*, 91–131.

Huestis, R. R., & Maxwell, A. Does family size run in families? *Journal of Heredity*, 1932, *1*, 77–79.

Kamens, D. H. Legitimating myths and educational organization. *American Sociological Review*, 1977, *42*, 208–219.

Lee, R. D. Demographic forecasting and the Easterline hypothesis. *Population and Development Review*, 1976, *2*, 459–468.

Markle, G. E. Sex ratio at birth: Values, variance, and some determinants. *Demography*, 1974, *11*, 131–142.

Messer, A. A. The only-child syndrome. *The New York Times Magazine*, February 25, 1968, pp. 90–101.

Mincer, J. *Schooling, experience, and earnings*. New York: Columbia University Press, 1974.

Moore, D. The only-child phenomenon. *The New York Times Magazine*, January 18, 1981, pp. 26–48.

Mott, F. L., & Shaw, L. B. *Work and family in the school-leaving years: A comparison of female high school graduates and dropouts*. Paper presented at the Conference on Young Women and Employment, Department of Labor, Washington, D.C., 1978.

Oppenheimer, V. K. *The female labor force in the United States*. Population Monograph Series No. 5. Berkeley: University of California Press, 1969.

Peck, E., & Senderowitz, J. *Pronatalism: The myth of mom and apple pie*. New York: Crowell, 1974.

Pines, M. Only isn't lonely (or spoiled or selfish). *Psychology Today*, March 1981, pp. 15–19.

Pohlman, E. The timing of first births: A review of effects. *Eugenics Quarterly*, 1969, *3*, 252–263.

Polit, D. F., Nuttall, R. L., & Nuttall, E. V. The only child grows up: A look at some characteristics of adult only children. *Family Relations*, 1980, *29*, 99–106.

Poole, A. Bythway's statistical trap. *Journal of Biosocial Science*, 1974, *6*, 73–74.

Presser, H. B. The timing of the first birth: Female roles and black fertility. *Milbank Memorial Fund Quarterly*, 1971, *49*, 329–362.

Presser, H. B. Perfect fertility control: Consequences for women and the family. In C. F. Westoff (Ed.), *Toward the end of growth: Population in America*. Englewood Cliffs, N.J.: Prentice-Hall, 1973.

Presser, H. B. Early motherhood: Ignorance or bliss? *Family Planning Perspectives*, 1974, *6*, 8–14.

Presser, H. B. Age differences between spouses. *American Behavioral Scientist*, 1975, *19*, 574–585.

Rosen, B. C. Family structure and achievement motivation. *American Sociological Review*, 1961, *26*, 574–585.

Russo, N. F. The motherhood mandate. *Journal of Social Issues*, 1976, *32*, 143–154.

Ryder, N. B. The future of American fertility. *Social Problems*, 1979, *3*, 359–370.

Ryder, N. B., & Westoff, C. H. *Reproduction in the United States*. Princeton: Princeton University Press, 1971.

Scanzoni, J. Sex roles, economic factors, and marital solidarity in black and white marriages. *Journal of Marriage and the Family*, 1975, *37*, 130–144.

Schachter, S. Birth order, eminence, and higher education. *American Sociological Review*, 1963, *28*, 757–768.

Scott, N. Working woman. *The Plain Dealer*, Cleveland, Ohio, July 20, 1979, p. 2.

Sewell, W. H., Haller, O., & Ohlendorf, G. W. The educational and early occupational status process: Replication and revision. *American Sociological Review*, 1970, *35*, 1114–1127.

Terhune, K. W. *A review of the actual and expected consequences of family size*. Washington, D.C.: U.S. Government Printing Office, 1974.

Thompson, V. D. Family size: Implicit policies and assumed psychological outcomes. *Journal of Social Issues*, 1974, *30*, 93–124.

Trussell, T. J. *Age at first birth and the pace and components of subsequent child-bearing*. Paper presented at the annual meeting of the Population Association of America, Atlanta, Georgia, April 1978.

Turner, R. H. Some family determinants of ambition. *Sociology and Social Research*, 1962, *46*, 397–411.

U.S. Bureau of the Census. Fertility of American women: June, 1976. *Current Population Reports*, 1977, Series P-20, No. 308. Washington, D.C.: U.S. Government Printing Office, 1977.

U.S. Bureau of the Census. Fertility of American women: June, 1977. *Current Population Reports*, 1978, Series P-20, No. 325. Washington, D.C.: U.S. Government Printing Office, 1978.

U.S. Department of Commerce. *National survey of family growth, cycle I, 1973, users guide*. Springfield, Va.: National Technical Information Service, 1978.

Waite, L. J. *U.S. women at work*. Washington, D.C.: Population Reference Bureau, 1981.

Westoff, C. F. Some speculations on the future of marriage and the family. *Family Planning Perspectives*, 1978, *10*, 79–83.

Westoff, C. F., Potter, R. G., & Sagi, P. C. *The third child*. Princeton: University Press, 1963.

Westoff, C. F., Potter, R. G., Sagi, P. C., & Mishler, E. G. *Family growth in metropolitan America*. Princeton: Princeton University Press, 1961.

Westoff, C. F., & Potvin, R. *College women and fertility values*. Princeton: Princeton University Press, 1967.

Williamson, N. Sons or daughters: *A cross-cultural survey of parental preferences*. Beverly Hills, Calif.: Sage, 1978.

Zajonc, R. B. Family configuration and intelligence. *Science*, 1976, *192*, 227–236.

AUTHOR INDEX

SUBJECT INDEX